DELIGHTS, DESIRES, AND DILEMMAS

DELIGHTS, DESIRES, AND DILEMMAS

DELIGHTS, DESIRES, AND DILEMMAS

Essays on Women and the Media

Edited by Ann C. Hall

Westport, Connecticut
London

Library of Congress Cataloging-in-Publication Data

Delights, desires, and dilemmas : essays on women and the media /
   edited by Ann C. Hall.
      p.   cm.
   Includes bibliographical references and index.
   ISBN 0–275–96156–7 (alk. paper)
   1. Women in mass media.   I. Hall, Ann C., 1959–   .
P94.5.W65D45   1998
302.23′082—dc21   98–4942

British Library Cataloguing in Publication Data is available.

Library of Congress Catalog Card Number: 98–4942
ISBN: 0–275–96156–7

First published in 1998

Praeger Publishers, 88 Post Road West, Westport, CT 06881
An imprint of Greenwood Publishing Group, Inc.

Printed in the United States of America

The paper used in this book complies with the
Permanent Paper Standard issued by the National
Information Standards Organization (Z39.48–1984).

10 9 8 7 6 5 4 3 2

Copyright Acknowledgments

The editor and publisher gratefully acknowledge permission to use the following material:

Chapter 10 is reprinted from Rosaria Champagne's book *The Politics of Survivorship: Incest, Women's
Literature, and Feminist Theory* (New York: New York University Press, 1996.). Reprinted by permission of New York University Press.

DELIGHTS, DESIRES, AND DILEMMAS

Essays on Women and the Media

Edited by Ann C. Hall

Westport, Connecticut
London

Library of Congress Cataloging-in-Publication Data

Delights, desires, and dilemmas : essays on women and the media /
  edited by Ann C. Hall.
     p. cm.
    Includes bibliographical references and index.
    ISBN 0–275–96156–7 (alk. paper)
    1. Women in mass media. I. Hall, Ann C., 1959– .
P94.5.W65D45   1998
302.23′082—dc21   98–4942

British Library Cataloguing in Publication Data is available.

Library of Congress Catalog Card Number: 98–4942
ISBN: 0–275–96156–7

First published in 1998

Praeger Publishers, 88 Post Road West, Westport, CT 06881
An imprint of Greenwood Publishing Group, Inc.

Printed in the United States of America

The paper used in this book complies with the
Permanent Paper Standard issued by the National
Information Standards Organization (Z39.48–1984).

10 9 8 7 6 5 4 3 2

Copyright Acknowledgments

The editor and publisher gratefully acknowledge permission to use the following material:

Chapter 10 is reprinted from Rosaria Champagne's book *The Politics of Survivorship: Incest, Women's Literature, and Feminist Theory* (New York: New York University Press, 1996.). Reprinted by permission of New York University Press.

For Sarah and Zachary

Contents

Acknowledgments

Foremost, I would like to thank Grace Epstein for suggesting this collection to me, as well as her many insights on feminism and culture throughout the years. No word of praise can reflect my gratitude to this volume's contributors who provided their time, talents, and patience. In particular, I would like to thank Katherine Burkman and Judith Roof who reviewed the manuscript, made suggestions on its organization, and offered me wondrous advice on everything from childrearing to cultural theory. To all my Ohio Dominican College colleagues especially Imali Abala, Jill Dardig, Godwin Duru, Darlene Erickson, Z. Fang, Steve Raglow-Defranco, Michelle Sarff, Joanne Vickers, and our Dean, Andy Keogh. In addition, I extend heartfelt thanks to Joan Franks for her ethical and philosophical insights and Ron Carstens for his generosity of spirit, suggestions, and good humor. Many thanks to Elisabetta Linton and Lynn Zelem of Greenwood Publishing for their patience, encouragement, and painstaking editing advice. John Calvert-Finn deserves a special mention because he good-naturedly took time out of his busy schedule to offer a final proof of this manuscript. And finally to Geoffrey C. Nelson for his support, affection, sense of the absurd, and ability to entertain toddlers for hours.

Introduction: Demystifying the Media

Ann C. Hall

In a recent ad campaign for Calvin Klein jeans, young people were placed in sexually suggestive postures and situations. While such a strategy may not surprise the advertising world, these promotions brought charges of child pornography:

These ads enter the heart of adult darkness, where toying with the sexuality of teens is thinkable. One of the most offensive segments poses a young man alone, his face in that dumb, deadened look associated with films that can be bought only in an adult bookstore. A man off-camera says, "You have a real nice look. How old are you? Are you strong? You think you could rip that shirt off you? That's a real nice body. You work out? I can tell." (Carlson 64)

As a result of pressure from large department stores, religious groups, and others, Klein pulled the ad campaign but not before he presented himself as a victim of censorship and an advocate of teenage sexual desire, a representative of "modern young people who have an independent spirit and do the things they want to do and can't be told or sold" (qtd. in Ingrassia 64).

Klein's comments and the public response to the ad campaign serve as an appropriate setting for a discussion regarding women and the media. First, Klein's response reflects the general trend of the media in a capitalist society: consumer culture co-opts the language of subversion and manipulates it to its own ends. Under such a system, mass-produced merchandise offers independence, not conformity; purchases make citizens, not consumers.[1]

Second, the scandal over his ads is telling in terms of what was not addressed during the controversy. That is, the scandal is predicated upon the fact that the campaign includes young men, not merely young women. Barbara Lipman of *Adweek* briefly raises the issue when she says "girls have been objectified forever. It's not shocking, sad to say. But an old man with a gravelly voice in a basement questioning a boy, that's creepy" (qtd. in Carlson 4). As many will remember, too, Klein catapulted his career to super-designer status through the purrings of a fifteen-year-old Brooke Shields. Sadly, Klein dismissed feminist attacks during a *Playboy* interview with a few profane words (Ingrassia 60). Sadder still, however, is the fact that the question of female exploitation did not even make it to newsprint in this recent reinKleination.

The silence over the Klein scandal, the mass murders of women in Montreal, and the justice system's treatment of sexual harassment and domestic violence in recent years are some of the issues that inspired this collection, which began as a series of panel discussions at the Midwest Modern Language Association's annual meetings. While numerous books have been written and much has been done to better the position, representation, and inclusion of women in the media, these events make it painfully clear that feminists still have a great deal of work to do. As the Lipman quote implies, women continue to be viewed as representation only, images for market consumption. Theorists such as Guy Debord, Jacques Lacan, and Fredric Jameson argue that ours is a spectacular culture, one based upon the visual. Debord even identifies twentieth-century culture as the "society of spectacle" which uses spectacle in many insidious and oppressive ways. As many feminists have demonstrated, women play an important role in this spectacle, generally serving as the objects of male speculation or the means by which men may indulge their scopophilia and narcissism.[2] The consequences for women are far-reaching, and at the very least it means that "a woman must continually watch herself. She is almost continually accompanied by her own image of herself . . . because how she appears to others, and ultimately how she appears to men, is of crucial importance for what is normally thought of as the success of her life" (Root 66).

As a review of women and media studies indicates, feminists have frequently modified their tactics to anticipate, refine, and elaborate their challenge to patriarchal oppression, most recently through anthologies devoted to the representation of women in the areas of film and television.[3] This collection not only attempts to include discussions on the visual image as well as the printed one, it also identifies and represents three major trends in feminist strategies: the "liberal feminist" method of analysis; the methods of resistance inspired by postmodernism and cultural studies; and the more recent attempts to identify the subtle and perhaps more offensive "backlash" which threatens to obliterate feminist gains.[4] As the collection illustrates, these trends afford a wide variety of approaches and theories, from psychoanalysis to new critical readings to cultural analyses of media texts. The trends are represented by essays that discuss the position of real women on and in the news, as well as fictional female characters. They afford opposing views regarding the media's inherent treatment of women: some essays, for example, view the media suspiciously; others see it as a possibility for evoking cultural change, "a critical view that can provide genuinely new insights into mass culture" (Modleski, *Studies*, xii). The title of the collection reflects these trends: the approach in the seventies took delight in exposing the question of the female as spectacle for male delight. That is, the media created women as objects of representation, and feminists exposed the frequently extraordinary means that the media went to to create these illusions. As a result of the postmodern movement, many feminists admitted that the media did appeal to them and their desires. And now, as a result of the backlash against women in general and women in the media in particular, feminists face new dilemmas regarding female representation in the media. All three trends and the essays clustered around them in this edition make it clear that whatever tack female viewers take when surfing the media wave, analysis must continue.

Early feminist attacks on the media argued that "real" women did not merely "stand in" for some platonic ideal necessary for the perpetuation of male domination.[5] Participants in the resurgence of feminist activity during the sixties and seventies were shocked to discover that their worst enemy was the media (Strainchamps xxv). In the United States and Britain, feminist anthologies logging the abuses of the media multiplied. Essays discussed the virtual absence of women in broadcasting, publishing, and film (other than actresses). Analyses appeared that demonstrated the manner in which the media perpetuated a myth of female incompetence, frequently under the guise of "helpful advice" or entertainment. Television's *Police Woman*, for example, offered a beautiful star, but men always came to her rescue. Women's magazines were linked with conduct literature and sermons of the nineteenth century and shown to be just as oppressive—advice columns actually imply that women cannot manage their lives without the help of experts. And perhaps most disturbingly, feminists unveiled the unforgivable representations of the female body. Female beauty in fashion magazines, for example, required a great deal of technological intervention. Inherently, the media implied, female bodies were fat, smelly, uncontrollable, and ugly.[6]

Many of these collections read like detective fiction: women uncover abuses and gleefully expose the culprits, their false promises, faulty logic, and ridiculousness. The collection format, too, reflects a feminist commitment to affording many women the right to speak, as well as reflecting the hydra-headed nature of the media in its multiple manifestations.[7] Frequently referred to as a "liberal feminist approach," these early collections depict men as manipulative patriarchs who oppress women and distort their experience through media presentations. Cultural theorists would identify this approach as similar to the "Frankfurt" school of thought which assumes that the media is a monolithic, oppressive entity that wreaks havoc upon its innocent, unsuspecting audiences.[8] Though frequently correct, inspiring, and entertaining, this approach sometimes results in distortions as a result of its overzealousness. Who determines, for example, what the "real" female experience is or who the "real" woman is? That is, for instance, this approach did not seem to take into account the women who liked some of the media representations. Works such as Modleski's *Loving with a Vengeance* demonstrated that soap operas, with their apparently stereotypical representations, had a feminist component. Postmodern feminists corrected this oversight and made "the uneasy connection between the pleasure of popular culture and the political aims of feminism" a "classic issue" (Zoonen 7).

The first three chapters in this volume approximate the "liberal feminist" approach, without some of the weaknesses of its earlier manifestations, thanks in part to their postmodern sensibilities. The chapters, moreover, demonstrate that this type of reading for feminists and media scholars is not "dated" but still inspiring, appropriate, and necessary. As the joke might go, just because feminists are paranoid does not mean that no one is out to get us.

First, the approach is well-suited to historical discussions, as in Jean Gregorek's "Horror Is What a Girl Would Feel: Narrative Erotics in Depression-Era Pulp Fiction." Through her analysis of female representation in the "pulps," Gregorek not only discovers female objectification and distortion but also how and to what end it occurs. In addition, through her observations regarding the nature of narrative, violence, pornography, sexual desire, and gender, her chapter has implications beyond the genre of pulp fiction.

Second, as the chapters by Carol Dietrich and Julia Keller indicate, the "liberal feminist" approach is essential, since many abuses by the media persist. While both essays avoid the simplistic dialectic of earlier essays, both authors clearly demonstrate the oppression and manipulation women face by a media that is still male-dominated. Dietrich's "Stalking Women's Stockings: Opaque Wisdom or Sheer Nonsense?" offers an encyclopedic look at hosiery ads, again offering an analysis of the methods, rhetoric, and means by which these ads construct femininity. Her readings uncover the technology of female representation in these ads and the effects the ads have upon audiences. Keller's "Getting Serious: Women at the Anchor Desk" exposes the realities of broadcast news for female journalists and uses the Connie Chung firing and the Jessica Savitch suicide as examples of the female news anchor image. To complicate her question of female representation, she also examines the made-for-television version of the Savitch story, thereby negotiating a feminist path through the media's hall of mirrors regarding female representation in terms of both a "real" television news event and a fictional biography of Savitch.

With the advent of postmodernism, theorists such as Jacques Lacan, Jacques Derrida, Guy Debord, and others identified the power relationships inherent to speculation, signification, and representation. Briefly, they argued that language was inherently dialectical and so oppression would more than likely occur even in subversive discourses such as feminism. Feminists like Luce Irigaray and Jane Gallop began reviewing feminist strategies. Irigaray, notably, took the practical effects of feminism into account: by challenging the status quo, feminists often wasted their energy and time; their attacks were often dismissed by the dominant culture.   While she tells women to "jam the patriarchal machinery" (78), she also tells them to "stop trying" (198–204). For her, the mere presence of women is enough to tear the apparently seamless fabric of patriarchal oppression. Other solutions such as a feminine writing appeared, but the crucial question that feminists felt compelled to address was the ability to make a difference—to be heard and taken seriously—in a dominant patriarchal culture, without reproducing the oppression of that culture.[9]

In Judith Roof's "Tracking Ida: The Bold, the Brash, and the Secondary in Hollywood Film," for example, she demonstrates how the character actresses Eve Arden and Mary Wickes create an alternative to the traditional Hollywood depiction of women.   In contrast to Laura Mulvey's important work on Hollywood cinema which demonstrates how women do not have a place in these narratives, Roof indicates a means for creating a feminist "stir" under the worst of conditions, a Hollywood romance. As Roof notes, two options for women are generally available: women are either good or bad girls; the good ones "get the guy" while the bad ones are left without a man. Eve Arden and Mary Wickes, however, find alternatives and ultimately serve as free female agents who may not play the leading role but make a feminist place for women through their performances and positions in the films' narratives.

Similarly, in "The Ideology of Heroism in *My Beautiful Laundrette*," Susan E. Lorsch argues that in a film about male homosexuality, female representation is not ignored but celebrated in ways unheard of in traditional cinema. Women are not merely objects of male desire but strong and even crucial to the film. Importantly, women's bodies are also represented in ways that violate patriarchal objectification.

Grace Epstein's "Resurrecting the *Ghost*: Innocence and Recuperation in American Popular Film" adds the dimension of race and ethnicity to the feminist analyses of popular Hollywood films. Using several recent films, particularly *Ghost*, Epstein illustrates how the films dismiss or ignore female desire. She also illustrates how films attempt to avoid racial bias but eventually participate in bigotry. In this way, her essay "deconstructs" claims of racial and female equality; but in the case of *Ghost*, it is not the narrative itself that highlights the film's sexism and racism—it is the performance by Whoopi Goldberg that calls the movie's ideological agenda into question.

One female reporter's rhetorical challenge to patriarchy and patriarchal discourse is the subject of James Boehnlein's "Meridel Le Sueur, Reportage, and the Cultural Situatedness of Her Rhetoric." Boehnlein shows how Le Sueur challenged patriarchal expectations through her independent life as a socialist and reporter, as well as her distinctive style, "reportage." This style, he argues, is particularly female and feminist, for it intermingles the personal with the political, thereby challenging a traditional patriarchal dialectic.

Given the fact that even waiters in restaurants have taken it upon themselves to monitor pregnant women's eating and drinking habits, the question of motherhood and abortion are this country's most volatile and important issues. "Maternity and the Masses: Drama, the Media, and Jane Martin's *Keely and Du*" shows how recent media coverage of the abortion debate does a disservice to both sides of this polarized issue. Jane Martin's recent play, however, shows the underside of the issue that the media will not depict.   Through her dramatization of nearly every significant argument of pro-life and pro-choice groups, the play creates an opportunity for significant debate, not sound bites or the pretense of conversation.

In the third and final section of the book, the chapters document an increasingly hostile attitude toward women in the media.   Susan Faludi's *Backlash* documents the movement through an exhaustive look at the media's representation of women.   While crucial, important, and perfectly timed, Faludi's book is quantitative rather than qualitative. The final chapters in this volume offer more detailed discussions regarding this backlash and its technology of oppression.   Further, these chapters imply some of the weaknesses we are beginning to see with postmodernism—that is, postmodernism's tendency to avoid or shy away from political action, to "sidestep the task of working through the constraining binary oppositions, including sexual difference" (Kaplan 4).

Katherine Burkman's "Misogyny and Misanthropy: Anita Hill and David Mamet," illustrates the unholy alliance between the media and drama in terms of sexual harassment, between art and public policy.   Supposedly written before the Hill-Thomas hearings, David Mamet's *Oleanna* promises to offer a balanced look at sexual harassment on a college campus.   But as Burkman illustrates, the play, like the trial, betrays its misogyny and that of our culture in significant ways through its narrative and the audience response to its production.

Rosaria Champagne's "Oprah Winfrey's *Scared Silent* and the Spectatorship of Incest" illustrates the pervasive and insidious distrust of women in culture through the response to incest narratives by such groups as the False Memory Foundation.   The determined and well-organized group represents one of the most institutionalized manifestations of the backlash against women and their claims of violation.   Champagne, however, singles out Oprah Winfrey's television documentary, *Scared Silent: Exposing and Ending Child Abuse,* as an effective and exemplary defense against such attacks.

Though very different, the final two chapters compare the ways women have historically and currently use the media or are used by it. Veronica Webb Leahy's "Women Who Have Dared but Deterred Other Women" exposes the thorny and frequently overlooked issue of women writing to oppress women. Through an analysis of eighteenth century writer Hannah More and contemporary Beverly LaHaye, Leahy examines the two authors' media tactics and their ability to market a message that they were both unable to live. That is, both women were highly successful hypocrites, able to sell women the idea of domesticity and subservience but who lived independent and surprisingly feminist lives.

Anne Marie Drew's "Elizabeth Tudor and Diana Spencer: Claiming an Image; Reclaiming a Life" began well before the death of Princess Diana in the summer of 1997. Consequently, she had to address the sad end to a woman who attempted to use the media to her advantage as successfully as her ancestor, Elizabeth Tudor. Sadly still, it appears that while the media may not have caused the Princess's death, as claimed by her brother and others, it did contribute to her untimely and tragic end. With these new developments, Drew's essay is especially timely and thought-provoking. The comparison between the two female royals remains, but the conclusion is all the more chilling as a result of Diana's death—in both cases, feminine sexuality is the issue which caused difficulty for both women, an issue that the media seems incapable of covering despite the centuries of progress in female equality.

In this way, this collection offers an eclectic and expansive view of the relationship between women and the media. The varying approaches and the identification of the three trends in feminist media studies also indicate that there are numerous means to combat the oppression inherent to the media's relationship to female representation. Importantly, the early chapters demonstrate that while liberal feminism may have had its weaknesses, identifying the oppression, analyzing it, and exposing it are still very valuable and worthwhile means of approaching feminist goals. Given the recent backlash, this collection might even serve as a call to action. At the very least, it is a reminder that feminism is still a viable and necessary movement in this country, one that should not be diluted but enhanced by greater understanding regarding culture, discourse, and the nature of representation.

NOTES

1. See Tania Modleski's Introduction to *Studies*, as well as the work of David Harvey.

2. See, for example, Woolf, Millet, D'Acci, De Lauretis (both books), Irigaray, Mulvey, Freedman, and Hart.

3. See, for example, Baehr and Dyer (*Boxed In*), De Lauretis (*Alice*), Mayne, Mumford, Press, Spigel.

4. Faludi coined the term, but George Grebner noted as early as 1978 that the media are staging "a counterattack on the women's movement as a social force for structural change. . . . And the gap between social reality and what is portrayed in the media is widening" (50).

5. Martha Banta's book is a significant study of the relationship between women and image during nineteenth century America, a time when "woman as type" was one of the "era's dominant cultural tics" (xxvii).

6. Perhaps one of the most surprising books is *Women in the Media*, a work commissioned by the United Nations which not only chronicles the distorted view of women presented by the media, but concludes that the tendency of the mass media to

reproduce stereotypes "is in direct contravention of the principles of the Declaration on the Elimination of Discrimination Against Women adopted by the General Assembly of the United Nations on 7 November 1967" (xx). The legal and international rhetoric illustrate power of and extent to which this feminist resurgence affected world policy.

Other examples of the "liberal feminist" approach include Ethel Strainchamps edition, which even includes an entire section on publishing firms and their attitudes towards women. Gaye Tuchman's collection includes the essay on magazines and identifies the treatment of women in the mass media as a "national social problem" (5). Josephine King and Mary Stott's volume is also extremely entertaining, particularly the remarks made by BBC executives to justify the exclusion of women from radio and television. Other representatives of liberal feminist approaches include Bentz, Dorenkamp, and Baehr's earlier works.

With *Turning It On*, an anthology of previously published essays, Elizabeth Baehr and her co-editor Ann Gray hope to move away from the weaknesses of liberal feminism which conclude that "males dominated media content," and one of the first essays in the book condemns liberal feminism's demonizing of men (Janus 5). Brown's collection also hopes to facilitate a new mode of approaching the question of female representation in the media by including chapters that reflect "resistance theory," a means of disrupting the dominant theory. Rowe's chapter also argues for the disruptive power of femininity, and Zoonen's book offers an overview of existing research, as well as the contributions of cultural theorists. She notes, "there seems to be no such person as the 'individual' communicator. She or he has to cooperate with colleagues, has to take specific needs, routines, traditions . . . into account, and is limited by the social, economic, and legal embedding of the media institution" (49). D'Acci uses a liberal feminist approach and television shows such as *Police Woman* to establish the difference *Cagney and Lacey* made in its fairly successful run as a feminist television program. Her book length study of the show, however, demonstrates that television production is fraught with compromise, dictatorial decisions from network sponsors and administrators, and so on, so the appearance of a show like *Cagney and Lacey* looks miraculous. Sochen is perhaps the most optimistic, arguing that strong, independent women do appear in the media, along with other less complimentary representations, of course. Rakow contributes to the discussion by including the issue of race in her collection.

Collections for classroom use or classroom development also abound. Works by Lont, Denmore, Dorenkamp, Baehr and Gray, and Creedon are all meant to help facilitate classes on women and the media. Lont is noteworthy because her contributors frequently include "do-it-yourself" exposes on the representation of women and the media (24).

7. Sochen, Zoonen, and Faludi are some of the few single-authored books on this subject. Faludi represents a liberal feminist approach, while Sochen and Zoonen tend toward postmodern.

8. Modleski's "Introduction" to *Studies in Entertainment* offers an overview regarding the various approaches to the media including the Frankfurt school and the Birmingham school which countered the monolithic representation of the media espoused by the Frankfurt school. As Modleski notes, "desirous of showing that people are not 'cultural dopes,' the Birmingham critics and their followers have attempted to demonstrate the complexity of the audience's potential response to mass culture" (xi).

9. See Jones.

BIBLIOGRAPHY

Baehr, Helen, ed. *Women and the Media.* New York: Pergamon Press, 1982.

Baehr, Helen, and Gillian Dyer, eds. *Boxed In: Women's Television.* New York: Pandora, 1987.

Baehr, Helen, and Ann Gray, eds. *Turning It On: A Reader in Women and the Media.* New York: St. Martin's Press, 1996.

Banta, Martha. *Imaging American Women: Idea and Ideals in Cultural History.* New York: Columbia University Press, 1987.

Bentz, Valerie Mahorta, and Philip Mayes, eds. *Women's Power and Roles as Portrayed in Visual Images of Women in the Arts and Mass Media.* Lewiston, N.Y.: Edwin Mellen Press, 1993.

Bordo, Susan. *Unbearable Weight: Feminism, Western Culture, and the Body.* Berkeley: University of California Press, 1993.

Brown, Mary Ellen, ed. *Television and Women's Culture: The Politics of the Popular.* London: Sage, 1990.

Carlson, Margaret. "Where Calvin Crossed the Line." *Time* 11 September 1995: 64.

Creedon, Pamela, ed. *Women in Mass Communication.* 2nd ed. Newbury Park, Calif.: Sage Publications, 1993.

D'Acci. Julie. *Defining Women: Television and the Case of "Cagney and Lacey."* Chapel Hill: University of North Carolina Press, 1994.

Debord, Guy. *The Society of Spectacle.* Trans. Donald Nicholson-Smith. New York: Zone Books, 1994.

De Lauretis, Teresa. *Alice Doesn't: Feminism, Semiotics, Cinema.* Bloomington: Indiana University Press, 1984.

De Lauretis, Teresa. *Technologies of Gender: Essays on Theory, Film, and Fiction.* Bloomington: Indiana University Press, 1987.

Denmore, Dana. *Syllabus Sourcebook on Media and Women.* Washington, D.C.: Women's Institute for Freedom of the Press, 1980.

Derrida, Jacques. *Of Grammatology.* Trans. Gayatri Chakravorty Spivak. Baltimore: Johns Hopkins University Press, 1976.

Dorenkamp, Angela, John F. McClymer, Mary M. Moynihan, and Arlene C. Vadum. *Images of Women in American Popular Culture.* New York: Harcourt Brace Jovanovich, 1985.

Faludi, Susan. *Backlash: The Undeclared War Against American Women.* Garden City, N.Y.: Doubleday, 1991

Freedman, Barbara. *Staging the Gaze: Postmodernism, Psychoanalysis, and Shakespearean Comedy.* Ithaca: Cornell University Press, 1991.

Gallop, Jane. *The Daughter's Seduction: Feminism and Psychoanalysis.* Ithaca: Cornell University Press, 1982.

Grebner, George. "The Dynamics of Cultural Resistance." *Hearth and Home: Images of Women in the Mass Media.* Ed. Gaye Tuchman et al. New York: Oxford University Press, 1978. 46–50.

Hart, Lynda. *Making a Spectacle: Feminist Essays on Contemporary Women's Theatre.* Ann Arbor: University of Michigan Press, 1992.

Harvey, David. *The Condition of Postmodernity.* Cambridge, England: Blackwell, 1990.

Howell, Sharon. *Reflections of Ourselves: The Mass Media and the Women's Movement, 1963 to Present.* New York: Peter Lang, 1990.

Ingrassia, Michelle. "Calvin's World." *Newsweek*, 11 September 1995: 60–65.

Irigaray, Luce. *This Sex Which Is Not One*. Trans. Catherine Porter. New York: Cornell University Press, 1985.

Jameson, Fredric. *Postmodernism, Or the Cultural Logic of Late Capitalism*. Durham: Duke University Press, 1994.

Janus, Noreen. "Research on Sex Roles in the Mass Media: Toward a Critical Approach." *Turning It On: A Reader in Women and the Media*. Ed. Helen Baehr and Gillian Dyer. New York: St. Martin's Press, 1996. 5–10.

Jones, Ann Rosalind. "Writing the Body: Toward and Understanding of *l'Ecriture feminine*." *The New Feminist Criticism: Essays on Women, Literature, and Theory*. New York: Pantheon, 1985. 361–78.

Kaplan, E. Ann. "Feminism/Oedipus/Postmodernism: The Case of MTV." *Turning It On: A Reader in Women and the Media*. Ed. Helen Baehr and Gillian Dyer. New York: St. Martin's Press, 1996. 3–43.

King, Josephine and Mary Stott, eds. *Is This Your Life? Images of Women in the Media*. London: Virago, 1977.

Lacan, Jacques. *Feminine Sexuality*. Ed. Juliet Mitchell and Jacqueline Rose. New York: Norton, 1982.

Lont, Cynthia. *Women and Media: Content, Careers, and Criticism*. New York: Wadsworth, 1995.

Mayne, Judith. *Cinema and Spectatorship*. New York: Routledge, 1993.

Millett, Kate. *Sexual Politics*. New York: Ballantine Books, 1970.

Modleski, Tania. *Loving with a Vengeance: Mass Produced Fantasies for Women*. New York: Routledge, 1990.

Modleski, Tania. *Studies in Entertainment: Critical Approaches to Mass Culture*. Bloomington: Indiana University Press, 1986.

Mulvey, Laura. "Visual Pleasure and Narrative Cinema." *Visual and Other Pleasures*. Bloomington: Indiana University Press, 1989. 14–28.

Mumford, Laura Stempel. *Love and Ideology in the Afternoon: Soap Opera, Women, and Television Genre*. Bloomington : Indiana University Press, 1995.

Press, Andrea Lee. *Women Watching Television: Gender, Class, and Generation in the American Television*. Philadelphia: University of Pennsylvania Press, 1991.

Rakow, Lana F., ed. *Women Making Meaning: New Feminist Directions in Communication*. New York: Routledge, 1992.

Root, Jane. *Pictures of Women: Sexuality*. London: Pandora Press, 1984.

Rowe, Kathleen K. "Roseanne: Unruly Woman as Domestic Goddess." *Turning It On: A Reader in Women and the Media*. Ed. Helen Baehr and Ann Gray. New York: St. Martin's Press, 1996. 81–86.

Sochen, June. *Enduring Values: Women in Popular Culture*. New York: Praeger, 1987.

Spigel, Lynn, and Denise Mann, eds. *Private Screenings: Television and the Female Consumer*. Minneapolis: University of Minnesota Press, 1992.

Strainchamps, Ethel, ed. *Rooms With No View: A Woman's Guide to the Man's World of the Media*. New York: Harper and Row, 1974.

Tuchman, Gaye, Arlene Kaplan Daniels, and James Benet. *Hearth and Home: Images of Women in the Mass Media*. New York: Oxford University Press, 1978.

Women in the Media. Paris, France: UNESCO, 1980.

Woolf, Viginia. *A Room of One's Own*. New York: Harcourt Brace Jovanovich, 1957.

Zoonen, Liesbet Van. *Feminist Media Studies*. Thousand Oaks, Calif.: Sage, 1994.

Section I

Manipulating Females: Negative Images of Women in the Media

Chapter 1

Horror Is What a Girl Would Feel: Narrative Erotics in Depression-Era Pulp Fiction

Jean Gregorek

Dear Editor:
Don't go soft on us. I want more blood and thunder than you've been printing lately. How about some more yarns like *The Bath of Blood*, that Appel wrote some time ago? That's the type of story I mean; something that'll really freeze my arteries, and jolt me from head to toe! Hard boiled? Perhaps, but after all, a story only lasts a few minutes, so why not put the steam on?

Yours truly,
Chuck
New York City

The fan letter above, which appeared in the "Chamber of Horrors" column (or, to the non-initiated, the Letters to the Editor) in the pulp magazine *Horror Stories*, offers some evidence of the physical responses to such tales which were registered—and valued—by the readers of this long-extinct popular subgenre of gothic fiction. Pulp magazines, named for the cheap pulpwood paper on which they were printed, were the predominant medium for formulaic genre fiction, including science fiction, detective fiction and westerns, between the World Wars.[1] First appearing on American newsstands in 1933, the line of "shudder pulps" or "weird menace pulps" advertised tales of "pulse-chilling terror" and "spine-tingling weirdness" to thrill-seeking readers. This pulp trend was initiated by *Dime Mystery Magazine* and was soon followed by Popular Publications' titles *Horror Stories*, *Terror Tales*, and *Thrilling Mysteries*, and then the even more explicit line by Culture Publications, *Spicy Mystery*; all told, fifteen different weird menace titles were published during the thirties (Jaffrey, *The Weirds* 9).[2] The shudder pulps created a successful new mix of suspense and sexual titillation, characterized by distinctive plots in which a strange, seemingly supernatural phenomenon turns out to have a perfectly rational explanation. This particular line of pulps was distinguished from its more popular and longer-lived competitor, *Weird Tales*, by the non-supernatural nature of the endings of its stories. With an all-male editorial staff and, with one or two exceptions toward the end of the decade, an entirely male crew of writers, these pulp magazines offered a predominantly male audience luridly illustrated short fiction for ten or fifteen cents an issue throughout the thirties. The heyday of the shudder pulps ended in 1941, in part as a result of threatened legal action from public censors scandalized by their sexual content.

The weirds' appeal to what Robert Kenneth Jones refers to as "pronounced sex sadism" has led to their characterization by mainstream (i.e., with no overtly feminist bent) specialists in popular culture as a kind of soft-core pornography for a more strictly regulated era. Fans of this genre openly recognized that in these stories "horror" serves as a pretext for explicit representations of sexual situations. Sheldon Jaffrey, the editor of two recent collections of shudder pulp stories, refers to them affectionately as "T and A for us" (*The Weirds* 8). And pulp historian Robert Kenneth Jones explains that after 1937 the sex sadism of the pulps became even more graphic, and that "many refer to this period as the high point in the magazines' careers" (3). As Jaffrey recounts this late period in the history of the shudder pulp:

During most of their publishing histories, the weird pulps' covers had been lurid, depicting women, in various states of undress, being menaced, in one way or another, by mad scientists and cretinous, cowled creatures. . . . The contents of the stories were not nearly as lurid, seldom completing the promises [!] offered by the covers. Injury rarely befell the threatened, voluptuous, innocent young things. Perhaps the mild nature of the fare and unfulfilled promises began to pall the readers. . . . Women who had been merely menaced in the past began to be brutally tortured and sadistically mutilated by bestial villains. It wasn't uncommon for the vilest and most sadistic details to be minutely described by the writers; women's breasts were routinely burned off with hot irons, whippings and flayings occurred routinely, and general madness appeared to be the order of the day. (*The Weirds* 8)

It may at first seem paradoxical that pulp fiction, acknowledged by its popularizers as heavily "sadistic" in content, provokes what appears to be a "masochistic" response on the part of the pulp reader. Yet many theorists of horror genres have pointed out that horror involves playing with the idea of relinquishing a sense of agency, a "thrilling exploration of what it would feel like to be on the brink of disaster, but momentarily deprived of active control" (Grixti 164). This experiment is of course carefully monitored by the limits of genre; the fantasy of the loss of power takes place in a context of presumed security. In this regard, horror can always be characterized as inciting a masochistic pleasure. To date, most scholars interested in the appeal of horror genres have focused on abstract sociological explanations—catharsis models, behaviorist models, games theories, media violence studies, and the like—which do not attend to psychosexual experience. But in Freud's well-known studies of male masochists, masochists seeking pleasure "invariably transfer themselves into the part of a woman; that is to say, their masochistic attitude coincides with a *feminine* one" ("A Child Is Being Beaten" 126). It therefore seems important to consider the role of gender in the construction and reception of horrific effects—in other words, the specifically gendered dynamics at work in the fantasies of the male horror aficionado.

Certainly the writer of the above letter describes his indulgence in horror fiction in sexualized terms: his every reading experience is an encounter with a *phallic* text: "don't go soft on me," he pleads. This kind of fictional pleasure "only lasts a few minutes"; it should therefore be as intense as possible: "put the steam on." Although we note that Chuck immediately attempts to emphasize his masculine toughness by defining himself as "hard-boiled," nevertheless his position with regard to the "jolts" of the text seems to be a passive and receptive one. Chuck describes a masochistic ritual in which the "masculine" text compels the hapless male reader to respond with an apparently much-relished mixture of desire and "terror."

D. A. Miller proves a noteworthy exception to the universalizing approaches to horror genres. As Miller notes, the mark of a successful horror story is the effect registered on the body of the reader; particularly, as the editors hoped, the impact on the reader's "pulse." (A typical pulp blurb addresses this issue directly: "a pulse-speeding mystery-terror novelette of unearthly menace!") Exploring the complicated ways in which Collins's sensation novel triggers, and then "manages," homosexual panic in the nineteenth-century male reader, Miller observes that these male readers of sensation fiction deliberately placed themselves in a metaphorically feminized reading position. Miller assumes that this sensational appeal to gender dysphoria induced a sustained anxiety or "nervousness" which became part of the overall thrill of the Victorian reading experience: "The drama in which the novel writes its reader turns on the disjunction between his allegedly masculine gender identification and his effectively feminine gender identification (as a creature of the 'nerves'): with the result that his experience of sensation must include his panic at having the experience at all" (163).

While pleasure of any kind may appear natural and spontaneous, film theorists Linda Williams and Richard Dyer have noted that genres aimed primarily at eliciting visceral reactions and "moving the body"—pornography, along with "thrillers, weepies, and low comedy"—have not been fully recognized as historical phenomena with specific and diverse forms of address. As they point out, the very fact that pornography has such a variable history shows that forms of "excitement and desire are mutable, constructed, cultural" ("Idol" 49). It is not my intention to attempt any simple or definitive definition of the highly contested term "pornography" in this essay; instead I will draw upon Annette Kuhn's psychoanalytic observation that "pornography produces meanings pivoting on sexual difference" (qtd. in Williams 30) and state that in their formulaic obsession with proving that men are not women, discussed below, as well as in their open appeal to moving the body of the reader, the shudder pulps do subscribe to Williams's conception of the "pornographic." Direct descendants of the Victorian illustrated papers and Penny Dreadfuls, the shudder pulps occupy a generic niche which combines elements of detective fiction, sensation fiction, and what we could now describe as soft-core print pornography.[3] This essay will seek to investigate the pleasures of these peculiar Depression-era texts—Chuck's particular kind of pleasure—and further, work to uncover what constitutes "terror" in these narratives, along with the ideological uses to which this terror is being put. I claim that while these texts offer a surprising multiplicity of perverse pleasures, neither pleasure nor perversion can here be unproblematically translated into a progressive sexual liberationist agenda, as these texts ultimately operate in the service of the reactionary economic forces that were changing the shape of the U.S. workforce in the 1930s.

Perhaps the most clear-cut example of the typical shudder-pulp formula is found in a tale called "Dance of the Bloodless Ones" (1937).[4] In this first-person narrative, several young American couples are vacationing on a remote island inhabited only by Portuguese fishermen. Their hoped-for idyll turns into a harrowing nightmare when they are menaced by a slimy and foul-smelling octopus monster. The creature first murders all of the American women, mutilating their faces horribly with its beak; later it steals the naked female corpses in order to bring them back to life and romp on the beach with them to the ostensible horror and shame of the American men. The once demure wives, now apparently transformed into sex-crazed zombies, are whipped into a lascivious frenzy by the octopus monster's tentacles. This part of the text is of course accompanied by illustrations. By the end of the story, the monster turns out to be the device of a young college-educated Portuguese fisherman in a rubber octopus suit. Corrupted by a mixture of genetic deficiency and higher education (one wonders which did more) the evil Portuguese youth had developed this elaborate plot in order to scare the Americans off the island so that he could begin to mine the valuable tungsten ore with which the island turns out to be laden. He had actually kidnapped the wives, rather than killing them, and replaced their "bodies" with the corpses of Portuguese village girls who had recently died, savagely and completely mutilating their faces so that the switch would not be noticed. Through the use of mysterious mind-altering drugs, he had managed to evoke "unnatural sex impulses" in the captive women and force them, through "the power of suggestion," to take part in lewd dances. When the drug wears off, they cannot remember any of this, and so cannot be held responsible for their shocking behavior. Ultimately, the sinister Portuguese threat is destroyed and all American husbands and wives are happily reunited.

This formulaic plot is enacted repeatedly in the pulps with local and supernatural variations. In the story "White Mother of Shadows" (1941), voodoo demons take the place of the octopus monster and Haitians substitute for

Portuguese. The secret villain turns out to be a white plantation foreman cleverly manipulating the natives, as persons of African descent are apparently beyond the realm of believability in the minds of pulp writers as the inventors of complicated evil plots. In "A Beast is Born" (1940), a similar scenario is played out in an asylum for "mental unfortunates," also described as "mewling cretins," who are being guided by a diabolical ward attendant in a hairy suit. An interesting plot twist occurs in "Mistress of the Blood Drinkers" (1940) in which a seemingly fatherly family doctor, with the eager assistance of an "oriental temptress," uses marijuana to drug a loving husband into a murderous frenzy and attempts to induce him to kill his own wife and drink her blood; fortunately the wife escapes at the last minute and the hero vents his blood lust on the treacherous doctor and a "brutish" Mongolian servant instead. In all cases, the villain, once unmasked, turns out to have purely economic motives for his elaborate scheme of terror: money or power is his real object.

These cartoonish stories are riddled with the most flagrant contradictions. For example, the exotic male Other is intellectually inferior and sub-human, yet also diabolically clever and superhumanly powerful. This racial or ethnic Other is the antithesis of the white male, yet his desires are exactly the same—wealth and status, marked by the acquisition of a young white female. And the terrifying spectre of the anarchic, uncontrollable (yet, often, secretly controlled) mob of slaves, workers, or "mewling cretins" which makes its appearance in many popular horror films of the twenties and thirties (*Metropolis*, 1926; *Frankenstein*, 1931; *Freaks*, 1932) is frequently raised in these narratives as well.

Since, as we always learn, the villain's real motives are not sexual, but pecuniary, the desire for the female is merely a secondary consideration, her ravishing just a "perk." The real contest lies between the two males, and the body of the female absorbs the violent impulses which are, it turns out, directed at the hero. However, the plot device of torture is almost exclusively reserved for the female body. Pulp narratives invariably revolve around the spectacle of female bondage and rape:

In the shadows, two figures gleamed, luminously white. I cried out in sheer horror at the sight of them . . . they were women, nude, bound upright to stone pillars.

One of them was Bonny. Bands of adhesive covered her mouth. Had I found her—too late? I went crazy mad, tried to force the steel bars that kept me from her, shouted insane challenges to the thing that had done this to us. . . .

The butler said, "Sir, the master wishes you to witness an exhibition. He trusts it will bring you around to his way of thinking." He retreated, and while my heart went berserk in my throat, I saw him unbind one of the struggling nude figures, and strap her to the plain wooden chair. ("Corpses on Parade"192–193)

While the typical pulp plot relies on the spectacle of the vulnerable female, the male body may be rendered temporarily impotent through such generic strategies as bondage or a different, less sexualized kind of penetration—the injection of a mysteriously paralyzing drug:

> Slowly he moved his right hand along the seat to where the thing had pricked his leg. His fingers touched something small and cylindrical. For thirty seconds John Hewitt sat without moving, frozen by abject terror. Horror such as he had never known flooded his body. He knew what the thing beneath his hand was even before he snapped on the dash-light.
>
> Strapped to the seat with black adhesive, the point raised so that it had jabbed his leg when he slid inside, was a hypodermic. ("The Tongueless Horror" 122)

The male reader is then "terrorized" in three ways: through immediate identification with the immobilized hero who is forced to watch his beloved tortured by the sadist; by an indirect identification with the body of the beloved who serves to absorb the violence that is always aimed, in reality, at him, and by the nerve-wracking suspense of reading of horror fiction itself.

A recurring assumption in these texts is that masculinity, far from having a masochistic component, is in fact inherently sadistic. As in much detective fiction, male sexuality, even the hero's, has a dangerous, brutal edge. Male sexuality always seems to be at the risk of becoming "degenerate," as these stories abound with characters who are described as sexual "deviants." The hero must be distinguished from more threatening males, and placed temporarily at their mercy—yet not seem permanently "unsexed." In "Mistress of the Blood-Drinkers," his overtly violent sexual desires are depicted as having been artificially aroused through the machinations of the villain, who eventually receives the brunt of the hero's righteous anger. The blurring between sadism and masculinity allows for ample play with "sex sadism": the sexual nature of female victimization clearly separates the female and male characters, and the villain is a rapist and torturer whereas the husband merely has violent reactions when drugged or threatened. The narratives also display an obsessive interest in characters known to be guilty of "sex crimes." In "The Mole Men Want Your Eyes" (1938), hardly anyone in the story escapes this charge; the story includes a village "idiot," two doctors, a criminologist, and a howling horde of naked lunatics who are all described as "sexual degenerates," as well as a federal agent who is a suspected "pervert." In these stories the potentially ambiguous term "degenerate" means "rapist"—never, for example, "male homosexual": the men of the town fear for their "sisters, wives, and sweethearts," not themselves. It then becomes the function of these narratives to sort out, not the gays from the straights, but the decent guys from the sex sadists. However, the narratives derive much of their suspense from the assumption that male sexuality is constituted along a continuum of sadism, and that these categories are, in fact, indistinguishable.

Another noteworthy contradiction occurs in the space between the bulk of the narrative and the formulaic ending. The rational explanation at the end of the story is not only predictable, it is always ridiculously far-fetched and always underemphasized. The solution is usually wrapped up in a paragraph or two, inevitably leaving glaring holes and many inconsistencies. While some editors, as well as some readers, regard such incomplete resolutions merely as poor storytelling, they are of course a standard feature of gothic genres; in the weirds, a tremendous gap exists between the psychic reality of the conflict with the supernatural horror and the patched-up "real" ending. This distance is, in fact, celebrated even when ostensibly criticized. Jaffery informs us that a particularly prolific pulp writer was "highly thought of by the editors of the weirds . . . notwithstanding his wild flights of fancy when resolving his stories, often ignoring plausible resolutions just to get the job done" (Jaffrey, *The Weirds* 66).

And while the editor-in-chief of the shudder pulps actually listed "credibility" as one of the requirements for the stories published in his magazines, his definition of credibility seems about as flexible as that used for "historical authenticity" in romance fiction. A nod in that direction is all that is required, for the interest of most readers clearly lies elsewhere. Obviously, credibility is in the eye of the beholder; however, even if one suspends disbelief long enough to accept the probability of a man sneaking around unnoticed wearing a cumbrous and smelly octopus suit, the possibility of husbands mistaking the naked bodies of dead Portuguese women for their own wives, especially when so much else in the story rests on the visibility of ethnic difference, seems singularly problematic. In these tales only protagonists and antagonists are constructed as ethnically marked, while "wives" figure merely as token objects of exchange.

However implausible, the economic rationale for the sadism described insures that any sense of paranoia is located on a different plane by the end of the story, transferring the sexual anxieties raised to a safer, more externalized province. These texts are probably unique in the way that their formulaic plots deliberately displace psychosexual anxieties with those of class. As we have seen, the narratives shift from an eroticized drama of sex sadism to an open contest between men, a "fair fight" in which the best man always wins. The private anxieties of the stories are brought into the arena of public competition—the threat is not to the hero's or reader's *body*, but merely to his status, a class status which in a competitive society is of course constituted by the fact that other men covet it. The "real" enemy is always the man who wants to *be* the hero. Thus what seems to be a personal threat is in fact a complimentary affirmation of the hero's social power.

But it is worth noting that this "rational" explanation is never very detailed or very convincing. While these male gothics pretend to be responding to and neutralizing the anxieties caused by the danger of the male rival, as they invoke these psychic perils they refuse to provide a fully worked out narrative resolution. It seems that in terms of unconscious fears, these fictions provoke and reinforce more anxieties about masculinity than they relieve. The successful male gothic is one in which the reader is left more paranoid, uneasier, than before; and this left-over paranoia is directed, at the end of the narrative, toward other males.

Pulp fantasies readily and, one suspects, given the time period, quite consciously, lend themselves to a kind of popularized Freudian analysis. There is no question that these texts allow the guiltless expression of hostility toward women, especially "sisters, wives, and sweethearts"; an aggression which the male reader, at the story's conclusion, can safely disavow. The blurb from "Sleep With Me—And Death" will stand as a particularly unsubtle example: "I could no longer deny that I was a beast . . . that my soul was black with murder-lust! . . . the bruised and torn flesh of my young wife in the next room—was that not evidence enough?" But the fact that the real enemy is always a male, never a female or a supernatural force, demonstrates the homosocial dynamics of the rivalry here; according to Freud, "patients suffering from paranoia are struggling against an intensification of their homosexual trends, this pointing back to a narcissistic object-choice" ("A Case of Paranoia"). And these suspenseful stories are virtual parables of castration anxiety: the plots often literally translate "castrated" and "castrating" Medusa-figures of female sexuality, appearing as Octopus monsters or hairy beasts, into something that can be recognized and defeated. A close examination of the hairy monster inevitably reveals a penis—"Woman," once exposed, is always found to be a Man.

Both Linda Williams and Gertrud Koch assume that classic Freudian castration anxiety lurks behind much heterosexual pornography and in fact dictates the formal characteristics of the recently-evolved pornographic film. In Koch's analysis, the almost mandatory close-up of the ejaculating penis, or "money shot," in hard core films is required for male viewing pleasure as the sight of the penis is a psychologically reassuring verification of intactness after an encounter with a vagina, imagined as capable of permanently devouring the male organ (26).[5] The anxieties which later became a structural feature of pornographic film can also perhaps be located in forms of print media equally motivated by the need to articulate and inscribe sexual difference. Yet I would insist that specific social and historical factors, as well as the dynamics of reader response, need to be taken into account alongside manifest Freudian content which registers a psychic fear of castration. It is my contention that the pulps' generic reliance upon the depiction of female rape and male immobilization, combined with the evidence of Chuck's letter, leads us back to a more or less conscious obsession with male *penetration* as the recurring anxiety which underlies these particular "pornographic" texts.

The bulk of twentieth century pornography offers a simple, morphological version of masculine sexuality—"real" men are not penetrated, they do the penetrating. Commercial images of the *Penthouse-Gallery-Hustler* type deliberately situate the male consumer in a masterful, voyeuristic subject position. Mass-produced sexually explicit fantasies of male powerlessness are in fact relatively rare and still largely confined to underground subcultural publications. Critic David Pendleton links the contemporary preoccupation with such masterful images, and more specifically, the denial of the possibility of male penetration with its implications of "feminization," to the need to uphold an increasingly precarious sense of modern male selfhood. In his view, the lack of such representations in straight male porn perpetuates a twentieth-century "myth of masculine inviolability."[6] Looking at pornographic representations from a historical perspective, he notes that fear of penetration has not always been characteristic of male erotic literature, and that its absence is a fairly recent phenomenon.   The penetration of males was a mainstay of Victorian pornography, and Steven Marcus's famous study, *The Other Victorians*, amply documents the popularity of a range of fantasies of male sexual submissiveness in the nineteenth century: "sado-masochistic literature, and particularly the literature of passive flagellation, was produced in great quantities," posing a striking contrast to standard Victorian ideals of manly "solidity, certitude of self, singleness of being" (261–263).   However, most of the erotic scenarios Pendleton and Marcus describe are fantasies of male submission to women, and their relative availability suggests that such masochistic fantasies were—and perhaps remain—more permissible, more within the sphere of what can be articulated, than fantasies of male sexual submission to other men.

Writing in 1937, Freud notes that desires for humiliation and submissiveness are not uncommon among his male patients, who often display a "masochistic attitude—a state that amounts to bondage—towards women," yet what they reject most energetically is "not passivity in general, but passivity towards a male" ("Analysis Terminable" 252n). According to Freud, the transferential relationship intrinsic to the process of analysis itself is likely to founder on the nearly-insurmountable obstacle of male resistance to assuming the "feminized" position of a subordinate attitude toward other men. For many of Freud's male patients, this passive identity is the subject-position they refuse most adamantly, and therefore they remain impervious to attempts at analysis: "At no other point in one's analytic work does one suffer more from an oppressive feeling that all one's repeated efforts have been in vain . . . than when one is seeking to convince a man that a passive attitude to men does not always signify castration and that it is indispensible in many relationships in life" (252). Here we have arrived at an impasse involving the very definition of masculinity; for many men, a successfully-achieved masculine identification cannot consciously tolerate a deferential or passive relation to other men and still consider itself "masculine."   Freud goes on to entertain the possibility that the vehemence of this response derives from its roots in male biology: "We often have the impression that with . . . the masculine protest we have penetrated through all the psychological strata and have reached bedrock" (252).

It is not necessary to follow Freud to such essentialist conclusions to agree that this is a particularly fraught area of male psychology—indeed, the very strength of the masculine protest would seem to indicate the presence of an extreme psychic need which is all the more resistant to conscious verbalization. I would like to note that in Freud's own account, everyday social situations of power inequity, such as those between patient and therapist, and by implication, worker and boss, become those most likely to trigger the state of contradiction that results in the refusal to acknowledge the possibility of submission. There is no reason to suppose that such troublesome and conflicted impulses don't exist in 'normal' men, nor that they lie outside of the parameters of 'normal' heterosexual masculinity. To attempt to locate traces of such contradictory desires and resistances in the realm of popular culture we need to look, not to the idealized fantasy content of mainstream pornographic film or magazines, but perhaps to less obvious places—for example, horror genres. Here, the masochistic and somatic pleasures of reading sensation fiction undermine, at least temporarily, the ideal of male invulnerability and self-control. As D. A. Miller comments:

If every sensation novel necessarily provides an interpretation of the sensations to which it gives rise in its readers, the immediacy of these sensations can also be counted on to *disown* such an interpretation. It may even be that the nonrecognition that thus obtains between our sensations and their narrative thematization allows the sensation novel to "say" certain things for which our culture—at least at its popular levels—has yet to develop another language. (148)

It seems relatively easy, after Eve Sedgwick's pioneering work in *Between Men*, to read what pulp fiction is leaving unsaid as the equally homosocial and homophobic impulses through which males both fear and desire other males ("For a man to be a man's man is separated only by an invisible, carefully blurred, always-already-crossed line from being 'interested in men'"); and more specifically, that in a culture fractured by race and class, extra-charged currents of unconscious fear and desire run across these boundaries (89). The chief pleasures of these texts circle around a rape fantasy that permits men to play with dominant, submissive, and voyeuristic positions; yet these erotic scenarios always take place from the organizing standpoint of the white middle-class male subject, and ultimately at the expense of the defeated exotic Other.

If the meaning of masculinity in this culture is to *not* be feminine, and to be feminine is, as Catherine MacKinnon implies, to be "rapable,"[7] then these texts deliberately toy with the idea that the masculine reader can also be vulnerable to forcible penetration. The male reader is constantly being "feminized" by physical reminders that he, too, is susceptible to the shocks administered by the terrorizing text. On the conscious level, only the female body is dramatized as the object of assault and sexual penetration—and this is clearly a point of textual obsession. The male reader, however, cannot escape some degree of more or less conscious fear of a similar assault on bodily integrity. What Miller claims for readers of nineteenth-century sensation fiction seems to apply equally to readers of twentieth-century gothics: these texts not only articulate a deep-rooted fear of "female" sexuality, they inscribe this fear of the woman-in-man into the body of the reader; they construct the very dynamics of reading in terms which replicate the narrative thematic. The masochistic reader is pleasurably menaced by the threat of the "feminine" both literally and figuratively, and from within and without.

Interestingly, there is a tacit acknowledgement of this "feminized" reading position in the texts themselves, where moments of gender confusion can occasionally be observed. Popular Publications editor-in-chief Rogers Terrill described the concept of "horror" for his writing staff in an oft-quoted official definition which, oddly, depended upon a conception of a *female* reader/spectator, despite the fact that the vast majority of his readers were male: "Horror is what a girl would feel in watching something from a safe distance. Terror is what she would feel if she knew she were the next victim" (qtd. in Jones 4). Built into the genre from its inception, then, is the assumption that the paradigmatic victim of "terror" is female; to be "terrorized" is to be feminized. The title of the pulp story, "The Mole Men Want Your Eyes," directly addresses the male reader, and draws upon well-known castration imagery; however, in the story, the mole men want only female eyes. The male reader is here clearly invited to take the female position, and this creates a double-edged fantasy which allows the reader to participate vicariously in the scenes of rape and torture of young girls, and simultaneously to fear for his own eyes/genitals. Again, in the conclusion of "Dance of the Bloodless Ones," a similar kind of figurative slippage occurs: "But some nights, I feel her cuddle closer to me and then as she winds her arms tighter around my neck, I know that she is dreaming of the crawling touch of those black tentacles over her flesh." Here the woman-as-octopus is momentarily resurrected, and the husband is her victim as she clings threateningly to his neck. Yet again, in the story only women are the desired prey of the octopus monster; and, as the octopus is "really" a man in disguise, the homoerotic connotations seem unavoidable.

Despite these disquieting alternations of gender which take place almost subliminally, the disjunction between the "masculine" weird stories reader and the "feminine" position of reading horror and sensation fiction necessitates an adherence to strictly defined sexual boundaries on the surface of the stories. The possibility of male rape is never overtly raised although there are occasional "feminized" male characters who endure symbolic mutilation (Danny in "The Mole Men Want Your Eyes" is a "mentally deficient" boy whose eyes are cut out). This is because the homosocial thematics of the stories are so deeply ingrained: ever-present in the dynamics of reading horror itself, the possibility of men being penetrated for pleasure must be banished completely from the surface of the text. Ultimately these texts perform a metaphoric ritual of opening up the male body only to seal it off again. Other men exist only as enemies, and women, after all, must be proved safely different. At the end of each narrative, the heterosexual couple, defined as phallic hero with devoted wife, stand alone.

"Terror," as it is constructed in the shudder pulps can thus be loosely defined as "fear of rape" or fear of "rapability." This fear appears to carry more complex unconscious psychological anxieties for male subjects than for females as it inverts normative sexuality and gender roles, rather than corresponding to them as it does in the case of women—traditional constructions of femininity are, according to MacKinnon, largely coterminous with vulnerability. This is not to say that rape and its constant threat are not terrifying to women, but that this threat does not involve the experience of gender dysphoria, which only shows the extent of the damage of a sexist and heterosexist society. It therefore seems important to highlight the implications of this kind of fantasy for women; the most effective and compelling vehicle for the fantasy of male powerlessness turns out to be the *female* body.

While women were and remain the prototypical victims of "terror," increasingly in late twentieth-century culture, "terror" is everywhere. "Horror" and "terror" have steadily come to be almost synonymous with sexual violation, and this phenomenon has accelerated in recent years. The shudder-pulp definition of "horror" is thus revealing in that it sheds some light on the rather bizarre preoccupation of contemporary U.S. society with representations of female rape—and, with very few exceptions, its absolute ban on representations of male rape—and why menaced women are so regularly splashed across movie screens, billboards, print advertising, and television sets every evening. If males are seeking out "what a girl might feel," then we need to consider the possibility that this disturbing deluge may have as much to do with currently "unspeakable" male desires for other men as well as an ahistorical, generalized concept of male misogyny.

With our unprecedented national emphasis on privacy, self-reliance, and self-determination, the traditionally male model of the inviolable self seems as entrenched as ever as an American ideal. However, when, as Freud has asserted in *The History of Sexuality*, sex comes to be regarded as "that secret which seems to underlie all that we are" (155), then sexual attack serves to symbolize the most utterly destructive and ultimately terrifying threat. In its powerful negation of the autonomy of self, sexual assault seems a particularly charged relation to American individualism. Thus rape has emerged as a sensational and sensationalizing metaphor for any abuse of power; it has taken on a discursive life of its own far removed from the specific and widespread practice of sexual violence. Rape-as-victimization can be traced in the rhetoric of both left and right, as the term is now shorthand for any imposition of lawless force upon a "feminized" victim. Examples abound: "The Rape of Kuwait," "The Rape of Bosnia," the "rape" of the Earth. Yet even as the casual use of rape metaphors trivializes the reality of sexual assault, its very frequency points to a newly-heightened level of cultural susceptibility to such "terrors."

Certainly the closeted rape fantasies of 1930s pulp fiction seem ripe for a contemporary queer reading as they deliberately flirt with expressions of male same-sex attraction, if in a demonized and disguised form. And the abundant absurdities and hyperbolic rhetoric of these stories undoubtedly lend them a kitschy appeal.   However, "queer" as these texts are, there is nothing progressive about them—despite their playfulness, that textual play is based upon premises which are fundamentally misogynist. In this regard these texts may serve as a classic example of how a violation of strict norms of heterosexuality often necessitates maintaining and policing rigid concepts of gender roles. The flirtation with male masochism in these narratives becomes possible in the first place because 1) it is displaced onto female bodies, thus maintaining the myth that females are the more "natural" victims and 2) it is done in the service of re-establishing a heterosexual norm through the mobilization of hostility and paranoia towards males of other races, ethnicities, and social classes.[8] The temporary destabilization of heteronormativity that occurs in this context can hardly be considered subversive. As Sedgwick reminds us, to understand the seemingly axiomatic binary oppositions of heterosexual/homosexual and feminine/masculine as "irresolvably unstable is not, however, to understand them as inefficacious or innocuous" (*Epistemology* 10).

And we should not forget that these particular rape fantasies surfaced during the worst period of the Great Depression, when unemployment was in the millions and the potential for revolutionary activity was real; when the structure of the most male work required a more complex level of cooperation among men; when the idea of the rugged, self-made individual was taking a beating; when the damaged self-image of American masculinity needed reinforcing but in such a way that was not genuinely threatening to the state apparatus or the interests of capital. One could hypothesize that as Fordist practices in this country dramatically reorganized patterns of work and leisure time, male bonds came under increasing scrutiny. A major shift implemented by bureaucratic modern societies in the service of industrial efficiency, according to Foucault, was the problematizing of male comradeship, a social category which came to be perceived as "inimical to the smooth functioning of institutions—the army, bureaucracy, administration, universities, schools—which therefore attempted 'to diminish, or minimize, the affectional relations.'" [9] Craig Owens points to the most successful weapon in this long campaign against male friendship: homophobia, "the imputing of a homosexual motive to every male relationship" (230–231). In a general sense, much so-called escapist popular culture aimed at men in this century could be said to further facilitate this nineteenth-century movement away from male affectional bonds, replacing them with overtly homophobic constructions.

One can readily observe that many such cultural productions function to allow the simultaneous expression of intra-gender hostility and desire, sports being the most obvious example.   And like sports, popular pulp fiction ultimately justifies the existence of individual "winners" and "losers" in a cutthroat, post-Darwinian world.   As we have seen, the hero in these texts is nearly always portrayed as the upwardly mobile middle-level manager who is in some way being threatened by his subordinates.   The pulps target other aspiring males, rather than the vicissitudes of a capitalist economy, as the most immediate challenge to the middle-class way of life.   In this analysis, pulp fiction becomes just one of a variety of mass cultural apparatuses which operated to preclude collective social and political action among men during a potentially revolutionary period.   Such "titillating" fictions, far from being emancipated flashes of healthy eroticism in a bleak landscape of sexual repression, as many commentators assert,[10] are more accurately characterized as mechanisms for narrating the relationships of individual males to each other in terms of competition rather than in terms of desire, cooperation, or friendship.

The rise of pulp fiction in fact helps to mark the beginning of a new era of consumer culture.   The pulps were, after all, a formative and transitional chapter in the advent of what Stephen Heath calls the culture of the "novelistic," of mass-produced and commodified fictions, a society largely regulated by the "constant narration of the social relations of individuals" and the invention of a narrative "fabrication of sexuality" on a mass scale.[11]   Following Heath, Miller points out that the novel and the novelistic as cultural institutions work to construct the illusion of bourgeois private space, an exclusive realm of personal feelings and motivations which exist apart from the "contaminations" of the economic and the political (162).   Yet this private space is, of course, anything but divorced from the ideological, as the whole notion of "horror" demonstrates.   The success of the strategies of popular horror depend upon an ability to mobilize anxieties on a mass scale, not an individual one.   In these texts, the notion of a protected private sphere (a man's home is his castle, a haven in a heartless world, etc.) so necessary to the preservation of a capitalist regime, is threatened with violation again and again, and this violation is equated with and figured by sexual violation.   These texts "frighten" by suggesting that masculinity is not protection enough by insinuating that privacy is never absolute.   But this illusory privacy is of course both constructed by, and already penetrated by, mass culture itself.[12]

NOTES

1.   While an exact profile of the overall pulp readership is difficult to determine, some revealing details emerged from the industry itself: one publisher calculated that 125 different pulp titles were shipped to 10,000,000 fans a year in the mid-thirties (qtd. in Peterson 309).   And one experienced editor noted that, in his observation, the largest volume of pulp sales was in the Middle West, the typical pulp reader was not college educated, and that many were juveniles, although the general editorial rule was to assume "a juvenile anywhere from sixteen to sixty" (Hersey 6).

2. For a useful survey of the history of various weird menace pulps, see Weinberg (370–397).

3. I would like to stress that my provisional use of the term "pornography" will here refer only to heterosexual male porn; I am not discussing erotic materials produced by or addressed to gay or lesbian audiences. Some interesting speculations as to narrative differences between gay and straight male porn can be found in Pendleton and Dyer.

4. All pulp fiction referred to in this essay come from Jaffrey's edition, *Selected Tales of Grim and Grue.*

5. Koch (26). Koch observes that the expectations of the 'ideal' heterosexual encounter, which would involve ejaculation inside the female body, are here superseded by castration anxiety. See also Linda Williams's *Hard Core* for a similar discussion.

6. Pendleton, (160–161); see also Leo Bersani (197–222). Bersani's analysis critiques both the homophobic and misogynist cultural impulses which recoil from "the seductive and intolerable image of a grown man, legs high in the air, unable to refuse the suicidal ecstasy of being a woman" (212) and leads him to recommend gay male sex, and particularly the position of 'bottom' in anal penetration, as a deliberately anti-phallocentric practice: "The self is a practical convenience; promoted to the status of an ethical ideal, it is a sanction for violence. . . . Male homosexuality advertises the risk of the sexual itself as the risk of self-dismissal, of *losing sight* of the self, and in so doing it proposes and dangerously represents *jouissance* as a mode of ascesis" (222).

7. MacKinnon notes, "Vulnerability means the appearance/reality of easy sexual access; passivity means receptivity and disabled resistance, enforced by trained physical weakness; softness means pregnability by something hard. . . . Masochism means that pleasure in violation becomes her sensuality." Whether or not one accepts the inevitability of MacKinnon's admittedly sweeping generalizations that male sexuality is defined through sexual domination and female sexuality through sexual subordination, there still seems to me to be some descriptive and diagnostic force to MacKinnon's work. However, the determinist elements of her views have now been subject to a number of critiques: see for one of many recent examples, Judith Butler's Chapter "Critically Queer" in *Bodies That Matter: On the Discursive Limits of "Sex."*

8. For a useful and extremely pertinent discussion of the nearsightedness of celebrating the liberatory potential of male masochism, see Tania Modleski's critique of Bersani in her chapter, "Lethal Bodies," in *Feminism Without Women* in which she notes that "masochism in the *guise* of powerlessness is, I have argued, frequently the luxury of empowered beings . . . social power and sexual humiliation may coexist quite easily" (149).

9. Foucault, qtd. in Owens (230). It should perhaps be noted that while Foucault locates this cultural break primarily in the late eighteenth century, Owens, following Eve Sedgwick, believes that this tactic of systematically deploying homophobia as a tool of social regulation was ongoing throughout the nineteenth century and continues into the present day.

10. Jaffery, his introduction to *The Weirds* (8–9); see also Tony Goodstone, (141). An identical claim, similarly based on the catharsis model, is made for horror genres in general by Stephen King in his influential *Danse Macabre* (47; 203–205). It seems worth emphasizing again that the repressed emotions being "liberated" in all of these essays are inevitably constituted as sadistic ones.

11. Heath (85). According to Heath, the novelistic is characterized by "the commodification of a phallocentric sexuality in which woman remains both object and

other." One could find few more blatant examples of this historical phenomenon that the weird menace pulps.

12. Many thanks to Ann C. Hall, Susan Ritchie, and Francesca Sawaya for their patient reading of drafts of this essay; and special thanks to Joel Woller for introducing me to "the Weirds."

BIBLIOGRAPHY

Bersani, Leo. "Is the Rectum a Grave?" *October* 43 (1987): 197–222.

Butler, Judith. *Bodies That Matter: On the Discursive Limits of "Sex."* New York: Routledge, 1993.

Dyer, Richard. *Only Entertainment.* London: Routledge, 1992.

Dyer, Richard. "Idol Thoughts: Orgasm and Self-reflexivity in Gay Pornography." *Critical Inquiry* 36 (1994): 50–62.

Foucault, Michel. *The History of Sexuality Vol 1.* Trans. Robert Hurley. New York: Vintage, 1980.

Freud, Sigmund. "A Case of Paranoia Running Counter to the Psychoanalytical Theory of the Disease." *Sexuality and the Psychology of Love.* Ed. Philip Rieff. New York: Collier Books, 1963. 97–106.

Freud, Sigmund. "A Child Is Being Beaten." *Sexuality and the Psychology of Love.* Ed. Philip Rieff. New York: Collier Books, 1963. 107–132.

Freud, Sigmund. "Analysis Terminable and Interminable" in *The Standard Edition of the Complete Psychological Works of Sigmund Freud* (24 vols.). London: The Hogarth Press and Institute of Psychoanalysis, 1964. Vol.XXIII. 216–243.

Goodstone, Tony, ed. *The Pulps: Fifty Years of American Pop Culture.* New York: Bonanza Books, 1970.

Grixti, Joseph. *Terrors of Uncertainty: The Cultural Contexts of Horror Fiction.* New York: Routledge, 1989.

Heath, Stephen. *The Sexual Fix.* New York: Schocken Books, 1984.

Hersey, Harold Brainerd. *Pulpwood Editor: The Fabulous World of the Thriller Magazines Revealed by a Veteran Editor and Publisher.* New York: Fredrick A. Stokes Company, 1937.

Jaffrey, Sheldon, ed. *Selected Tales of Grim and Grue from the Horror Pulps.* Bowling Green, Ohio: Bowling Green State University Popular Press, 1987.

Jaffrey, Sheldon, ed. *The Weirds: A Facsimile Selection of Fiction from the Era of the Shudder Pulps.* Starmont Popular Culture Series, Vol 1. Mercer Island, Washington: Starmont House, 1987.

Jones, Robert Kenneth. "Popular Weird Menace Pulps." *Selected Tales of Grim and Grue from the Horror Pulps.* Bowling Green, Ohio: Bowling Green State University Popular Press, 1987.

King, Stephen. *Danse Macabre.* London: Futura Press, 1982 .

Koch, Gertrude. "The Body's Shadow-Realm" *October* 50 (1989) : 3–29.

MacKinnon, Catherine. "Feminism, Marxism, Method, and the State: An Agenda for Theory." *Signs: A Journal of Women in Culture and Society* 7 (1982): 515–544.

Marcus, Steven. *The Other Victorians: A Study of Sexuality and Pornography in Mid-Nineteenth Century England.* New York: Basic Books, 1964.

Miller, D.A. *The Novel and the Police.* Berkeley: University of California Press, 1988.

Modleski, Tania. *Feminism Without Women: Culture and Criticism in a "Postfeminist" Age*. New York: Routledge, 1991.

Modleski, Tania. *Loving with a Vengeance: Mass-Produced Fantasies for Women*. New York: Methuen, 1982.

Owens, Craig. "Outlaws: Gay Men in Feminism." *Men in Feminism*. Ed. Alice Jardine and Paul Smith. New York: Methuen, 1987. 219–232.

Pendleton, David. "Obscene Allegories: Narrative, Representation, Pornography," *Discourse* 15 (1992): 154–168.

Peterson, Theodore. *Magazines and the Twentieth Century*. Urbana: University of Illinois Press, 1964.

Sedgwick, Eve Kosofsky. *Between Men: English Literature and Male Homosocial Desire*. New York: Columbia University Press, 1985.

Sedgwick, Eve Kosofsky. *The Epistemology of the Closet*. Berkeley: University of California Press, 1990.

Weinberg, Robert. "The Horror Pulps, 1933–1940." *Horror Literature: A Core Collection and Reference Guide*. Ed. Marshall B. Tymm. New York: R. R. Bowker, 1981. 370–397.

Williams, Linda. *Hard Core: Power, Pleasure, and the "Frenzy of the Visible."* Berkeley: University of California Press, 1989.

Chapter 2

Stalking Women's Stockings: Opaque Wisdom or Sheer Nonsense?

Carol E. Dietrich

When the obdurately unliberated male gaze focuses on a female leg—ogling over one bit of body and enacting an ancient erotic routine—it likes to find the leg smooth, glossy, without blemish, slim yet curvilinear, with its shape delineated. High heels can induce the desired contours, but for surfaces and outlines stockings are essential. Stockings make female legs different from men's. They also render flesh visible but untouchable—at least for the moment—thereby provoking the senses.

—Margaret Visser, "Silk Stalkings"

Margaret Visser's one-page history of "silk stockings" is a fascinating portrait of a product that has come to embody completely the notion of planned obsolescence. This form of obsolescence is not only the reality that women's hose never last a human lifetime, but also the cultural definition of femininity, which has been craftily expressed in the advertising themes and motifs of hosiery.[1] The advertising of women's stockings creates an image of femininity; addressed primarily to women, these ads tell women how they ought to feel and behave if they are attractive women. They create a visual vocabulary that cleaves to the civilized body with an intimacy akin to the very products to be sold. Visser's description of ideal legs transformed in stockings ("smooth, glossy, without blemish, slim yet curvilinear, with its shape delineated") is an image that few women can attain; yet the advertisers assure it is a goal worth pursuing, thus hoping to create a market for the products forever.[2] The images of women show females as sexualized bodies, whose status in the world, and position in the advertisements, is dependent on how they look rather than on what they do. Advertisers, in fact, seem to have no compunction about capitalizing on gender stereotypes to sell products, especially for an industry, such as pantyhose, that garners $3 billion in yearly sales (Staples 77). At the same time, many businesses rely on the consumer's adherence to these stereotypes to sell their products ("sex sells"). The entire manufacturing and marketing strategy behind such products is tied to the exploitation of gender-specific behaviors. Thus, the reinforcement of traditional gender stereotypes has an important economic motivation for business, and this is seen nowhere better than in the portrayals used in print advertisements of hosiery.

Historically, the values and preoccupations, the fantasies and aspirations, the actual conditions and behaviors—that is, the conventionalized portrayals of gender—are not subverted in advertising but sustained. Advertisements not only sell products but also aggressively sell gender stereotypes.[3] Ads are meticulously designed, photographed, airbrushed, computer generated, and laid out to convert potential consumers into actual consumers and to reinforce current consumers. The ads are carefully crafted bundles of images, frequently designed to associate the product with feelings of pleasure stemming from deep-seated fantasies and anxieties. To be successful, an advertised message must invoke consumer reaction. Advertisers manipulate these fantasies and exploit our anxieties, especially those concerning our gender identities, to sell products. As *The Boston Women's Health Collective Book* notes:

Every society throughout history has had standards of beauty, but at no time has there been such an intense media blitz telling us what we *should* look like. Magazine covers, films, TV shows, billboards surround us with images which fail to reflect the tremendous diversity among us. Never before have there been hundreds of businesses that profit by convincing us we don't look good enough. Whole industries depend on selling us products through slick ads depicting "beautiful" women, playing on our insecurities and fears of imperfection. (23–24)

Advertising has created and continues to create a significant part of the female image in the twentieth century. The ways in which women are pictured in print advertisements, for example, reveal an interplay, at once subtle and extravagant, ostentatious and austere, between fashioned images and so-called natural behaviors. For women these depictions of gender hold the potential for psychic confrontations. Advertisements embody an artificial pose/posturing in which consumers are led in some (un)conscious and ineluctable way toward some great tenacious image that establishes an iconography of femaleness. Hosiery ads, in particular, present vexing problems in defining feminine cultural identity, discretion, and social reality.

In this chapter, I examine the representation of women's hosiery in selected print advertisements from the 1920s to the present. My search, however, is not historical. Rather than providing a content analysis of selected print advertisements in a chronological manner, this chapter uses an episodic form, more a montage of attractions, a spectacle inspired by Guy Debord's *The Society of Spectacle* that "epitomizes the prevaling mode of social life" (13). In identifying the matter of my gaze, I paid attention to my everyday responses and experiences to these preserved cultural artifacts known as print advertisements. As I microfilmed my way through more than four hundred odd ads of hosiery, I noted which images/metaphors/patterns returned most insistently. I make no claim that the same formulations impress themselves on the attention of all women equally; I can only describe what I myself found. Just as I am not using a traditional conceptual framework, I wish to emphasize that in referring to an advertisement, for example, from the 1930s, I intend to make no historical claim about that period. While it would be relatively easy to situate each ad in its respective age, I have instead straddled the issue of historicity/historicism as Higonnet argues is possible:

Most critics and historians, however, have at least identified two positions they wish to avoid: at one extreme, an essentialist stance that seeks to posit a sensibility or esthetic common to all women regardless of class or race; at the other extreme, a deconstructive strategy so relativist that it forecloses political agency. For feminist critics and historians, and for artists as well, theory and practice must work together toward changes in the ways that permit both understanding history and making sense of the present. (390)

It is entirely consistent with my analytical project that I take the text of each ad "out of context"—out of its own historical context and *into my own*—for that is precisely the way in which I encountered it. As Debord states, "Images detached from every aspect of life merge into common stream, and the former unity is lost forever. Apprehended in a partial way, reality unfolds in a new generality as a pseudo-world apart, solely as an object of contemplation. The tendency toward the specialization of images-of-the-world finds its highest expression in the world of the autonomous image, where deceit deceives itself" (*Society* 12). Advertising as a spectacle of choice and detached, disseminated images reveal that consumers prefer the sign to the thing signified, the copy to the original, the representation to reality, the appearance to the essence. I chose advertisements published after 1920 for a number of reasons, chiefly that it was not until 1914 that advertising became an established and integral part of the mass-circulation magazine format.

Women's magazines, whether traditional or modern or postmodern, proclaim that it is alright for a woman to "be" and "do" as long as she retains her "femininity." That "femininity" might be demonstrable through her fashions and wardrobe or through her domesticity and/or career wizardry. According to *Wall Street Journal* reporter Susan Faludi's *Backlash: The Undeclared War Against American Women*, it is a conspiracy concocted by the reactionaries and the media, seeking to drive women back into the safety of confining stereotypes, through the use of "myths." Myths about motherhood, domesticity, chastity, and passivity that were challenged by second wave feminism have been supplanted by the beauty myth that influences women to measure their worth against unrealistic standards of physical attractiveness and also encourages men to want to possess beautiful women (Wolf). One of the ways that "femininity" of the beauty myth is promoted is through the display of *genderisms* in advertisements. Essentially, the purpose of a print ad is to get the message across at a glance; thus, considerable control is exercised to make the picture appear *natural*, no matter how outlandish it may be.

In a brilliant analysis of "gender advertisements," Erving Goffman analyzed some of the concrete visual components in ads that create the appearance of "gender naturalness." He labeled these components gender themes or genderisms; they include relative size, ritualization of subordination, function ranking, the family, licensed withdrawal (the woman's greater freedom to be psychologically "not there"), and feminine touch.   For purposes of this discussion, the final gender theme, the feminine touch, is observable in many advertisements of hosiery. In a 1960 advertisement for Belle-Sharmeer stockings, the main caption reads, "There are times when you want to be all things feminine . . . when only Belle-Sharmeer will do." A woman whose face and upper torso have been obliterated/fuzzed out/muted is seated. Her left leg is fully extended, her right leg bent at a 90-degree angle, and her hands are gently sliding the hose up to her knee. The language of the ad is alliterative and tactile:

SLIP ON BELLE-SHARMEER. HMMM—NO ORDINARY STOCKINGS THESE. What fit! What feel! Sure and snug at the ankle. Caressing at the calf. Sleek at the knee. Scarcely more than an eloquent echo whispering wonderful things about your legs. Exclusive legsize-knit spins the spell. Means magical fit. Individual leg-sizes make it your own. These extra steps in the making and shaping mean more dancing, more strolling, more romantic encounters from every single pair of Belle-Sharmeer. Your choice of seamless or full fashion styles in all of the season's most desired shades, high or low lustre. At finer stores everywhere. . . . when you want to be all things feminine.

The entire experience of the model dressing is made into an intimate act of defining the person, so that life becomes what she wears and the issue of choice is made to seem moot. Who could disassociate herself from this intimate part of her material possessions when she is told to think of her clothing as she does her body? For the woman viewer, the visual can never be totally separated from the tactile.

In a 1957 Hanes ad, the high-heeled half-torso of a woman is delicately and sensually (un)dressing, her left hand barely touching the clothing she is removing/putting on. Both ads of the half-torso present as a fundamental fact that a woman enjoys adorning/displaying herself. For her, dressing may be a privileged ritual: a re-enactment of that primordial interweaving of look and touch which is the fabric of the maternal space.

In many similar advertisements, women are shown cradling, tracing, just barely touching, and caressing the surface of objects—including their own bodies—with their fingers and hands. Their hands are not prehensile; they do not grasp, hold, manipulate, or reach. Other parts of the body, including the face, can touch and do the work of the "feminine" hands. Such advertisements portray women as narcissists, touchers, and adorers of their own semi-nude bodies; they appear turned inward, relating to men only as "props," as the female is situated, for example, in the 1927 Allen A hosiery ad with her head turned away from the male gaze and toward her own legs. Perhaps this is done to undercut the one-way sex gaze. If the woman admires herself, it's only "natural" that a man would admire her, too.

Images that encourage women to look at other female bodies are also common: practically all women's magazines are full of glossy and provocative advertising photographs of women's bodies, faces, and parts of bodies. The similarity between some of these images and those aimed at men is in some ways mystifying—are women really being encouraged to fantasize about the control and sexual consumption of other women? It seems more likely that some advertisers do not bother to address their male and female audiences separately, because in this culture women grow up learning to look at themselves in the way that men do. This argument about perception, particularly regarding women and contemporary fashion, is premised on Simone de Beauvoir's thinking and reflects two recurring charges against the culture of femininity. First, fashion is enslavement; women are bound by the drudgery of keeping up their appearance and by the impediments of the styles which prohibit them from acting in the world. Second, fashion "may disguise the body, deform it, or follow its curves;" but ultimately "puts it on display" (de Beauvoir 529). Central to this argument is de Beauvoir's understanding of female narcissism in which the looker is implicated, since female display always depends, as she expresses it, on attracting the attention of another. That is, women are socialized to learn to appraise themselves through the eyes of the male. In *Ways of Seeing*, the art historian John Berger extends and reinforces de Beauvoir's position, arguing that men act and women appear. Men look at women. Women watch themselves being looked at. This determines not only most relations between men and women but also the relation of women to themselves. The surveyor of woman in herself is male, the surveyed female. Thus she turns herself into an object and most particularly an object of vision: a sight.

Berger's ideas have been taken up by feminists and elaborated into a theory of gender and representation. "To be born a woman," he states,

has been to be born, within an allotted and confined space, into the keeping of men. The social presence of women has developed as a result of their ingenuity in living under such tutelage within such a limited space. But this has been at the cost of a woman's self being split in two. A woman must continually watch herself. She is almost continually accompanied by her own image of herself.

As a 1938 Se-Ling Hosiery ad states, "Mirrors are Friendly to Legs in SE-LING. And admiring glances will confirm your mirror's tale of loveliness when you wear Se-Ling hosiery. They cling, they flatter, they slenderize. . . . And yet you'll find them unbelievably durable. Ask for Se-Ling by name at your favorite shop." The qualities that are considered beautiful and desirable are merely symbols of female behavior.

Thus, the image a woman conveys is what gives her status and power. A 1922 advertisement for Burson fashioned hose entitled "Speaking of Ankles" suggests that fashion change has a direct relationship to the degree of freedom and status assigned to women in society:

On the sidewalks of the city, up-and-down Main Street, where'er milady walks, eyes pay constant tribute to the slender, graceful ankle. If one is so fortunate as to boast a well-modeled pair she can accentuate their beauty by carefully chosen stockings and should *never, never!* mar their gentle curving by crooked, ungainly seams. And, even if one's ankles are not quite perfection, one may still make amends by avoiding crooked seams, wearing Burson stockings, which fit perfectly and have no seams whatever to annoy the eye.

When the woman is confined to the more or less graceful bondage of a societal role, her contours become more softly rounded and her style of dress and hose becomes relatively static; given her public presence, however, the feminine mode moves much more swiftly toward a different image, an alternative female world with its own laws, economy, religion, sexuality, education, and culture, each element as repressive as any that had gone before.

While many writers have persisted in denigrating an interest in fashion as proof of vanity, vacuity, or worse, and are critical of those who take more than a fleeting interest in appearance, Annette Kuhn has explored some of the basic questions feminists ask about how images make meaning: what relation spectatorship has to representations of women; what sort of activity looking is and what looking has to do with sexuality, power, and knowledge; how images of women speak to the spectator, and whether the spectator is addressed as male or female; whether femininity is constructed in certain ways through representations; and why images of women's bodies are so prevalent in our society. The answers to these questions, she argues, cannot be found only through examining and analyzing images, because meanings do not reside in images. Images have use, value, and exchange value based on context, on the particular time and place of their consumption. "All representations," Kuhn concludes, "are constructive in their own right: . . . they construct meanings through their own particular codes and conventions." In *The Devil's Dictionary*, Ambrose Bierce presents the image of men and women using a traditional mind/body dualism:

> To men a man is but a mind. Who cares
> What face he carries or what form he wears?
> But woman's body is the woman. (15)

The message here is self-evident, but the implication of this simple verse is powerful: Is a man "but" a mind? Who cares? Is woman's body the woman? Is *a* woman's body *the* woman? Consider Bierce's maxim in light of a 1965 Hanes ad that appeared in *Harpers Bazaar*. A female's leg is in the foreground, diagonally positioned across the right side of the page. Behind the leg are a pair of female eyes. A tear is forming and falling out of one of the eyes. The text above the eye says, "How to make 96,906,500 women very, very sad." The text that runs down the left of the leg, almost touching it, says, "Wear Hanes Sheer Extravagance. Only a handful of women can own these troublemakers! And while they're driving the male population out of its mind . . . other women will simply have to dry their eyes. So, hasten." One powerful message is that woman is doomed to envy the embodiment of desire that will forever elude her, unless she purchases the product. Desire in women thus appears as envy— perhaps only as envy. And women's power is derived from their ability to drive the male population "out of its mind." As Jessica Benjamin notes, "The 'sexy' woman—an image that intimidates women whether or not they strive to conform to it—is sexy, but as object, not as subject. She expresses not so much *her* desire as her pleasure in being desired; what she enjoys is her capacity to evoke desire in the other, to attract" (89). More recently, Susan Rubin Suleiman advances Annette Kuhn's argument by proposing that the female body is itself a symbolic construct that exists in some form of mediated discourse (2).

So what is the symbolic construct of the female body? Is a female, in Simone de Beauvoir's terms, not born, but made? In a 1951 Gotham ad, a woman dressed in a pillbox hat and tightly fitted outfit, wearing long white gloves, is walking two poodles. With her right hand she is holding the dog leashes and touching the bottom of her dress. Her right hand is poised at the hemline of her short dress just below her crotch; her left is angled just below her hip. The brand of hosiery is labeled "the Sensation Color of '51 Gotham Gold Stripe Cheesecake." "Cheesecake . . . Gotham's exciting new, sunlit-beige . . . gossamer as a shaft of ligh . . . perfect for Spring and Summer Fashions . . . Cheesecake is the most traffic-stopping, camera-clicking nylon stocking color in America!" It is easy to read this ad as blatantly sexist (the term cheesecake, after all, refers to a photograph of a pretty girl scantily clothed), and while her index fingers serve to point our gaze to her legs, the subtext of the hand placement can be read as if she is about to lift her skirt, that is, revealing her *real* site of femininity. The hose, therefore, "stand for" her. Print ads such as this do use images to demonstrate the effects of the commodities they offered, effects not always clearly caused by the product itself but which are insistently associated with new feminine ideals. It is a commonplace to say that ads encourage women to identify themselves as objects, objects of adulation and of commercial exploitation. Has the symbolic construct of the female body changed at all, or is the female model, the most glorified among consumer goods, still enforcing and serving some societal standard of beauty, offering consistent, repetitive emblems for ad-miration?

The images of women in advertisements show females as sexualized bodies, whose status in the world, and position in the advertisements, is dependent on how they look rather than on what they do. Achievement is primarily visual achievement, and perfection is the attainment of physical beauty. In a 1927 ad, we see a drawing of a man seated, a package poised precipitously on top of his knees, presumably a gift for the "girl." Opposite him is a pair of woman's legs in a lounging position, stretched out. Her hand holds a cigarette, aimed erectly in his direction, from which a few smoke rings are visible. The text states, SHEER AUDACITY, "The beauty of silken sheerness on slender, shapely legs. . . is it this that gives the owner such assurance, such audacity . . . is it this that fills even the timid man with admiration?"

Presumably, this line drawing model is blessed with shapely, well-formed legs, an excess that inscribes her image as different from that of the reader; the reader can only *have* such legs with McCallum hosiery. This dichotomy is the mark of a properly feminine lack, the failure of the woman to identify fully with an image that can never be entirely her own, her "self." This moment of lack is effaced by an agenda that promises to transform looks into accomplishment ("legs" into "lifestyle") through product usage. Consequently, the ads aimed at women frequently offer the chance to create such effects by the purchase of a particular product.

As a 1995 Smooth Silhouettes™ from L'eggs ad advises, "Don't do leg lifts when you can buy them. The shape you've been killing yourself for comes naturally with new Smooth Silhouettes from L'eggs. Slimming and smoothing every crucial inch between your tummy and your toes. Don't be afraid to show off!" Looks can be transformed into accomplishments through consumerism. Through the advertisements, the woman is encouraged to enjoy a fantasy of power. A 1967 ad expresses the power this way. A woman is seated at the back of a motorcycle. "Kayser's Panty Hose. You shouldn't sit down without them."

Today's short, short skirts make Kayser's Panty Hose a must. You need that sheer, silky look all the way up your legs. With no stocking tops or garters peeking out.

Tall or short. Slim or not-so-trim. You should own a pair of Kayser's Panty Hose exactly proportioned for you. So you don't get stood up. For exactly $2.50, you can be sitting pretty.

But, unlike ads directed at men, this is not power over people and things, but the power to become a perfect sight, the ultimate to-be-looked-at woman, a Pretty Woman. As an ornament on the back of the motorcycle, the female's positioning confers status on the man. This ad is about men's institutions and institutional power.

The public shape of femininity has not lessened the conflicting admonitions addressed to women: "Gentlemen prefer Hanes." "Ladies with L'eggs Have Choices," and the ad promises "The more you choose L'eggs, the more you get chosen." Even here, certain contradictions can be seen. The most pervasive of these is that old conundrum: women are invited, or told, to form their bodies in order to attract (men's) attention—to dare to be sexy (Barthel 70).

In most ads of hosiery, the message is that the legs need care and attention so that eventually they can become as perfect as the picture. Typically, beautiful legs are proclaimed a natural quality, while being promoted as a packaged illusion. "Veiled Illusion," as a 1950 Berkshire ad states, "Just as a fine veil flatters your face, so does the 'Veiled Illusion' of Berkshire's exclusive Nylace stockings beautify your legs with a subtle, dull flattery . . . and they cannot run!" No attempt is made by the advertiser to represent true reality, but the similarity is close enough to urge the reader to make such a leap of imagination. This is really no different from the way "realism" functions in other art forms: the denotational verisimilitude of the aesthetic object is achieved by means of conventional signifying devices consensually held to achieve such verisimilitude. In other words, we know it is not reality, but agree to accept temporarily the illusion that it might be. The legs, therefore, become eroticized and sexual, to be looked at and marveled in. The whole outer surface of the body is transformed into an exquisite, passive thing.

Advertisers wish to make print ads a pleasurable experience for the intended audience. They construct the ads in ways that reinforce the image of gender most familiar to and comfortable for their target audience. Sigmund Freud's own analysis of narcissism rehearses the process whereby feminine pleasure is fixed by the masculine gaze. His own definition of narcissism corresponds to popular usage today: "The term narcissism is derived from clinical description and was chosen by Paul Nacke in 1899 to denote the attitude of a person who treats his own body in the same way in which the body of a sexual object is ordinarily treated—who looks at it, that is to say, strokes it and fondles it until he obtains complete satisfaction through these activities" ("On Narcissim," 173).

Freud's understanding of narcissism can be applied to a 1932 ad for Roman Stripe Hosiery that features a seated woman looking at her face in a hand-held cosmetic mirror, surrounding by caricatured (disengendered/genderless?) eyes. The caption reads, "THE EYES HAVE IT." "We're sorry to have to report this, but it looks as though legs would just have to keep on being looked at. Eyes—feminine as well as masculine—have an instinctive way of dropping an appraising glance below the hem-line." This text exemplifies the treatment of feminine auto-eroticism, which can be spoken to the degree that the woman is addressed, interpellated, as a narcissistic subject who is contained through the masculine gaze and consumerism. Feminine narcissism as a polymorphous auto-eroticism (the pleasuring in having great legs—or some other, any other, part of her body marked out as such by some consumer item) affords the woman the opportunity of constructing (or perhaps more accurately buying) a position of autonomy in which she takes control of her imageness as a source of pleasure for herself. The fact that she must construct herself as an image suitable to be looked at leaves open the possibility that this image will be appropriated by the masculine gaze. Or, as an ad for Rollins Runstop Stockings shows, the woman must conform to the man's imagining—how to pose, how to apologize for flaws, how to "change" to be acceptable, and so forth—all captured and contained and controlled through the lens of, in this case, a male photographer. Masculine appropriation is not the only outcome for the work of beauty—as the Rograin ad goes on to state: "That's why so many people who want sheer smartness within today's budget keep asking stores to insist on having ROGRAIN. Once you a try a pair of ROGRAIN stockings you're likely to insist on having ROGRAIN from then on. And that, as we say, makes life hard for us. But we're no quitters; we'll knit until our fingers drop off." The message is that knitters never quit; and smart buyers always buy ("Shop 'til they drop!"). This embodiment of beauty is an imperative for women because it is biological, sexual, and evolutionary.

The grounding of the pleasurable image in product usage positions feminine narcissism within a consumer economy. A 1956 Hanes ad juxtaposes a woman's eyes, exaggerated in proportion to a pair of female legs. The heavily lashed (mascaraed) eyes are behind and between the legs. There is little literal text in the ad, aside from "No seams to worry about—Hanes seamless stockings," which is positioned in the left corner aslant. The possibility of the woman taking pleasure in herself, for herself, is circumscribed by the necessary contingency of the masculine gaze and the demand that she function as a consumer, even if that means consuming herself with her own eyes. Here the corporeal surface is a sartorial skin, a second skin of fripperies and colors which detains the gaze. Essentially, it is a double arrest, as both viewer and viewed become immobilized, and by the advertiser's intent, the eyes of the reader of the ad are captured.

In a 1951 Kayser ad, the injunction is that it is a woman's duty to feel attractive to others. The ad shows a female leg, skirted just above the knee. The leg forms a large diagonal across the page. Behind the leg is a five-framed "film" clip of four partial faces, three male and one female. The eyes of each face are focused on the female leg. They watch her at a distance—a familiar scenario of voyeuristic pleasure. She is beautiful—framed in the gap—an image. They are framed too, and their eyes are looking up. They may only see her leg but the visual movement travels under her skirt back to the leg/hose standing for her. The visual presence of the eyes freezes the flow of action in moments of erotic contemplation. As Walter Benjamin has suggested, looking through the camera is an acceptable, if not the dominant, way of perceiving "reality." The idea is to make one's appearance unforgettable, so that one's actions become redundant. The eyes seemingly slide over the corporeal surface, detailing its particulars as if it were part of the picture it composes. The caption reads, "You owe it to your audience to bare the beauty of your leg through the near nude beauty of Kayser's sheer, sheer 75 gauge, 10 denier nylons with patented 'strait-on' heel that never, never twists. $1.95 the pair. Other stockings from $1.15. Stockings by Kayser a beauty treatment for your legs." In essence, the message for the female is "Hey, look at me so we'll both be delighted/excited." By purchasing and wearing this product, you will fulfill your injunction to be an ornamental female who sees herself (and is seen) as a decorative object. To be seen as a sexual object, however, she must first be seen as a decorative object. The ad illustrates what Mary Ann Doane has described in the classical Hollywood cinema as "the overwhelming intensity of the injunction of the feminine spectator-consumer to concern herself with her own appearance and position—an appearance that can only be fortified and assured through the purchase of a multiplicity of products" (30).

After all, beauty is "so central to femininity, and packaging the feminine image often requires preoccupation with endless details of appearance" (Freedman 221). According to Naomi Wolf, we need to examine the political construction of the concept of beauty itself:

"Beauty" is a currency system like the gold standard. Like any economy, it is determined by politics, and in the modern age in the West it is the last, best belief system that keeps male dominance intact. In assigning value to women in a vertical hierarchy according to a culturally imposed physical standard, it is an expression of power relations in which women must unnaturally compete for resources that men have appropriated for themselves.

J. C. Flügel suggests that the pleasure afforded by sartorial display derives initially from such narcissistic investment in one's own body, which is later metonymically displaced onto the clothes and other decorations that the body wears. In a 1954 Hanes ad, a woman wearing a short frilly skirt has her legs widely spread. The woman's head appears upside down between her legs, as if she is giving birth to herself. The ad states, "head over heels in love with Hanes Seamless Stockings. No seams to worry about. They're smart coming and going. They make my legs look slimmer and trimmer." For Freud, the pleasure of self-display is a vicissitude of the scopophilic drive. Exhibitionism originates in the auto-erotic activity of looking at a part of one's own body—an activity initially coincident with pleasurable bodily sensations—which will later evolve into looking at someone else's body by a process of comparison. The scopophilic drive will then once again be turned around upon part of one's own body, but this time with a new passive aim, that of being *looked at*. A 1946 ad "eyes are on Kayser nylons" depicts a woman's legs walking on a fuzzy surface, which reveals two large eyes, and in a 1947 Kayser ad ("eyes are on Kayser Fit-All-Tops"), a young girl (presumably a daughter) is looking at her scantily clad mother who is hammering a nail, her eyes gazing at the younger girl. Freud insists that "anyone who is an exhibitionist in his unconscious is at the same time a *voyeur*" (*Three Essays*, 167).

These images of looking and being looked at are of special interest. The pleasure in looking is no less a female than it is a male preserve, but it is diversely inflected by sexually differentiated relations to the body. Biology, including the female body, is not meaningful in and of itself but only in a social context that has gender at its center. By arguing simply to revalue the female body and all it stands for, feminist writers unwittingly help to reconstitute the patriarchal system that privileges the notion of sexual difference. In a 1966 Kayser ad , a standing, smiling suited man is holding a woman (her face is masked as is the case too often in these ads, with no upper torso at all) whose legs are quite visible. The ad says:

Kayser Cantrece. The only stocking that behaves the way you do. A disciplined stocking for devils. A sheer evening stocking to dance with ease in, behave as you please in. Cantrece nylon is the luxury stocking that moves with you . . . naturally . . . without binding above or wilting below. It conforms to the tiniest ankle, hugs the knee, and breathes at the top for active movement, perfect fit. Go ahead. Let him sweep you off your feet. Now you can afford the one stocking that behaves. Even if he won't. Now only $1.35.

Among other things, this ad is reenacting a drama of romance, socially constructed with attendant norms and rules for behavior. That clothes are burdened with so many moral provisos is proof of their power and significance within society. The ad spotlights the sexism of the man-girl inequality, the sex-object status of women, and the implied conflict between attractiveness and attraction. Diane Barthel observes this ritualistic pattern:

Even well into the twentieth century, men initiated romance and carried it through. They made the dates, conceived romantic gestures, spoke in acceptable phrases of their desires. Women assented or refused.

Although in recent decades this one-sided pattern has been slowly changing, most advertisements still conceive romance as an adventure in passivity. But, although a woman cannot openly approach the male, this does not mean that she is sitting back and doing nothing. There is instead a great deal of emotional work and beauty work going on. (58)

For Christine Delphy, gender-based thinking is itself problematic, and must be acknowledged as cultural and historically specific. It testifies to the pervasiveness of patriarchal ideologies in Western thought, which posit a natural hierarchical heterosexual order. More importantly, however, it draws attention to the fact that the sexed body is inseparable from discourses about it. Post-structural analyses suggest that we question the notion of an unchanging, biological/sexual identity that stands apart from our thinking about it.

In exploring the ways in which thinking about the body is conditioned, Mary Douglas draws attention to the relationship between the literal and the metaphorical body. She observes that "just as it is true that everything symbolizes the body, so it is equally true (and all the more so for that reason) that the body symbolizes everything else" (122). She calls this social definition of the physical, and the "physical" definition of the social, the "two bodies." What she means by the former is that although we exist physically in our bodies, we actively and physically construct and reconstruct ourselves and our bodies in accordance with social and individual norms and values, and for various purposes.

One persistent construction of the female form in Western culture is that of The Three Graces, a motif from Greek mythology of three sister goddesses, Aglaia, Euphrosyne, and Thalia, who dispense charm and beauty. The image of the three female forms has appeared in artwork through the ages. The Three Graces have also surfaced in many advertisements: In a 1936 ad for Gordon hosiery, three legs serve as pillars for the three women who stand beside them. The ad itself is written as if it were announcing the latest dramatic production:

The Play: The Three Gordons. The Cast: Petite, Princess and Regal. Gordon's famous trio of individually proportioned stockings in three lengths. Now playing in all good stores. Ask for PETITE for short, PRINCESS for medium and REGAL for long and you will get stockings fashioned to fit you at the top, calf, ankle and instep, as well as correct in length, assuring smartness and long, luxurious wear. In lovely sheer chiffons and service weights . . . in all the new shades of spring . . . and for every costume and occasion.

Three females appear in a Belle-Sharmeer ad with the caption, "Do you know that your leg size has a name?" These Three Graces, identical in appearance except for their height, are featured; their names are Duchess (the leg size for talls), Modite (the leg size for middlings), and Brev (the leg size for smalls). So as not to leave anyone out, yet maintain the image of Three Graces, a small sign, appearing to the right of the three females, says in small print "also Classic the leg size for plumps." And in a Kayser ad, "Everybody's having a perfect fit," as three women of varying heights identically dressed appear as if in a chorus-line strolling/dancing on an oversized stocking that serves as a type of runway. Another Kayser ad features three women straddling a fence in a rural setting; with rings of flowers in their hair, one nibbling on a blade of grass; they are lined up, their legs jutting through the slats of the fence. The ad says, "3 Proportions are we—but we rely upon Kayser's famous 'Fit All Proportions' to reveal superbly fitting nylons!" All of these depictions of the recurring three women are used to emphasize form, uniformity, and conformity/harmony—characteristics not unlike those attributed to the Greek goddesses.

The literary idea of the Three Graces, in fact, goes back to a treatise on liberality by Chrysippus in the third century BC, who might have been emulating Epicurus. His lost work was quoted by Seneca (first century AD); it shows that Chrysippus was the first to associate ideas of giving, accepting, and returning with the Graces. These three phases were to be represented as interlocked in a never-interrupted circle of dance to symbolize the return of thanks. Seneca saw them as wearing transparent, ungirdled garments. Pausanias (second century AD) said they were nude, but he didn't know the origin of this. Servius (fourth century AD) was the first to view them as an antithetical group, with one seen from the back. Horace (first century BC) speaks of the "knot of the Graces," suggesting the interlaced gestures. According to the Neo-Platonist Ficino in his *De Amore*, Voluptas (on the left) symbolized *abundant pleasure*, Castitas (in the center position) stood for *juvenescence* or *growing young*, and Pulchritudo (on the right) for *splendor* (Wind 28-34). Pleasure, youth, and splendor/beauty—these attributes are certainly integral to the advertisements of hosiery, or any other feminine product for that matter.

In the characterizations of the Three Graces, the feminine body became the site where desire and the impulse to order, to categorize, and ultimately to master, came together. The three females are typically seen as full bodies, but a more frequent characterization of women in hosiery ads reflects the more common breakdown of the whole body into its parts. The breakdown into body parts is a theme echoed in advertisements for makeup "for eyes, lips, cheeks, and nails" and for selling hosiery. Or as Mary Ann Doane points out in *The Desire to Desire*: "Commodification presupposes that acutely self-conscious relation to the body which is attributed to femininity. The effective operation of the commodity system requires the breakdown of the body into parts—nails, hair, skin, breath—each one of which can constantly be improved through the purchase of a commodity" (32). The objects are given, in the imaginary, the status of body-parts insofar as they too are detached from the body: the sigh and the tear are expelled from the body; the clothes are stripped from the body; and the mirror is but a reflected fragment of that body. In an ad from Burlington's Cameo, the female body is cut in half, and the upper portion of the ad contains four boxes, each with a fragmented version of femininity, a synedoche. The accompanying text that describes each illustration reads,

Soft as the feathered tips of a plume . . . long-lived as the memory of precious hours . . . as subtly seductive as a mischievous glance . . . these are Bur-Mil Cameo Just Fabulous stockings, the dress sheers *that give up to twice the wear of other sheer nylons.* Know them by their effective run guards . . . their fluted tops that hug your thighs with blissful comfort. In the shiny black Cameo box. Seamed and seamless. $1.50 the pair. Other Cameo styles, $1.35 the pair.

As Elspeth Probyn in "Theorizing Through the Body" notes:

Living within the dominant Western culture, women and men are used to seeing women's bodies separated from themselves. Indeed, we are accustomed to seeing bits of women's bodies—a leg on this billboard, a headless torso on another, a pair of lips blindly looking out from the magazine page. The political activity of reclaiming these fragments has been crucial within feminism. (84)

In other instances, the fragmentation is more deceptive and the message more misleading. The expressions, poses, and settings belong to a rhetoric of art rather than to a more succinct, objective, and strictly illustrative intention. In a 1968 Burlington ad, a leg appears in the middle of the page in front of a cloudy background. The main caption reads, "You can even bend over and still be a lady. Put on our pantyhose." The text goes on to say, "You can also let the wind blow. Get out of a car. Reach. Lounge. Climb an open stairway. In Burlington-Cameo proportioned pantyhose you're up to your waist in glorious colors. Opaques are $3, sheers, $2.25. Put them and forget to remember to be careful to be a lady. Just be. Burlington-Cameo." The moral issue is raised in this ad: the pantyhose are protective, sensible, and comfortable, but the age-old question of whether the body is more seductive clothed or unclothed is suggested. Nudity viewed outside passion is normally only attractive if the body conforms to the current ideal of physical beauty and sex appeal. In another advertisement, from 1922, a woman is depicted with her dress blowing up in the wind, her hand shielding her face, her umbrella/kite (?) turning to protect her. The text says simply, "You just know she wears them." In both ads the concern is with sensory functions, the hide-and-seek, innocence and knowledge, sexual seduction. It is the dress that encourages men to be shameless, yet the shift is on the woman's role in maintaining the shame/order (being "careful," being a lady). As James Joyce said, men want their women to be half whore and half nun. For Flügel, the auto-erotic pleasures arising from the contact of the skin with certain fabrics, or the comforting feeling afforded by tight garments, are inferior to the sensations arising from the play of air and wind upon the surface of the skin, or the free-play of the muscles. He writes, "on the whole, therefore, muscle-eroticism, like skin-eroticism, loses rather than gains by the wearing of clothes. It is therefore to displacements of the Narcissistic rather than of the auto-erotic elements that clothing must look for psychological support of a directly pleasure-giving kind" (89). Flugel's emphasis on the pleasure-giving qualities of attire becomes the means by which a woman demonstrates her self-control and autonomy, rather than submission to the gaze of a masculine subject. This position, however, is not without contradiction; it depends on a rereading of old models so that femininity is not grounded in patriarchy and consumerism. This rereading is especially difficult, as the entrenchment of the past is evident in this passage from Sarah Mower:

The truth is American women have become used to having things—in fashion, at least—their own way. Choice, not uniformity, is the operative force now. Just as you can choose this summer to wear long or short when and if you please, so you now have the option to like sheers, or stay away from them, or just wear them *sometimes*. Never, thank goodness, are we going back to the time when every woman wore regulation skin-tone sheers everywhere and always, whether they did anything for her or not. Since, to its credit, the hosiery industry saw the writing on the wall for sheers, it has set about anticipating and satisfying our every whim. Now, due in part to microfiber technology, there are pantyhose that fit and caress and support better than the dreamiest dreams of the 1950s. (180)

"Anticipating and satisfying our every whim" is not the hallmark of a liberated femininity that does not depend upon fit and caressing and support. The transcendence of "whim" is the real choice, but is this choice possible? As Radner suggests, the body is "a contested terrain, attacked from within and without, the cite at which both victory and defeat are negotiated" (64). The print ads examined here are brutally direct, some are blatantly obvious, and some are subtly and perversely complex. Despite changing attitudes in the broader culture, images of women remain remarkably consistent—and conservative. Each ad, too, builds ideology, image, and identity. Without question, gender portrayals in the media influence the ways that we, and others, see us. If Margaret Mead is right and gender identity is culturally constructed, then we can begin to understand the importance of gender portrayals in print advertisements. Women made into an image is the outcome of the tensions between the imaginary and the symbolic, between a subject that wants itself whole and a subject that can only exist as split. Although advertisements do not always reflect cultural reality, they do reinforce existing values by repeatedly presenting these values to the public. The power to image and fashion women has traditionally been a male prerogative, and the creators do imprint their conceptions on their creatures. If some of the central aims of feminism were "to protect women from sexual assault and economic exploitation" (Patai and Koertge 207) and "to transform traditional attitudes about gender roles," (Patai and Koertge 207), then we must conclude that these aims—though recognizably noble and urgent—have yet to be completely fulfilled. At present, run-less nylons remain only a figment of Carol Higgins Clark's fiction, *Snagged*, and stereotypes persist. Anti-feminists argue that revised gender roles have created as many problems for women (including psychological and physical stress) as they have resolved. But Susan Faludi rejects these arguments and believes that such objections constitute a "backlash" against feminism rooted in a fear that equal treatment for women threatens the status quo. Traditionalists, who are threatened by hard-won feminist gains, wish to make "a preemptive strike that stops women long before they reach" their goal of full equality with men.

Although the history of women's hosiery can be characterized as a quasi-progression in technology and invention, the more insidious history of women as depicted in hosiery ads is static and frayed with exploitation. With the advent of new technologies, women do not need to show how representation is ideological; they do need, though, to assert their freedom not to be appropriated by spectator-owners. Women need to resist and reject the messages, "Half of you is leg"; "Clothes aren't sexy, women are"; "Think of hosiery as makeup for your legs"; and "The last thing to go in a woman are the legs." Furthermore, women need to be lightened from and enlightened about the powers of planned obsolescence. As Naomi Wolf urges, "If women are to free [them]selves from the dead weight that has once again been made out of femaleness, it is not ballots or lobbyists or placards that women will need first; it is a new way to see" (19). The new way to see is a new realization that truth is not detatched like a finished article from the instrument that shapes it. In the words of Debord, such a move involves change of deep structure of knowing and being and doing: "In contrast to the passing *fashions* that clash and fuse on the frivolous surface of a contemplated pseudo-cyclical time, the grand style of our era can be ever recognized in whatever is governed by the obvious yet carefully concealed necessity for revolution" (*Spectacle* 116). If women can "lastingly free themselves from the crushing presence of media discourse and of the various forces organized to relay it," then women can progress from "spectacle" to "respectable" (Debord, *Comment* 19). In the meantime, women can choose to "induce," "produce" or "reproduce" their images. They can broadcast their own potent messages. They can see; they can wisely admonish, "Stop pulling our legs!"; and they can walk in their own visionary ways.

NOTES

1.   The word "hosiery" is derived from the Anglo-Saxon word "hosa," a term designating a garment made of cloth, similar to very tight trousers that covered the legs and lower part of the body. The term was generally used in the plural "hosen." "Stocking" comes from the Anglo-Saxon word "stoka," meaning stump; that is, the part that remains. Stockings, therefore, are the parts that remain when the garment "hosen" is cut, the upper part becoming knee breeches. "Strumpf," the German word for stocking, is traced to a similar origin.

2.   Before the turn of the century, silk was a luxury commodity available only to the wealthy; but with the invention of artificial silk—later known as rayon—in 1892, garments with the appearance of silk became accessible to the masses. This was followed in rapid succession by the development of other man-made fibers and synthetic

materials which not only simulated the qualities of costly status items but introduced a whole new field of fabrics that influenced the design of the finished product. So great was the impact of nylon, invented in 1934 in the United States by William Carothers of Dupont, on the women's hosiery industry that the common name for stockings was changed to "nylons." Full-scale manufacture of nylon began in 1938. By 1939, 64 million pairs of nylon stockings were sold.

3. A stereotype is less a representation of "real" human beings than it is a representation of a particular belief about human beings. Basically, a stereotype represents a set of ideas or beliefs about people, and in the case of gender roles, "beliefs about the ways in which men and women differ" (Broverman et al. 1972). As Masters, Johnson, and Kolodny point out, stereotypes "held by many people and based on oversimplified evidence or uncritical judgment," can be harmful "because they lead to erroneous judgments and generalizations and can thus affect how people treat one another" (274).

BIBLIOGRAPHY

Barthel, Diane. *Putting on Appearances: Gender and Advertising.* Philadelphia: Temple University Press, 1988.

Benjamin, Jessica. *The Bonds of Love. Psychoanalysis, Feminism, and the Problem of Domination.* New York: Pantheon Books, 1988.

Benjamin, Walter. "The Work of Art in the Age of Mechanical Reproduction." *Illuminations.* Ed. by Hannah Arendt. Trans. Harry Zohn. New York: Schocken, 1969.

Berger, John. *Ways of Seeing.* London: Penguin, 1972.

Bierce, Ambrose. *The Devil's Dictionary.* Cleveland: World Publishing, 1911.

Broverman, I. K., et al. "Sex-Role Stereotypes: A Current Appraisal." *Journal of Social Issues 28* [2] (1972): 59–78.

Clark, Carol Higgins. *Snagged.* New York: Warner Books, 1993.

de Beauvoir, Simone. *The Second Sex.* Trans. H. M. Parshely. New York: Knopf, 1953.

Debord, Guy. *The Society of Spectacle.* Trans. Donald Nicholson-Smith. New York: Zone Books, 1994.

Delphy, Christine. *Close to Home.* London: Hutchinson and Company, 1984.

Doane, Mary Ann. *The Desire to Desire.* Bloomington: Indiana University Press, 1987.

Douglas, Mary. *Purity and Danger.* New York: Praeger, 1966.

Faludi, Susan. *Backlash: The Undeclared War Against American Women.* New York: Doubleday, 1991.

Flügel, J. C. *The Psychology of Clothes.* London, 1950.

Freedman, Rita. *Bodylove. Learning to Like Our Look—and Ourselves. A Practical Guide for Women.* New York: Harper & Row, 1989.

Freud, Sigmund. "On Narcissim: An Introduction." *The Standard Edition of the Complete Psychological Works of Sigmund Freud.* (24 vols.) Trans. James Strachey. London: Hogarth Press and Institute of Psychoanalysis, 1955. Vol. XIV. 163–190.

Freud, Sigmund. "Three Essays on the Theory of Sexuality," *The Standard Edition of the Complete Psychological Works of Sigmund Freud.* (24 vols.). Trans. James Strachey. London: Hogarth Press and Institute of Psychoanalysis, 1955. Vol. VII. 123–246.

Goffman, Erving. *Gender Advertisements.* London: Macmillan, 1979.

Higonnet, Anne. "Women, Images, and Representation." *A History of Women in the*

West.   Toward a Cultural Identity in the Twentieth Century.   Ed. by Françoise Thébaud. Cambridge: Harvard University Press, 1994. 343–401.

Kuhn, Annette. *The Power of the Image: Essays on Representation and Sexuality.* London: Routledge & Kegan Paul, 1985.

Masters, William H., Virginia E. Johnson, and Robert C. Kolodny. "Gender Roles." *Human Sexuality.* 3rd ed., New York: Harper Collins, 1988. 274–287.

Mead, Margaret. *Male and Female: A Study of the Sexes in a Changing World.* New York: William and Morrow Co., 1967.

Mower, Sarah. "Quantum Leap: Legwear Isn't What It Used to Be." *Harper's Bazaar* April 1994: 180, 230.

Patai, Daphne and Noretta Koertge. *Professing Feminism.* New York: Harper Collins Publishers, 1994.

Probyn, Elspeth. "Theorizing Through the Body." *Women Making Meaning New Feminist Directions in Communication.* Ed. by Lana F. Rakow. New York: Routledge, 1992. 83–99.

Radner, Hilary. *Shopping Around. Feminine Culture and the Pursuit of Pleasure.* New York: Routledge, 1995.

Staples, Kate. "Sheer Determination." *Working Woman* February 1995: 77–78.

Suleiman, Susan Rubin.   *The Female Body in Western Culture.*   Cambridge, Mass.: Harvard University Press, 1986.

Visser, Margaret. "Silk Stockings." *Saturday Night* 107[9] (November 1992): 52.

Wind, Edgar. *Pagan Mysteries in the Renaissance.* Rev. Ed. New York: W. W. Norton, 1968.

Wolf, Naomi. *The Beauty Myth: How Images of Beauty Are Used Against Women.* New York: Morrow, 1990. 9–19.

Chapter 3

Getting Serious: Women at the Anchor Desk

Julia Keller

In May, 1995, after repeated assurances from CBS News management that she was doing a bang-up job (generally the kiss of death in the television news business), Connie Chung was demoted from her position as co-anchor of *The CBS Evening News.* Chung, who had worked alongside Dan Rather for approximately two years, was one of only two women to hold, however briefly, the top spot in a weeknight broadcast network newscast. (The other was Barbara Walters, who was momentarily paired with Harry Reasoner on ABC's nightly newscast in 1976, much to Reasoner's quite public displeasure.) CBS executives said that things simply weren't working out; Chung and others charged sexism.

The topic of media images of women is most often examined in the context of motion picture and television roles: Will gay-themed plot developments on *Ellen* represent a leap forward for lesbians? Was Alfred Hitchcock a misogynist? Yet a far more pervasive and influential arena for image-making than the entertainment world is the quotidian broadcast network newscast, a place to which, on the local and national level, millions of Americans habitually turn for an authoritative-sounding summary of the day's events—neatly ranked in order of presumed importance, and presented by a well-dressed person who seems singularly on top of it all.

That is why, I believe, the Chung affair is significant for feminist scholars as well as for the casual student of broadcast network decision-making and image-proffering: Chung's fate provides an ideal opportunity to study how illusions of "authority" (or the lack thereof) are used as weapons against female ascension in the media, and to demonstrate the burden placed upon women by a business whose predominantly male decision-makers still have not decided if women are either legitimate contributors, fully equal to their male counterparts, or window-dressing for ratings—distressed newscasts. A corollary to these issues is the reaction of some television critics at the nation's daily newspapers, a group charged with reporting and commenting on the activities of the television news and entertainment business. From this community, which typically delights at the chance to castigate network executives for their cynical, profit-driven and myopic agendas, the failure to put Chung's fall in the larger context of gender-specific image-making is illuminating.

The Chung affair, I will argue, hinged not upon issues of journalism or even economics, but upon assumptions about imagery: which images do television news executives anoint, and expect viewers to accept, as authoritative? Why is broadcast network television news one of the last bastions of male direction and domination, both in front of and behind the camera? More to the point, why has the situation been allowed to exist with little comment or opposition from the nation's television critics and other interested observers? Perhaps an issue such as the Chung debacle may, in the fullness of time, eventually rouse us from our passive acceptance of the imagery set forth by television networks as authoritative. Perhaps, in that light, Chung may prove to be a martyr for the next wave of television criticism: criticism that will analyze the imagery underlying what passes for authority in a network newscast.

By now, most Americans know the awful truth: television newsreaders, unlike newspaper reporters, do not personally gather information and then write it down for presentation. (Some do so early in their careers, but promotion to anchor status—which brings a larger salary, more prestige and usually a clothing and makeup allowance—means release from those prosaic chores.) For the difficult and time-consuming drudgery of actually seeking and writing news, stations employ less photogenic people. Thus, contrary to the image of the hard-driving, "street smart" journalist/anchor that many stations attempt to perpetuate with commercials showing their newsreaders racing around the newsroom or propping a phone against an upraised shoulder while typing the final details on a late-breaking story, anchors don't "report" the news. They read it. Reading aloud can be challenging, as anyone who has participated in a high-school speech contest can verify, but it is a far different challenge from doggedly acquiring information and shaping it into clear, accurate, compelling prose.

I mention these details because, in the wake of Chung's ouster, one of the more irritating reactions was the charge that she was a journalistic lightweight, a pretty bauble set down beside the serious, capable Rather. She was only brought in to boost the ratings, many observers sniffed with high-minded disdain, as if *anything* done by network television news executives is done for any purpose other than increasing the ratings. (Television news is one of those peculiar enterprises forced to display interest in a "higher good," a noble calling, while also paying strict attention to a fiscal bottom line; universities face the same paradoxical mission, a mission that practically guarantees hypocrisy in the contrast between public statements and private behavior.) Such a derogatory picture of Chung's achievements and abilities is very much at odds with the actual facts of her career—yet even if it *were* true, it would be irrelevant to the issue of authoritative imagery. A lightweight? No more and no less so than her colleague Rather. Yet Rather has been, as they say, dining out on his reputation as a journalist—a reputation forged in 1963 when he found himself in Dallas at the time of the assassination of President John F. Kennedy—long after he had ceased to do more than show up at disaster scenes and read other peoples' words about the events. His "coverage" of Hurricane Opal in south Florida in early October 1995 is a case in point; a wild-haired Rather stood in the midst of a pounding rain and tearing wind, clinging to a post, while excitedly informing the audience that yes, hurricanes are rough. Rather frequently indulges in such pointless on-air spectacles. I can only imagine how a female anchor who engaged in such theatrics would be vilified for melodramatic histrionics at the expense of real news—a typically hysterical "female" response to a situation requiring logic and calm, some observers doubtless would charge.

Many observers, however, continued to insist in the wake of Chung's demotion that she was an inept—yet comely—bumbler hardly fit to sit next to the avuncular, accomplished Rather. Naturally, they claimed, she could only have been brought aboard the newscast to improve the ratings, to lure those shallow, ill-informed viewers who choose a newscast based on a pretty face rather than more responsible inducements such as thorough, unbiased news coverage. Certainly, they opined, it could not have been Chung's professional track record.

How, then, to explain a 1986 memoir in which former NBC News anchor Linda Ellerbee called Chung "one of the hardest working journalists I know" (112), and described Chung's incisive investigative report on abortion clinics in the Los Angeles area? Ellerbee's book takes pains to ridicule many other television news reporters, anchors and executives—in fact, that seems to have largely been the point of Ellerbee's tart-tongued memoirs—hence the praise for Chung rings with uncommon sincerity. I have no special regard for Chung; she is one of a number of competent newsreaders who are able to communicate with viewers with an impressive degree of pseudo-intimacy that is the hallmark of the contemporary broadcast style. Yet to dismiss her work as trivial is to ignore a respectable record of achievement in the light of recent reverses. Chung's fate at CBS managed to do, I think, what such headlong pitches from high places always tend to do: distort the record, calling forth the sort of smug, ill-informed hindsight that delights in the misfortunes of others.

Chung's abilities, however, are really beside the point, since journalistic ability has nothing to do with the anchor position. Whether or not she was a competent journalist whose credentials are easily the match of Rather's—and I believe the record shows that she is and they were—Chung was dumped for reasons that have nothing to do with getting that big story on deadline.

Commentators on the Chung affair, both inside and outside the television news business, pretended that the issue was one of journalistic acumen, but it wasn't and isn't—the issue is image-making. The image of a television news anchor is one of grave and steady authority, of attaining power over events by virtue of having delivered details about them to ignorant multitudes, of being "in the know." Whether or not that image is accurate—whether, that is, the person reading the news actually knows anything at all about the subject under discussion—is, as I have argued, irrelevant: television news anchors aren't journalists, anyway. Image is preeminent. Authority, the image in question, is one of those coveted commodities that have defined the feminist quest in the public sphere. She or he who defines the parameters of "authority"—what does it look like, sound like?—will be graced with the mantle of success: title, salary, the implication that such authority is inevitable and "natural."

Marlene Sanders, a former ABC News executive producer and now a journalism professor at Columbia University, told *Los Angeles Times* reporter Jane Hall: "Women still are on the fringes as evening news anchors. The networks regard these newscasts as their symbols of seriousness, and they're reluctant to give a woman the job" (12). Symbols of seriousness. Note that the issue as defined by Sanders, who has been privy to high-level network meetings, is not *actual* seriousness of purpose or approach, as might be manifested in the choices of words, pictures, or perspectives that constitute the newscast, but one of symbol, of imagery. The *Times* article also quoted Cokie Roberts, ABC News reporter and commentator: "I'm sure there are still a lot of viewers who would prefer to see a man sitting there when they turn on their TV set in a time of national crisis. It's father in charge" (12).

Interestingly, then, Sanders and Roberts observe the same phenomenon—the historical lack of women in anchor positions in network television newscasts—and cite utterly different origins: Sanders blames the (predominately if not exclusively male) news executives for their prejudice against women as symbols of authority; Roberts claims that the executives are only reflecting audience desires and expectations. This classic, chicken-or-egg debate infuses a great deal of commentary about decision-making in the television industry: Do network chieftains select and air inane programs because that is all the public will watch, or does the public watch inane programs because those are all that network chieftains select and air? Likewise, might one attribute the lack of female anchors to network news presidents' conviction that viewers see males as symbols of authority, or to the fact that viewers see males as authority symbols because males have historically been assigned such symbolic status by virtue of the convictions of network news presidents?

Sanders and Roberts do agree, however, that the issue of selecting and promoting anchors indeed is one of "authority," of a knowledgeable and reassuring presence during the recitation of what may prove to be depressing, surprising or inconvenient information. NBC News anchor Tom Brokaw, interviewed on the June 7, 1995, edition of *Larry King Live* shortly after the Chung ouster, mused that the Rather-Chung tandem failed because viewers were accustomed to a "single line of authority." The important word in Brokaw's phrase, I think, is not "single" but "authority." (Brokaw attempted to claim that Chung's demotion came because of a crowded anchor desk, not because she is female; under Brokaw's scenario, one of the anchors just had to go, *ergo* former CBS News President Eric Ober must have flipped a coin—and Chung, unfortunately, lost.) Authority—a fictional contrivance at best, an illusion composed of vocal tone, garb and perhaps the amount of silver in the hair—is the criterion upon which critical decisions about the staffing of news delivery systems are made. (How have women fared in the on-air authority sweepstakes? According to a 1993 study by Joseph Foote of the School of Communications at Southern Illinois University which was cited in *The Los Angeles Times*, women deliver one-quarter of the stories on network television newscasts, and one-third of network on-air personnel are female, figures that have remained stable for the past decade.)

Despite attempts to cast the lack of female anchors as a simple reflection of audience desires, the idea that a woman lacks the seriousness of mind to interpret and deliver major news stories would seem to be rooted in the basest and most reprehensible sort of prejudice—much like the earlier, equally false and odious notion that the lack of blacks in positions of responsibility in business and government was due to an inherent intellectual inferiority. Such demeaning prejudices always seem to be based on "truth" and "reality"—until they are proven wrong.

It was not until the early 1970s, in fact, that women were featured as regular contributors to local newscasts, much less national newscasts. Among the first was Jessica Savitch, the late NBC correspondent and occasional anchor whom some regard as a pioneer in the profession—and, ironically, a victim of the very energy and ambition that accounted for her success. *Almost Golden*, a 1995 made-for-cable movie, dramatizes Savitch's swift rise and even swifter tumble (due to, the movie theorizes, low self-esteem, bad relationships, and cocaine dependency), but not before she had worked as the nation's first female co-anchor of a weeknight newscast in a major television market. Judy Girard, vice-president of programming and production for Lifetime Television, the cable network that aired the Savitch biography, said, "Prior to that [Savitch's work], it really, really was believed that people did not want to hear news from a woman—they wanted to hear weather and maybe a little reporting was OK, but the serious stuff, they didn't want to hear from a woman. They couldn't take a woman telling them about a Jonestown massacre live, which she [Savitch] did. And she did that quite effectively on the night that it happened."

Yet Savitch's employment history, which in some ways prefigured Chung's, is emblematic of the exploitation women routinely encounter in the television news business: According to *Almost Golden*, NBC hired Savitch because she was attractive and because viewers responded positively to her, not because of her reporting skills, the standards by which her male correspondents were evaluated and hired. When the ratings did not show growth, Savitch was dropped. Bernie Sofronski, producer of *Almost Golden*, said her story is one of "a network using someone for the ratings and simply throwing them away." Likewise, Sofronski said, Chung "was also dumped because she didn't deliver. It wasn't up to Rather to deliver the ratings, it was up to her to deliver the ratings, right? And that's why she was dropped."

The treatment of Chung and Savitch by network television executives reflects a discouraging truth about the business: Women, indisputably, often are hired for reasons other than their professional abilities—superficial, cosmetic reasons, reasons that have more to do with luring viewers than providing quality news reports. The real culprits in such situations, of course, are the executives who make the hiring decisions, not the women who aspire to careers in broadcast journalism and who must live within a set of rules they neither made nor, I suspect, condone.

Moreover, if a thwarted desire for increased ratings indeed was behind the demotions of Savitch and Chung, a curious double standard is at work: Why is it the woman's responsibility to boost newscast ratings? If, indeed, as some observers claim (but CBS executives denied), Chung *was* hired to help the slumping CBS News broadcast—a slump that began during Rather's solo tenure—why, if the ratings didn't respond, was *Chung* dumped? Logic and fairness would seem to dictate that the person whom viewers had rejected initially, that is, Rather, be let go instead of Chung. Women, however, are always more expendable.

Among the several television critics whom I polled informally about the Chung matter during the Television Critics Association semi-annual meeting in Pasadena, July 14-23, 1995, all but one blamed, in effect, both Chung and CBS: Chung for letting herself be used as a ratings ploy, the network for using her thusly. Only one critic termed Chung's demotion sexist.

Sandy Smith, formerly a television critic for *The Nashville Tennessean*, called Chung a "scapegoat for all the mistakes the network made," yet "her firing was no more sexist than her hiring was." Smith added, "Chung may have had a problem working with Dan Rather, who made things hard for her, but there are women anchors all over the country working with male anchors who make it hard for them." Scott Pierce, television critic for *The Salt Lake City Desert News*, blamed public relations: "The whole thing was handled dishonestly by CBS," yet "she got the job because she was a woman. They never would've hired a man as a co-anchor." *The Wichita Eagle's* television critic, Bob Curtright, called Chung "a fall guy," adding, "The network's problems run deeper than Connie Chung." Gail Pennington, television critic for the *St. Louis Post-Dispatch*, concurred: "I blame the network more than Chung. They put her in there to lighten up the broadcast, then complained that she had undermined her credibility with fluff pieces." Hal Boedeker of the *Orlando Sentinel* called the Chung affair "rather sad." Her hiring "backfired, because it wasn't done for the right reasons in the first place. She was the wrong woman for the job. If they had put a more qualified woman in the job in the first place—a woman with journalistic credentials—they wouldn't have had this problem." Barry Garron, formerly television critic of *Kansas City Star*, was equally dismayed with Chung: "If she'd been a male, she never would have been seated next to Dan Rather. Given that opportunity, she made the least of it." Susan Young, television critic for *The Oakland Tribune*, echoed his disgust: "She was at the top of the heap. She could've done any story she wanted to do. And what did she do? Fluff. Plus, she made too many mistakes."

Chung's so-called "mistakes" supply an interesting commentary on the expectations for male and female television personalities. Chung was chided for provoking Speaker of the House Newt Gingrich's mother into a potentially embarrassing on-air admission by telling Mrs. Gingrich the remark would be "just between us," a strategic, obviously coy, and deliberately disingenuous rhetorical flourish often used by male interviewers; and for allegedly insulting rescue personnel after the bombing of the Oklahoma City federal building in April 1995 by asking them if their departments were capable of handling the emergency. Male reporters asked the same questions at the scene, and were praised for their hard-hitting, no-holds-barred truth-seeking. Mistakes? Missteps? Perhaps by the interpreters of these harmless incidents; certainly not by Chung.

The only critic who called Chung's treatment sexist was Ron Miller of *The San Jose Mercury News*: "It was a clear case of a double standard. Look at all the things Rather has done—walking off the air just before a newscast because a tennis match had run long, causing the network to go to black, and the comments he's made about the network to outside groups—and there was incredible tolerance. When something goes wrong at CBS and there is a problem between a man and a woman, they dump the woman."

What of Chung's ethnicity? As an Asian-American woman Chung is, of course, heir to two separate strains of prejudice: racism and sexism. Those prejudices are daily, undeniable presences in the workplace, but they are especially meaningful in a job such as network anchor, a job that carries a tremendous load of symbolic import. To be a figure of authority, one must assume power; assuming power means subverting a social order built upon the silencing of women. Few commentators have expressed this more cogently than Carolyn Heilbrun in *Writing a Woman's Life*:

Women of accomplishment, in unconsciously writing their future lived lives, or, more recently, in trying honestly to deal in written form with lived past lives, have had to confront power and control. Because this has been declared unwomanly, and because many women would prefer (or think they would prefer) a world without evident power or control, women have been deprived of the narratives, or the texts, plots, or examples, by which they might assume power over—take control of—their own lives. (16)

Heilbrun is speaking of women's biographies and autobiographies, but I think there is a discernible and significant link between the concept of personal narrative—biography and autobiography—and the performative narrative of events presented by the anchor of a television newscast. In both cases, the power belongs to the narrator; whether one is telling the story of one's own life, or telling the world's story, the tale is owned by the teller. Image-making in the anchor ranks, then, is an issue of power and control, of who decides what constitutes "news," of who will do the speaking.

Yet many people—television critics, network executives, Chung's colleagues—have gone to great lengths to deny that authority and imagery are at the heart of networks' failure to hire and support female main anchors. That is, women usually are relegated to weekend and late-night broadcasts, less visible arenas. Witness an exchange on the aforementioned *Larry King Live* broadcast, which featured Brokaw, CBS anchor Mike Wallace, and Walters. Brokaw and Wallace agreed that a nightly newscast was simply ill-equipped to deal with the dual-anchor format; thus the Chung demotion, they concluded with mutual self-satisfaction, was a reflection of venue rather than any other factor. Walters gently chided them: "Huntley and Brinkley did all right." Her allusion to perhaps the best-known and most successful news team in broadcasting history—and *their* convenient ability to block it out—reveal the extent of the cultural denial that power and authority are the salient issues. If it was indeed the presence of two anchors, and not Chung's gender, that doomed her, then how does one explain the Huntley-Brinkley success? Brokaw and Wallace also failed to explain why the dual-anchor format has worked so well for local television newscasts, in which the presence of one male and one female anchor is virtually an institution. How, moreover, does one explain Rather's unwillingness to take responsibility for the ratings slump? Since Chung's banishment, by the way, *The CBS Evening News* has failed to improve its ratings position.

The broadcast network news anchor is a position of unique and perhaps unparalleled authority in contemporary America—a "symbol of seriousness" entrusted to set the national mood in times of crisis or celebration, elation or despair. The fact that no woman has been permitted to hold that position for more than two years is rather astonishing. Admittedly, women are more visible in upstart cable news operations; yet to the majority of Americans, "the news" still refers to the nightly broadcast newscast. Equally astonishing, moreover, is the fact that the situation has been allowed to continue without significant challenge for so long, even as women have made strides for full representation in other highly visible fields. The media industry is always swift to point out the ways in which other businesses fall short of important social goals such as equal opportunity; thus the house from whose threshold it throws that particular stone, ironically, seems to be constructed entirely of glass.

Perhaps the Chung demotion and its aftermath will highlight, as nothing else quite has, the degree to which authoritative imagery has eluded women in this most prominent and crucial of venues. For messengers matter; they matter most of all in a medium in which the message itself is so often trivial, redundant, and primitively stated, that is, television news. The authority of a broadcast television news anchor may indeed be mostly illusory, an unholy alliance of marketing and makeup, yet that authority is a symbol that might transcend the specific circumstances from which it arose. A female news anchor, that is, might prove influential far beyond the self-selected range of the audience for a particular television broadcast.

Television news, for all of its shallowness and inanity, for all of its obvious inferiority to print news in terms of thoroughness and sophistication, still is regarded by a vast segment of the public as a legitimate source of information, as the purveyor of a valuable perspective on the world. Much as that may make media critics shudder with distaste, it is true, and because it is true, its power must be respected. Indeed, while network anchors may be little more than glib, well-dressed mouthpieces for the media conglomerates that now own each of the three major networks, they are also symbols—symbols of power, success, prestige—and images, as we know, suggest and finally embody their own stubborn reality.

BIBLIOGRAPHY

Ellerbee, Linda. *And So It Goes: Adventures in Television.* New York: G. P. Putnam's Sons, 1986.

Girard, Judy and Bernard Sofronski. "July 1995 TCA Press Tour: July 9, 1995." Unpublished transcript.

Hall, Jane. "Why No Women Anchors?" *The Los Angeles Times* 17 July 1995: 12.

Heilbrun, Carolyn G. *Writing a Woman's Life.* New York: Ballantine Books, 1988.

Section II

Causing a Stir: Women's Ways of Subversion

Chapter 4

Tracking Ida: The Bold, the Brash, and the Secondary in Hollywood Film

Judith Roof

Eve Arden and Mary Wickes are both "character" actors whose atypically strong sidekick personae translated into screen longevity. Arden's career lasted from the 1929 *The Song of Love* to 1982's *Grease 2* and included the successful radio and television series *Our Miss Brooks* (1952–1957). Wickes began acting in films in 1941 and is still cavorting as a gawky nun in *Sister Act II.*[1] Playing the buddy, the savvy confidante, the wise-cracking cynic with the heart of gold, the bus-driving nun, the capable, clunky woman who represses dreams of marital bliss, Arden and Wickes provide the filmic equivalent of a spinsterish Shakespearean fool who is, of course, no fool. Both portray insightful characters of uncertain (or very mobile) class, seemingly extraneous gender, and detached (but really deeply involved) affections who are shrewd, loyal, utilitarian, self-denying, and likeable. Able to cross the bounds of social groupings, gender expectations, and sometimes propriety, these versatile and omnipresent *femmes audacieuses* are privy to the main character's introspection, perform a meta-commentary on the film's action, double the female protagonist and the audience, and mediate between film and viewer in various ways. Intercessors and interpreters, the bold, brash, and singular are independent and parasitic; they are imaged only insofar as they perform their functions, but they promise so much more in the seductive intermittence of their screen appearance and the aura of safety that surrounds them.

How these wise jesters with their astute estimations of plot, character, culture, and life are translated into the "tough" spinster figure in films of the 1930s, 1940s, and 1950s is an effect of the way Hollywood cinema negotiates the politics of the "loose" woman—that is, the woman who is not moored to any specific coupling (either real or imaginary). Insofar as the prototypical narratives of many film genres are linked to a heterosexualized disposition of female characters—women are married, tragically not, fallen, recovered, all in relation to men—those females who present only a distant or secondary relation to such hetero fates seem to fall out of narrative consideration. While the good pretty woman gets married and the bad pretty woman gets what she deserves, the really smart but gawky woman gets nothing, posing a loose end problem for the romance plot that is visible not so much at the film's end where these characters more or less disappear, but throughout the film in their example of a chronically reluctant liberation. Stranded by their virtue, spinsters are the good whores, the ugly virgins, the female guys, the bachelorettes, who, because of their position outside the marriage market, are able to see the vagaries of love with the long-range insight of Teiresias. The larger function of secondary spinster characters in these narratives, as I hope to demonstrate, is not only to support, enable, and by contrast, make desirable the ends of the film's central narrative, but also to supply the hint of an alternative—a counterposition—to such coupling that is also both attractive and diegetically possible.

NOW YOU SEE THEM, NOW YOU DON'T

To read for these characters is to read against the grain of the film's spectacle and its narrative; wanting to watch Eve Arden instead of Joan Crawford in *Mildred Pierce* (1945), for example, has two effects: 1) it is impossible to find any sustained narrative that accounts for Ida Corwin (Eve Arden); 2) Ida's appearances are aligned with a kind of canny uncanny, a *heimlich unheimlich* that keeps reappearing, but which provides a solace point in the trajectory of the film's more melodramatic narrative. Unlike the uncanny which would supply the impetus for a momentary and frightening unrepression of repressed material, the homey (or homely) return of the canny spinster character provides moments of bliss.[2] This bliss is both the extreme delight of familiar and homey repetition—the more typical meaning of bliss—and an instance of Roland Barthes' more problematic textual "bliss" performed by the "text that imposes a state of loss, the text that discomforts, . . . unsettles the reader's historical, cultural, psychological assumptions . . . ."[3] Insofar as the female second goes along with, enables, and supports the film's narrative of productive joinder (marriage, financial success, knowledge), she is a canny text of pleasure in Barthes' terms; insofar as her appearance imports an alternate possibility, a sudden (if minor) break in the certainty of the romance or an interruption in its trajectory, her appearances are analogous to bliss. The point of this analogy to Barthes' textual distinction (which may not finally exactly fit the film experience) is to find some language to characterize how the female second's role and appearance are linked simultaneously to pleasure and scandal, with and against the narrative, to home and to an ejection from the domestic scene. Bliss approximates the complex delight arising from the pleasure, loss, mastery, and uncertainty of their appearances.

Like a text of bliss, Ida Corwin is difficult to track through *Mildred Pierce*. Tracing her scattered appearances is an exercise in interrupted pleasure and loss as well as an experience of the sustained anticipation of returning safety, insight, and humor. Ida weaves through Mildred's story, but is neither omnipresent nor central to the narrative's impetus; rather, she literally moves off screen where viewers either abandon her or are thwarted in their already counter-narrative *fort-da* game of narrative/spectacle mastery. *Mildred Pierce* begins with a murder in its film noir present and depicts the main character, Mildred, leading her friend, the crass Wally, back to a beach house where, having been abandoned by Mildred, he discovers the dead body of her husband Monte Beragon. The police investigate the crime, picking Mildred and her daughter Vida up from their opulent home and depositing them at the police station to await questioning. The film introduces Ida in the police station, where, dressed in furs and a toque, she tells her police escort to be careful, saying "Look, I bruise easy." Meeting Wally, she remarks, "Well, what is this, a class reunion?"

Her wisecracks already signal her as the beauty with the mouth, the woman who seems not to care too much about male opinion. This brief introduction also establishes Ida as a comic type in the film's framing melodramatic environment, the off-key wit whose sense of everyday proportion manifests itself even at the extraordinary site of police investigation. Her sarcastic resistance to the police make her immediately a character to be trusted, one who dislikes being pushed around but who realistically complies with the circumstances. Her presence in the police station raises the question of who she is and how she fits into any of what is happening, projecting a certain pleasure in the prospect of finding out. The film then proceeds through a series of happier, less stylistically film noir flashbacks in which Mildred recounts the narrative of her rise to success as a restaurant entrepreneur.[4] Having split with her husband, Bert, and conducting a long and fruitless search for a job, Mildred becomes a waitress in a restaurant Ida manages; Ida gives Mildred her first break and her first lessons in restaurant decorum. Ida's reappearance as Mildred's temporary savior in the everyday register of the flashback answers one question raised by her initial appearance; her reassuring figure stabilizes the film's flashback logic. In the depictions of Mildred's early, post-marital career, Ida is the surrogate for Mildred's first husband, supplying the equivalent of domestic companionship and care that Bert finally resumes at film's end.

Although Ida is present during much of the film's flashback exposition of Mildred's feelings and doubts and at the points of her public success, Ida has no existence of her own apart from Mildred. It is impossible to follow Ida consistently through the film except as she intersects with Mildred. While Mildred circulates through multiple environments—Wally's real estate office, Monte Beragon's beach house, her home—Ida stays at the restaurant, the primary site of Mildred's success. Linked to money and independence, Ida's appearance reinforces Mildred's sharp business sense, industry, and the rewards of hard work. At the end of Mildred's first day of business as a restaurant owner, Ida, who has been running the cash register, riffles a stack of bills and says, "Isn't that a lovely noise?" When Mildred comments that she didn't know what she would have done without Ida, Ida responds, "Probably had a nervous breakdown." During the same conversation, Ida's interactions with Wally, who unsuccessfully pursues Mildred, not only play out the spinster status of the singular second, but echo loudly Mildred's unspoken opinions about Wally. When Wally walks past Ida as she is adjusting her stockings, Ida quips, "Leave something on me, I might catch cold," to which Wally responds, "I was just thinking, not about you." When Mildred decides to get a ride home with Ida instead of Wally, leaving Wally to take care of the adolescent Vida, Wally complains, "I hate all women," to which Ida adds a "My, my." In a fit of pique, Wally snarls, "Thank goodness, you're not one."

As Wally's rejoinder suggests, Ida is not quite the "woman" Mildred is, neither as a gutsy businesswoman nor as a male focus. In all of her appearances Ida is witty, sardonic, and protective, treating and treated by Mildred as a friend and equal, one who is mildly hostile to the men who take advantage of Mildred's weakness for her daughter. As the first person Mildred checks in with after a month-long vacation, Ida tries to calm Mildred down, getting her a drink ("Hey, Gene, crack open the safe and get out some of that good bourbon"), and putting Mildred's male problems into perspective by recounting her own: "Oh men," she comments, "I never met one of them who didn't have the instincts of a heel. Sometimes I wish I could get along without them." Responding to Mildred's query about whether she had ever been married, Ida replies, "No, when men get around me, they get allergic to wedding rings. You know, big sister type, good old Ida, you can talk it over with her man to man. I'm awfully tired of men talking to me man to man."

Ida's only history is her narrative of her buddy relation to men, one that parallels her relation to Mildred; she marks herself as outside the romance plot. Man to man,woman to woman, Ida is the interstitial female denied romance but well supplied with confidences. And as she continues to appear to manage Mildred's difficult moments, this confidence is well earned as her perspective on events (which matches the audience's perspicacity) enables her to give timely but unheeded warning to Mildred and others. Presiding over Vida's birthday party on the night when Mildred's various male friends betray her and wrest control of the restaurant from her, Ida senses that something is wrong and warns Mildred to be careful. Ida is a canny reader of character, however, whose observations, like those of the fool figure, are most often ignored. When Monte becomes romantically entangled with Vida, she warns him: "Don't look now, Junior, you're standing under a brick wall." When he replies that he doesn't understand her, she predicts, "You will when it falls on you." If Monte doesn't get it, the audience does, Ida's sense of events reporting the film's dramatic irony. At Vida's party when Ida suspects trouble, she tells Monte, "Something's going on. I'm worried. I think she's in some kind of business trouble." When Beragon unfeelingly quips, "It happens in the best of families," Ida subtly indicts him for his probable part: "Don't look now, but you've got canary feathers all over your face." With her broader perspective Ida is linked with the audience; her insight into characters is that of a more omniscient presence. At the same time her mastery of such knowledge is clearly the result of her superior intuition and good sense, since she is plainly not witness to many of the events which clue the audience into the dubious characters' capacities.

Because her insight and sardonic but succoring role are clearly focused on Mildred, Ida's appearances in the course of the film are also comforting insofar as the audience identifies with Mildred. Ida is a resting place whose combination of humor and wisdom gives us all a moment of mastery as Ida evens scores (insulting Wally and, more subtly, Monte), tallies the day's take, and supplies sustenance. The pleasure associated with her appearances combined with her disappearance from the scene often during the unpleasant or tense moments, makes her a pleasurable figure both in herself and in her association with moments of repose and revenge. At the same time, Ida's way of cutting through the romance is analogous to a bliss that exists in the very possibility of destruction offered by the character who systematically disappears.

In addition to reverberations of textual bliss, tracking Ida provides a slightly different kind of pleasure than a fix on Mildred might. If part of Ida's charm exists in her trenchant commentary and rich ambivalence, part also lies in her seductive pattern of presence and absence and the pleasure/bliss her appearance/disappearance affords. While tracking the secondary character offers a position of symbolic superiority created by the secondary characters' wisdom, insight, and savvy about the very narrative that elides them, it also produces and is produced by a desire that results from the irregular appearances of these characters themselves. Following a secondary character produces a very different kind of spectatorial desire, one that will of necessity be thwarted by the exigencies of the film's dominant system, but a desire that is sustained because it is thwarted.

This desire is a desire connected to a perverse narrative if we understand the perverse, as Freud did, to be the spot where coherent sexual development, or by analogy, a story, falls apart. In Freud's account of the perverse in *Three Essays on a Theory of Sexuality*, perverse activity is a necessary part of sexual development, sexuality, and the story, serving its function as inhibition or dissociation only in relation to the sexual narrative's ultimate end in "the discharge of the sexual substances" (76). In other words, the perverse consists of sexual activities which don't have either reproduction (the proper "aim") or the genitals of a person of the opposite sex (the proper "object") as their goal or focus; even so, perverse activities are necessary to the impetus that enables individuals and the story to get to its proper end at the proper time. The perverse titillates, leads on, distracts, and finally gets us to a productive conclusion. In relation to *Mildred Pierce's* dominant narrative, Ida's appearances are perverse; necessary, beside the point, intriguing in their pleasure, they deviate from and lead back to the heterosexual romance plot and solution of the murder mystery that comprise the film's primary action.

As such perversity is linked to the desire that is generated by the sporadic appearances of Ida, the perverse economy might also be understood as a figuratively lesbian dynamic.[5] If we understand a lesbian dynamic as a desire for desire (the inherently perverse), then deliberately tracking a secondary, liminal spinster character becomes a kind of lesbian and/or perverse reading practice, whether the representation or the viewer is consciously lesbian or not.[6] Reading against the heteronarrative text, desiring the spectacle of that which is as often denied as it is provided, tracking the secondary spinster is a pleasurable activity associated with the counter-narrative such characters provide. Like the perverse, this counter-narrative is not really a counter-narrative in the sense that it works solely against the romance plot; it is a part of and necessary to such a plot. In so functioning, however, it counterposes a different economy of desire against the closure narratives of success and romance in the primary plot. If the protagonist of *Mildred Pierce* begins a successful restaurant only to lose it all because of her blindness about her daughter's greedy superficiality and her bad judgment about men, and ends up back where she started with the original nuclear familial male, Ida is, no less than Mildred, a victim of and contributor to this trajectory. But Ida is conscious, resigned, and perversely combative all at the same time; in relation to the film's narrative her consciousness of the narrative pattern provides an alternative position located both in the safe space of female friendship and support and in the provision of a superior knowledge of narrative patterns themselves. Ida's felicitous presence and final detachment suggest an ironically healthier relation to the extra-romantic interstices than Mildred's investment in production/reproduction provides.

In *The Man Who Came to Dinner* (1941) and *White Christmas* (1954), Mary Wickes's interstitial character mediates between film action and audience. A constantly flustered nurse in the earlier film, Wickes finally does what many other characters in the film have tried unsuccessfully to do: tell off Sheridan Whiteside. Her regular appearances with medicine (which she literally throws at Whiteside) function much like Ida's appearances function in *Mildred Pierce*: to provide a safe, recurrent ground for an alternate identification. Much more abbreviated that Arden's sustained supporting role, Wickes's nurse nonetheless manages to foment a small rebellion that represents both character and audience opinion about the imperious Whiteside.

In *White Christmas* Wickes is even more a mediating character who tries to control the narrative disposition of characters and events. Positioned as the spinster housekeeper in a winter lodge failing for lack of snow, Wickes manipulates events behind the scenes, listening in on telephone conversations and aiding Bob (Bing Crosby) and Phil (Danny Kaye) as they try to bring business to the hotel. She occupies the traditionally off-screen, behind-the-scenes locus where knowledge circulates. But unlike Ida Corwin, Wickes functions as a literal interrupter in the romance plot when she misunderstands a conversation she has overheard. Giving Betty Haynes (Rosemary Clooney) the wrong idea about Bob's motives causes Betty to quit the show and leave for New York. Since the happiness of all depend on Betty and Bob's getting together, Wickes functions as the impetus for loss and the possibility of the narrative's failure. She is, of course, also instrumental in the ploy that enables Bob to bring everything—show, soldiers, romance, and snow—to Pine Tree Lodge at the film's end.

In addition to her disruptive manipulations, Wickes functions as a chorus in the film, reflecting audience and character reactions to events hyperbolically, kissing Bob and Phil when they decide to bring their show to the inn, crying at engagement announcements. Her presence at these moments is necessary to mark the convergence of all narrative lines—the normal, the perverse, the possible, and the improbability of the pairings that constitutes the film's simultaneous movement toward matchmaking and healing leftover wounds caused by the war and obsolescence.

SPATIAL CASES

One reason these secondary characters perform effectively as counter-narrative agents is that they are both consistent and predictable; Arden and Wickes appear in the same type of secondary role across filmic genre and for a fifty-year span of Hollywood film history. That the same actresses regularly play wise-cracking second roles seems a logical extension of these particular actresses' personae even though their screen characters and our way of reading and interpreting them are defined by their roles in film. Their very presence in a film already signals their role and the way they should be read even if the films they are in vary from comedy to musical to melodrama.[7] While film narratives are fairly predictable, expectations vary from genre to genre; that these characters stay much the same from film to film suggests that the brash exceed genre and function instead within the more comprehensive working of narrative and gender ideology. Fools perform everywhere. The female seconds' interfilmic and pan-generic consistency is important in the face of film's more openly gendered narratives (narratives in which gender is an issue instead of narrative's typically gendered pretext[8]); no matter what narrative or environmental disturbance threatens the female lead, we can depend upon female seconds to assure the protagonist and audience that all is well, that there is always a place of escape, that within the difficulties of capitalist production and marriage there is another option for survival. Safe within the film, they suggest the possibility of life beyond the strictly hetero.

While they are narratively eccentric, these secondary spinsters occupy what is less a periphery than the figurative site of home. Neither the familial nor the domestic, this home is the center of operations—a kind of commercial home where business and camaraderie are mixed, the refuge of the already atypical, overly independent (or at least unmarried) woman. The quasi-public sites of their influence—*Stage Door's* theatrical boarding house, *Mildred Pierce's* restaurant, *White Christmas's* Pine Tree Inn, or *The Trouble With Angels'* and *Sister Act's* convent schools—signify both the liminal character of these side-kicks and the extent to which the films' female protagonists have eschewed the confines of a traditional patriarchal role and space. Some of these settings are all-female spaces, like *Stage Door's* Footlights Club, which in itself already captures the interactions among women as the film's primary locus; the same, of course, is true for convent schools, though *Sister Act's* school is coeducational.

In *Mildred Pierce* and *White Christmas* Arden and Wickes inhabit the centers of operations; Arden is cashier and trusted employee, Wickes is the housekeeper and conniving protector of the realm. Marginal to the more overtly public spaces to which they contrast—the theatre in *Stage Door*, the Inn's dining room in *White Christmas*—the offices, cash registers, and hotel desks simultaneously signify marginality and empowerment, sequestration and centrality. Their association with sites of control reinforces their ambivalent position as both inside and outside, dependent and independent, savvy and overlooked. These alternative spaces are also safe spaces emblematic of both struggle and respite, self-determination and pride no matter what film genre employs them. The female protagonists take a break in these spaces from narrative difficulties, catch up with themselves, ponder and reflect as Mildred Pierce does in the restaurant office with Ida or the aspiring actresses do in the living room of the Footlights Club, or, to a lesser extent, as the Haynes sisters do with Mary Wickes in *White Christmas*.

If we read how such spaces are articulated with the films' narratives, these marginal spaces of safety and control constitute a kind of on-screen off-screen space—the imaging of that which is traditionally minor in terms of its value in a patriarchal culture and omitted in the films' confluence of narrative and spectacle. The imaging of this space provides the illusion of a privileged view behind the scenes in spaces that are not directly attached to the protagonist's primary engagement in coupling, success, or the resolution of familial difficulties. In other words, this space seems to represent, in the films' narrative and spatial articulations, a kind of counter-ideological scene or perverse space (in the sense that it is the image of that which is extraneous, repressed, yet necessary to the narrative's emphasis on productive joinder). Imaging this space as part of these films' systems provides the opportunity for a visual mastery of what is narratively alternative—the women not bound up in romance—which in turn provides the illusion of a comprehensive mastery through the permitted vision of women alone—a vision of a space that delusively extends beyond patriarchy while resting safely within it.[9] Imaging such space appears to provide a locus for a complex identification with the margins (of both spectacle and narrative), defining a space that mediates among the film's onscreen space, its literal off-screen space, a species of alternative or "off"-narrative space, and the actual off-screen position of the viewer. This provides an alternate visual pathway into the film not necessarily identified with the protagonist or the impetus of dominant narrative, but still bound into the exposition of that narrative and the perspective provided by the apparatus itself.

Associated with safe, mediating, alternative spaces, Arden and Wickes combine independence with attachment and provide the terse care that makes these homes away from home homely. Like the spaces they occupy (and seem to have occupied forever), Arden and Wickes are tough and atraditional, substituting rough camaraderie for patriarchal protection, understanding for criticism, the bare truth for delusions of romance. Like the space they occupy, they function as go-betweens, co-conspirators, and modes of transport (Wickes is always the bus driver). Literally enacting their liminal privilege, Arden and Wickes get both protagonist and audience from one place to another.

Their generic polyvalence and perverse narrative position corresponds to the slight hint of sexual and gender ambivalence that typifies them, an ambivalence linked less to perverse narrative structures than to slight disturbances in the imaging of gender. Neither is what Karen Stoddard would define as a "saint" or a "shrew," nor are they versions of Kathleen Rowe's "unruly women," since neither is unruly or shrewish enough to pose any real threat to the dominant heteronarrative.[10] Instead there is a seemingly "natural" identification between role and actress linked to the ways they signal an ambivalence about power itself. They represent the category of the impermissibly able—the woman who is capable at stereotypically masculine tasks—but who pays for that capability by being barred from heterosexual commerce. This typing is not simply a matter of physical appearance where the female lead is somehow more beautiful than her single friend; Arden is as attractive as any of the actresses with whom she appears. Rather it is a self-contained but displaced lesson in female independence; while the female protagonist may assume power, her more atraditionally hard-bitten side-kick pays the price. But even as these female seconds pay, they signify the positive possibilities of exclusion from a system that the films, if read against the grain, already critique as disastrous to women. If, as both *Mildred Pierce* and *Stage Door* suggest, the dominant romance narrative is not necessarily healthy for women—Mildred's first husband leaves her, her second husband is a parasitic playboy who bleeds her dry and sells her out, and the men who squire the actresses in *Stage Door* are harassing opportunists or rubes from the sticks—then the alternative of the strong woman seems a possible answer. And insofar as the strong woman character is omitted from narrative disposition at the end of the film or, as in *Stage Door*, their disposition augments their image as ambivalent, the position they occupy is never quite discredited.

Cast as homely whether or not their appearance complies, Arden and Wickes are the feminine men, the strong women, the heterosexually ineligible, the unsuitable for suitors. Even the issue of sexual indeterminacy is indeterminate; imaged as primarily feminine, each displays signifiers—height, body language, tone of voice—that suggests an androgyny or slight cast of masculinity in addition to any cast of perversity their narrative function already conveys. Ruling over or at least imaged as strong and capable in more homogeneously female realms, they become, in an ineffable heterosexual logic, the masculine element among females, the surrogate men who provide straight talk and mechanical competence. But even a reading of sexual or gender indeterminacy depends upon their counter-narrative position within the romance plot; they are at one and the same time the women not chosen by men who are necessary to illuminate the fortune of the protagonist who is and the women who provide a substitute for heterosexual partnering in a less perilous female world.

GIRLS AMONG GIRLS

The safe economy of the perverse in films located within a predominantly heterosexual matrix such as *Mildred Pierce* and *White Christmas* changes slightly when these female seconds are relocated within primarily female worlds such as those featured in *Stage Door* and *The Trouble With Angels*. Where the female seconds were surrogate partners or parents to the female leads, in the more feminine world, they become more clearly the wise consorts, the protectors, and the handymen. Wickes, for example, consistently plays the bus-driving nun, the convents' surrogate male. This shift follows a heterosexual logic wherein some females take on characteristics typically defined as masculine in relation to other women; but as in *Mildred Pierce*, this assumption of strength or power again locates these characters in the interstitial position of the wise fool, the knowing seer who continues to provide a mediating metacommentary. Becoming, however, less spectacular in the film's increased economy of female presence, the Arden and Wickes characters are also more dangerous voices that mildly threaten while they support, and chastise while they protect.

In the 1937 *Stage Door*, Arden plays one of the Footlights Club's most vocal denizens. Performing the role of the acute critic and insightful commentator, Arden is also cast as the chief voice of opposition to Terry Randle (Katharine Hepburn), the Club's ingenue rich girl whose drive for success belittles the Club's long-struggling actresses. Imaged constantly with a cat she calls Henry, Arden critiques the boarding house food, Randle's intellectualism and ambition, the activities of the powerful and harassing theatrical agent, Anthony Powell, and the lumbermen who constantly call to date their hometown friend played by Lucille Ball. Part of an ensemble cast, Arden is the most acerbic voice of many critics including Ginger Rogers, Hepburn, Ann Miller, and Ball. But Arden stands out as the character who is notably not attached nor necessarily wishing to be attached to a male nor is she, like Hepburn, full of driving zeal.

Arden's metacommentary on the mating activities and thwarted ambitions of her companions provides a masterful view of the actresses' circumstances; at the same time, its sardonic quality is less homey and productive than it was in *Mildred Pierce* even though its very brusqueness serves to diminish the severity of the sometimes desperate straits of her companions.   When the homey—or what might traditionally be a periphery—becomes the film's center, the fool characters are displaced from a peripheral and openly perverse economy into a mainstream where their insight, because it is no longer perverse, becomes almost too painfully direct.   But even when these normally peripheral communities become central, the Arden and Wickes characters remain somewhat eccentric because of the penetrating quality of their insight and detachment—their slight difference marked as both knowledge and ambiguity. In films featuring women's communities, the female second is both central and marginal, taking again the role of protector.

Stage Door sets up a complex array of conflicts and rivalries among the boarding house denizens.   Ginger Rogers initially takes on Hepburn's Terry Randle, with Arden, chorus-like, sniping from the ensemble cast.   Echoing Rogers's difficulties with the pretentious Randle, Arden becomes Randle's primary verbal nemesis, doubling both Rogers and Hepburn in her detached, ironic way. Olivia de Havilland's character, the sensitive and talented actress, is championed by all, but particularly by Arden, who   serves as her protector. When de Havilland kills herself, Randle, who has won the part that should have been de Havilland's, doubles de Havilland, suddenly gaining the sensitivity she had previously lacked.   At the end of the film, Ball marries a lumberman, Randle has success, and Arden goes on as before, a communal constant, a watchdog of pretention, a check on the illusions and fantasies of fame.   While hints of any overt lesbian desire are quashed before they emerge in the communities' stolid preoccupation with things male (even in the convent), it is also as if such desires are there all along as we find out at the end of *Stage Door* when Eve Arden discovers that her beloved cat is really a female.

Tracking Ida or Mary Wickes or Thelma Ritter or any of several other "character" actresses forces the reversal of figure and ground. When characters who normally constitute ground become figures, their disposition, relations to dominant narrative, and mode of imaging often read counter to films' hetero-ideological impetus. Although these characters most often facilitate a film's primary plot, they also disturb its assumptions, at least in so far as those assumptions are linked to normative notions of gender and propriety. Clever, witty, insightful, the female second is a much more necessary player in the intrication of romance narratives than her sardonic manner would indicate. Tracking the second means seeing films anew.

NOTES

1. Eve Arden (Eunice Quedens) (1912–1990) acted in more than 25 films of all genres from *Anatomy of a Murder* (1959) to *Under the Rainbow* (1981). Mary Wickes (Mary Wickenhauser) (1916–) also appeared in more than 25 films.

2. Freud defines his notion of the uncanny in "The Uncanny" as the return of something once familar but repressed.

3. Barthes, *The Pleasure of the Text*, 14. Barthes distinguishes between pleasure and bliss as a function of their relative relation to what he calls "oedipal" narrative, or narrative that follows what is generally an oedipal trajectory. Pleasure goes along with the oedipal; bliss plays around it.

4. See Linda Williams, "Feminist Film Theory: *Mildred Pierce* and the Second World War," for a discussion of both *Mildred Pierce's* context and a useful summary of readings of the film.

5. In *The Practice of Love* Teresa De Lauretis maps out the relation between perverse desire and lesbian sexuality. In *Come As You Are: Sexuality and Narrative* I link the perverse to Barthes's bliss as well as to the representation of homosexualities.

6. In *The Woman at the Keyhole*, Judith Mayne discusses the possibilities of a lesbian desire in film regardless of overt content or the sexuality of the filmmaker.

7. Arden and Wickes play in everything from high drama to melodrama to musicals to fairly base comedy.

8. For an analysis of how it is that narrative is gendered, see De Lauretis, *Alice Doesn't*.

9. For discussions of off-screen space, see Noel Burch, *Theory of Film Practice* and Stephen Heath, *Questions of Cinema*.

10. Stoddard's study focuses on older women; while both Arden and Wickes age in their long careers, their characters' roles stay pretty much the same. Rowe defines unruly women as demonic and grotesque in a carnivalesque mode. While one might see both Arden and Wickes as countercultural, they are too much within the culture to really enact the carnivalesque.

BIBLIOGRAPHY

Barthes, Roland. *The Pleasure of the Text*. Trans. Richard Miller. New York: Hill and Wang, 1975.

Burch, Noel. *Theory of Film Practice*. Princeton: Princeton University Press, 1981.

De Lauretis, Teresa. *Alice Doesn't: Feminism, Semiotics, Cinema*. Bloomington: Indiana University Press, 1984.

De Lauretis, Teresa. *The Practice of Love: Lesbian Sexuality and Perverse Desire*. Bloomington: Indiana University Press, 1994.

Freud, Sigmund. *Three Essays on the Theory of Sexuality*. Translated by James Strachey. Rev. ed. New York : Basic Books, 1975.

Freud, Sigmund. "The Uncanny." *Standard Edition of the Complete Psychological Works* (24 vols). Trans. James Strachey. London: Hogarth Press and Institute of Psychoanalysis, 1919: 219–252.

Heath, Stephen. *Questions of Cinema*. Bloomington: Indiana University Press, 1981.

Mayne, Judith. *The Woman at the Keyhole: Feminism and Women's Cinema*. Bloomington: Indiana University Press, 1990.

Roof, Judith. *Come As You Are: Sexuality and Narrative.* New York: Columbia University Press, 1996.

Rowe, Kathleen. *The Unruly Woman: Gender and the Genres of Laughter.* Austin: University of Texas Press, 1995.

Stoddard, Karen. *Saints and Shrews: Women and Aging in American Popular Film.* Westport, Conn.: Greenwood Press, 1983.

Williams, Linda. "Feminist Film Theory: *Mildred Pierce* and the Second World War." *Female Spectators: Looking at Film and Television.* London: Verso, 1988: 12–30.

Chapter 5

The Ideology of Heroism in *My Beautiful Laundrette*: The Woman's Alternative

Susan E. Lorsch

The issues of race relations (in Thatcher's England and more generally) and of homosexuality arouse the most interest and comment at first viewing of Hanif Kureishi's *My Beautiful Laundrette* (1985). And this is as it should be. After all, the main story concerns a wealthy Pakistani community in London, unofficially led by Nasser, and the fortunes of his nephew Omar as he comes under Nasser's tutelage. Omar acquires a run-down laundrette; hiring Johnny, his homosexual English lover, Omar makes of it a going business. Ultimately Omar does not marry Nasser's daughter Tanya, contrary to Nasser's wishes; he has his relationship with Johnny. Obviously the current state of England, capitalism and jingoism, as well as homophobia and sexual relations, are at the forefront of the film's story if not its discourse.

But beyond these more volatile and controversial areas of concern, *My Beautiful Laundrette* takes up the issue of the gender/power nexus in contemporary British society. The film quietly reveals a vision of a world in which women are the most admirable and powerful forces, for they are active nonparticipants in a racist capitalist destructive system to which all others—that is, men—become either complicit or victimized. Using traditional gender codes or signs that are conventionally associated with women—the baring of breasts, the gathering and cooking of plants, even the activity of laundering itself—Kureishi deconstructs or attacks the traditional constructions of gender in a bourgeois patriarchal society as constricting and destructive. Running counter to patriarchal ideals of action and success, *My Beautiful Laundrette* uses such conventional signs of femininity to establish an alternative and feminist ideology of heroism.

In this remarkable independent film, women evade the alternate traps of being either participants in or victims of "the system," traps into which the men seem to fall—and often eagerly leap. Women are neither those who evict (think here of Nasser and Johnny) nor those who are evicted (think again of Johnny and the skinhead evicted with him—ironically by Selim—during the film's opening moments, or of the third-world poet evicted *by* Johnny later on); they are neither those who escape with cheap vodka (like Omar's father Hussein), nor those who celebrate with expensive champagne (like Nasser and Selim). Perhaps most importantly, women are presented in contrast to people who, like the main character Omar, are in awe of the money and success available to those who play society's game in a society where being successful is defined as going from evictee to evictor. What follows might be narrowly construed as a "feminist textual analysis" which, in the words of Annette Kuhn "in uncovering the processes whereby certain sets of meanings surrounding 'woman' are constituted in a film, opens it up to readings 'against the grain' and thus also in some sense finally transforms the film itself" (82). With *My Beautiful Laundrette*, however, Kureishi himself works counter to traditional cinema in quite explicitly criticizing and calling into questions the conventional "sets of meanings surrounding 'woman'" so as to create a highly ironic, subversive, and implosive film.

The women who collectively manage to reject society's values in *My Beautiful Laundrette* and elude its grip are Omar's cousin Tanya, Tanya's mother Bilquis, and his uncle's mistress Rachel. Notably all three are linked directly to Omar's uncle Nasser who represents, more than anyone in the film, society and its bourgeois, patriarchal values, for he has bought into those values wholeheartedly and "made it" on society's terms. The one other woman who belongs in this group is Omar's dead mother, of whom we hear only a few vital facts.

My Beautiful Laundrette tracks the initiation of Omar, son of a man who was an influential journalist in Bombay but is an ailing, widowed, homebound alcoholic in England. As nephew to Nasser, a more "successful" émigré to London, whose businesses include a garage and some real estate, Omar has a chance to enter the "family" businesses and become a part of this displaced Pakistani community. This community includes Nasser's rather shady partner, the young Selim, who smuggles cocaine to finance his lifestyle (and possibly Nasser's businesses— depending how one interprets some innuendoes accusingly cast at Nasser by his outspoken daughter Tanya).

Omar comes off the dole to work for Nasser (as, before him, Selim had been taken on by Nasser) and becomes a central figure to Selim and Nasser and the British Pakistani community which Nasser dominates, when Omar cleverly transforms a broken-down laundrette to a sleek, modern, and, he hopes, profitable enterprise.

As Omar flowers as a clever young businessman (bringing in his friend and lover Johnny to work for him) and simultaneously sells out to British notions of success (helping Selim smuggle drugs and cheating Selim along the way in order to further his own business interests), he must also choose between serving Selim's and Nasser's interests (and marrying Tanya to, in Nasser's words, "get her off my back") or being true to Johnny, the lover he really seems to love.

My Beautiful Laundrette is a film of such choices. Omar chooses to buy into British definitions of success (as monetary) while, at the same time, he tries to continue his relationship with Johnny. Johnny chooses to work for Omar in the laundrette and for Nasser in his apartment buildings, and to remain Omar's lover. Omar's father, Hussein, chooses to permit and even ultimately endorse Omar's association with Nasser. But of more interest, and even importance, if less straightforwardly stressed by *My Beautiful Laundrette*, are the choices faced and made by the women in the film. It is a woman, Selim's wife Cherry, who first sounds the theme of choice when she offers Omar the advice she herself fails to heed: "I'm sick of hearing about these in-betweens. People should make up their mind where they are." But the choices facing the characters in the film go beyond the British versus Pakistani choice she explicitly refers to here.

The main options for the characters here are cast in sexual and gender-related terms from the very start. The title implies that this will be a film about love and romance; "laundrette" could be confused with "laundress," suggesting female qualities with its "ette" ending (especially when spelled "laundrette" rather than the more conventional "launderette"), and indeed the title's speaker, Omar, is in love with this laundrette, if not instead of a woman, certainly to the exclusion of one. In fact, the film *is* about the romance between Omar and the laundrette, for it is a film about the British (specifically Thatcherian) romance with money and its acquisition.

The social alternatives in this world are also presented to us as choices of sexual preference. On the one hand one can choose the "success" of a Nasser that is cast as a heterosexual domination that implies using and abusing one's partner. Nasser instructs Omar: "In this damn country which we hate and love, you can get anything you want. It's all spread out and available. That's why I believe in England. Only you do have to know how to squeeze the tits of the system." To succeed in England is cast in terms of the sexual domination of a woman. What should be love-making, fondling, seems, rather, like milking the woman to have one's way with her and fulfill one's desires, or even torturing her (just how painful will this "squeeze" be?) to achieve complaisance from her. The "unscrewing" (evicting) that Nasser instructs Johnny in, is surely one more link between societal success and negative (hetero)sexuality.

Despite the fact that within the British society portrayed in this film (that is, exclusive of the women who are outsiders or opt out), homosexuality as portrayed by Omar and Johnny seems clearly the best and most humane and loving alternative, even this choice is linked with negative socio/sexual imagery. The alternative to the success offered in Britain through squeezing the tits of the system is the sexuality associated with the impotence and submission of Pakistan. Nasser diagnoses the ailment which has sent this Pakistani community to England in this way: Pakistan "has been sodomized by religion. It's beginning to interfere with the making of money."

The only answer to the sexual bullying of British financial success or the sexual victimization when money is not the primary measure of social success is to opt out of this sexual powerplay entirely, and in *My Beautiful Laundrette* it is only the women who have the strength to do this. Of course, not all women have such strength and insight. Selim's wife seems to relish her role in furthering Selim's power (and he is surely the worst, most morally culpable and abhorrent character in this film). Selim's wife Cherry (a perfect name for the woman who willingly subjects herself to the violent bully Selim) seems to believe, in contrast to everything we see enacted in the film, that she can have it all, Pakistani identity and British wealth and power. Though she clearly relishes the wealth England and Selim's drug dealing have brought her, she asserts of Pakistan, "It's my home," and says, mocking Omar's understandable confusion about her relationship to England and Pakistan, "How could anyone in their right mind call this silly little island of Europe their home?" But Cherry has clearly sold out to the worst sort of decadent British success. While asserting her Pakistani identity, she brags to Omar that "Every day in Karachi, every day, your other uncles and cousins come to our house for bridge, booze, and VCR." And in the scene at Nasser's annual party, we learn that she is pregnant. Like the affluent in British society, this Pakistani family, which buys into British values of domination and unscrewing and harvests British wealth, will certainly continue to flourish.

The means by which such wealth and success are harvested is also reflected in Omar's romance with the laundrette he aptly names "Powders," for the Pakistanis' success seems, at least in part, founded on the traffic in cocaine, white powders. Once Omar has engaged in this powder business to finance his other powder business, Selim astutely tells him, "You're one of us now, Omar." But Kureishi shows us that given the alternatives of unscrewing and sodomy, it is better to "take a powder" than to smuggle powder. And it is precisely the strong women in *My Beautiful Laundrette* who take a powder and simply opt out.

Before we look at how they opt out, it is only fair to note that it may be easier in some ways for them to opt out than it might be for the men because simply by virtue of their gender they are already and irrevocably outsiders. And, of course, Pakistani outsiders are doubly so. Nasser's wife is always seen on the fringe, observing but never participating; Rachel can have no legitimate place in Nasser's life since he is already married; and Tanya herself understands that she has never had a chance to be an insider, even while she ironically questions the insider's definition of success. When Omar tells her "Your father's done well," she replies, "Has he?" and goes on to say, "I think he wants you to take over the businesses. He wouldn't think of asking me," presumably because she is a woman.

Perhaps the most important feminist image in *My Beautiful Laundrette* is of Tanya, standing in scorn and mockery outside the men's club that runs her father's house and symbolically fuels English society, baring her breasts at the window. Besides the film audience—at whom she looks directly—only Omar, who Tanya hopes is still unformed and malleable enough to refuse initiation into this patriarchal world, sees her, and he seems both impressed with her nerve and embarrassed at what he sees. It is as if Tanya is saying to these wheelers and dealers, "You're no big deal; you're not as great and powerful as you believe.

We, women, suckled you; we attract you; we're the ones with meaningful power and you're just babies to us."

The gauge of subversiveness, the feminism, of Tanya's gesture is the degree of discomfort she forces upon Omar. He stands on the threshold of power, at the doorway leading to the inner sanctum, so to speak, where the monied Pakistani men make their deals. This is an all-male club Omar fervently wishes to join. But he has a choice to make. Inside here, in this room, is the male-bonded success he desires, but outside is Tanya, to whom he also feels an attachment, some allegiance as a cousin and a friend, and whose audacity he seems to admire even when—or perhaps because—he is unable to emulate it.

Tanya finds it easier than Omar to scorn the power of the inner sanctum since it is undeniably off-limits to her because of gender. She mocks Omar's desire to belong, baring her breasts and taunting him. Her breasts draw Omar's eyes and his embarrassment reduces him almost to a child who has both outgrown and still craves his mother's breast. More than sexual (Omar is, after all, most attracted to Johnny), Omar's gaze reduces him—and by extension all those Pakistani businessmen—to little boys, helpless before the power of women, their power to bear and suckle children. At the same time, this image of Tanya's bared breasts mocks not only this male society in the film but the very medium of film itself and the ideology of voyeurism and scopophilia on which traditional cinema is based (Kuhn 58–59, 159).

In "Visual Pleasure and Narrative Cinema," Laura Mulvey seems to write directly to this scene:

The alternative cinema provides a space for a cinema to be born which is radical in both a political and an aesthetic sense and challenges the basic assumptions of the mainstream film. This is not to reject the latter moralistically, but to highlight the ways in which its formal preoccupations reflect the psychical obsessions of the society which produced it, and, further, to stress that the alternative cinema must start specifically by reacting against these obsessions and assumptions. (7–8)

Tanya mocks and Kureishi thereby undercuts and challenges the traditional positioning of man as spectator and woman as object in society and the conventional objectification of women in mainstream film. Positioning Tanya so that she flaunts herself not only at Omar but at the audience directly, Kureishi alerts the reader to the ideological independence of the film to follow. However briefly, Kureishi allows Tanya to "own the gaze"(24), to use Kaplan's terms: "it is significant that . . . when the man steps out of his traditional role as the one who controls the whole action, and when he is set up as sex object, the woman then takes on the "masculine" role as bearer of the gaze and initiator of the action" (29).

In her honesty and forthrightness, Tanya stands in sharp contrast to the passive Omar who responds to his uncle's demand that he marry Tanya and Nasser's sharp question as to when this will take place, with "Yes—any day now," while Tanya responds to the idea by telling her father directly, "I'd rather drink my own urine."

Nor is Tanya taken in by her father's treatment of her mother. Tanya tells off her father's mistress, Rachel, refusing to allow Rachel to continue repressing her awareness of what that affair is doing to *other women*. And when Rachel points out that Tanya, too, lives off men ("But tell me—who do you live off?"), Tanya attempts to stop doing so, although in this patriarchal society one can only make one's escape on money borrowed from men.

At the end of the film Tanya leaves, opting entirely out of this decadent, competitive world. Tanya sets out to become independent so as not to get swallowed up by her family "like a little kebob," as she puts it. Despite her father calling her back ("Tanya, where the hell are you going?"), she boards the train which passes everyone else by. Tanya, in her truth-telling regardless of consequences, her independence, and her ability to break free and simply leave, seems to me the moral center of *My Beautiful Laundrette*.

The other candidate for moral center is, of course, Omar's father who, at least at the start of the film, has the right values. While his sympathies are with the working class (though it is, as he wryly puts it, "a great disappointment" to him), he wants Omar to go to college so as to avoid being an "underpants cleaner." He understands that his brother Nasser is a "crook" and, in his wish for Omar's future, speaks what is perhaps the most directly didactic line in the whole film: "He must have knowledge. We all must know—if we're to see clearly what has been done and to whom in this country." But unlike Tanya, Omar's father is unable to act upon his knowledge and we are clearly shown that knowledge without action is worthless. Omar's father sits and drinks, a man who can find no place for himself in the society of Thatcher's England, while the trains *which Tanya boards* pass him by.

Nasser's wife, like his daughter baring her breasts in defiance of male power, also fights back, using the only weapons available to the displaced, illiterate, uneducated Pakistani woman in England: the weapons of nature—magic. In the course of the film this woman grows from being passive, an omnipresent observer, to being active in that, with the help of her daughter, she uses the traditional female functions of gathering and cooking to fashion some sort of charm or potion against her husband's mistress. Thus the codes which conventionally signify woman achieve the power to critique and interrogate the patriarchal construction and the ideology it embodies. And the filmmaker means us to believe that even in the modern European rational, scientific, *male* world, such female magic, the woman's potion, has potency. It works—and enacts the required change. Her husband's mistress Rachel ends the affair. Interestingly, Tanya's mother, like Tanya herself, intends to break away from both Nasser and England. We are told that she is thinking of going back to Pakistan once she's hospitalized Rachel with her potion.

Even the unlikely figure of Rachel, Nasser's mistress so criticized by Tanya, is ultimately presented as an admirable woman, independently empowered. Though she has chosen (and her cool answer to Tanya's recriminations indicate that hers has been a well-considered choice) to put herself in the less than admirable position as Nasser's mistress, she also has the strength to choose to remove herself from it. It is to her credit as well that she seems to bring out the best in her lover—and also to her credit that she is another truthteller in this world. She points out to her lover's daughter that in this patriarchal society all women are forced, in one form or another, to live off men. It is a strong statement that in *My Beautiful Laundrette* these three strong women, each in her own way, withdraw or opt out of the system as it is embodied in and controlled by Nasser.

The fourth woman requiring serious consideration in *My Beautiful Laundrette* is Omar's mother, whose portrait, sitting beside Hussein's bed, is emphasized with a close-up. Though not a character in the film, she is a significant presence, particularly each time a train runs past the seedy flat Omar shares with his father. Though to leave she did not board a train like Tanya, her response to British society is equally active and defiant: she threw herself *under* a train to escape. This suicide is presented as an active gesture: "She died last year my mother. Jumped onto the railway lines." And it is presented as an act of supreme power: "Yeah, I heard. All the trains stopped." The death of Omar's mother is explicitly related both to Thatcherian capitalism (whose aim was, presumably, at least to keep the trains running—if not always on time) and to the patriarchal hierarchy: "Papa hated himself and hated his job. So he took it out on her and she couldn't take it."

Though these four women, Tanya, her mother, Rachel, and Omar's mother, seem so different, they are connected by their attitude toward the system, questioning its values and its definition of success; by their being inevitable outsiders of the system by virtue of gender; and by their response to that system, the ideology of heroism: in one way or another, to opt out. Indeed, where race and class are such important markers of distinction and separation among the men in Thatcher's England, as portrayed in the film, women are, regardless of class or race or age, united as outsiders and the real underclass. Though Rachel tries to justify to Tanya her behavior by invoking her differences from Tanya ("You must understand. We're of different generations—different classes."), even she recognizes the feebleness of such an excuse. The reality is how much each woman in this film, as outsider, has in common with the other. So it should not come as a surprise, though it does, when, after asking his surname, Rachel—affluent, middle-class, and classy—says to Johnny—poor, lower-class, and unrefined, "That's it. I know your mother." Though isolated, one from the other, the women in this film are linked and, in their separate though similar responses to this system, present us with the strongest, clearest-thinking, and most admirable characters in *My Beautiful Laundrette*. Kureishi cuts against the grain of mainstream filmmaking and bourgeois society, dramatizing noncomplicity in a racist and inhuman patriarchal world as the enactment of an alternate ideology of feminist heroism and resistance.

BIBLIOGRAPHY

Kaplan, E. Ann. *Women and Film: Both Sides of the Camera*. New York: Methuen, 1983.

Kuhn, Annette. *Women's Pictures: Feminism and Cinema*. London: Routledge and Kegan Paul, 1982.

Kureishi, Hanif, screenwriter. *My Beautiful Laundrette*. Dir. Stephen Frears. Prod. Sarah Radclyffe and Tim Bevan. London: Working Title Films, 1985.

Mulvey, Laura. "Visual Pleasure and Narrative Cinema." *Screen* 16.3 (Autumn 1975): 6–18.

Chapter 6

Resurrecting the *Ghost*: Innocence and Recuperation in American Popular Film

Grace A. Epstein

[T]he hero, the mythical subject, is constructed as human being and as male; he is the active principle of culture, the establisher of distinction, the creator of difference. Female is what is not susceptible to transformation, to life or death; she (it) is an element of plot space, a topos, a resistance, matrix and matter.

——Teresa De Lauretis, *Alice Doesn't: Feminism, Semiotics, Cinema*

Ghost films have been a staple of American cinema almost since the beginning of film-making. Time-honored favorites like *The Christmas Carol* (1938) or *It's a Wonderful Life* (1946) are only two of the most popular Hollywood classics. From suspense thriller to romantic comedy these films attest to America's continued interest in the idea of life after death. In the thriller genre, however, ghostliness provides a device for veiling cultural anxieties concerned with issues not only of death, but of unchecked sexuality.[1] Clearly, in less serious films, where spirits are often friendly or at least civil, the trope of ghostliness offers, at the very least, an opportunity for imparting a transformed perspective on human behavior, be it humorous, satiric, or moralistic. In a handful of these films, it is the ghost who is center of the dramatic action. Here, the spirited self must be transformed in order to gain appropriate heavenly reward, not simply through the completion of a task on earth—usually of romantic significance—but, in classical tradition, by enduring some anguish or spiritual pain that imparts heroic status. The enormously popular 1990 *Ghost* which became that year's highest grossing film falls into this particular genre of part romance, thriller, and comedy.

In addition to the obvious question of what "ghostliness" represents in contemporary American culture, such a narrative that positions the ghost as the protagonist begs another question: What, exactly, has died and for what purpose has it, by necessity, returned? These are the questions that I want to consider here by identifying structural elements that foreground the thematics in *Ghost*. In so doing I hope to open up some possible readings of both the film and its historical moment.

Ostensibly about Sam Wheat (played by Patrick Swayze), a rich heterosexual white man, who posthumously awakens to the shortcomings of his life, *Ghost* stakes out its narrative trajectory with the ghost's attempt to reclaim his unfulfilled life and to transform his death via the mediation of a black woman, Oda Mae Brown (played by Whoopi Goldberg) whose psychic powers make her an unwilling, if not unexpected, mediator. *Ghost* is a web of signification that guides Sam and the audience into an "other world" of chaos and violence, into which the deceased hero, seemingly through no fault of his own, has fallen.

On the surface, the real object of Sam's desire is his white heterosexual girl friend, Molly Jenson (Demi Moore) to whom he never professes his love. Yet, as the movie progresses, much of Sam's attention and that of the camera's, is directed to the ethnic woman, splitting the terrain of eroticized desire between two objects: one well-off, white, Anglo-Saxon, and heterosexual—traditionally, as De Lauretis's quote above implies, the topos, the sign of white male success; the other, poor, black, African-American, and apparently non-heterosexual—a sign no less traditional, even if slightly less articulated.

Before examining the pairing of eroticized signs, assessment of this film's historical context may reveal the appeal that generated its blockbuster reception. Produced literally on the heels of the Savings and Loan scandal, the year of the film's production, 1989, produced a deluge of information about the ensuing fiduciary crisis. When the banking institutions collapsed because of the poor judgement and greed of business people like Charles Keating and others, the crisis of innocence was obvious (Morganthau 35). Those who were powerful, wealthy, and privileged were the perpetrators. Stunned at the federal government's complicity,[2] middle- and working-class Americans were inundated by images of rich white men, ushered in and out of limousines, mansions, and private hearings, only to be informed that it was taxpayers, not the guilty elite, who were expected to pay the bill. Into this climate of discovery, of scandal and cynicism, *Ghost* was conceived and produced. Like the white upper-class bankers he represents, Sam desperately seeks reunion with the Others from whom he has been so abruptly separated.

As the movie opens, Sam installs himself in his upper-class New York loft fashioned by his own spit and polish. It is no coincidence that he reconstructs the parameters of his living space, because, once he passes to the other side, a reconstruction of space is essential to executing his desire. As the unwitting accomplice to his best friend's (a second level loan officer) banking swindle, Sam is murdered to prevent him from discovering the fraud. His posthumous discoveries of the friend's betrayal and his own failure to articulate his love for Molly plunge him into confusion and disorientation—literally a spectator to a kind of "third world" experience, in which all his efforts, words, and beliefs are traded for an entirely new set of realities.

This new world order confronts Sam in death with what he failed to do and see in life: the profession of his love for Molly (the ultimate signifier of his material success and moral zeal) and the betrayal by his trusted male friend. The narrative obstacle to Sam's desire is also split between the doubled representation of white friend who executes the swindle and a mysterious black man who executes the body. Thus, this plot's forward movement is to restore credibility and righteousness to the white heterosexual man's life refracted through the lens of race, class, gender, and ethnicity represented by the split objects: Molly/Oda Mae and white/black villain. There is little doubt that in the late 1980s of the film's inception such a restoration of privilege was momentarily threatened.

The reception of the film, however, as is sometimes the case, came at a slightly different historical moment. With the banking scandal receding from the national headlines, *Ghost* hit the box offices in mid-July of 1990, amid a panoply of movies that were high on action and violence, and by extension, guilt and innocence, such as *Total Recall, DieHard 2, Robo Cop 2, Days of Thunder, Air America,* and finally, *Young Guns II* ("Battle," 86–89). These law and order thrillers testify to a cultural preoccupation with guilt and innocence, in which justice is recovered through extraordinarily violent means by extraordinary white men. Most of these films were expensive ventures that anticipated windfall returns. For Paramount studios, the substantially small budget *Ghost* became the unexpected bargain of the year (Travers 20), not because its hero or violence was any less extraordinary—he had, after all, returned from the dead—but because he too had proven to be vulnerable to a devastating betrayal of trust.

In contrast to the big-budget, high-impact offerings, *Ghost's* violence was more metaphysical than physical with allusions to a traditional Christian iconography of good and evil (Novak 8). In addition, Goldberg's parodic performance is engaging and funny, which brings me to a feature of the historical context that is especially relevant to the film's reception: the looming Desert Storm crisis.[3]

As American armed forces began flexing their muscles in the Middle East following Iraq's invasion of Kuwait on August 2, 1990, movie-goers may have felt like a little "other-world" escape. Given what was eventually a prelude to the existential reality of world war and the hovering prospect of loss of life, it is hardly surprising to see why American audiences responded so favorably to a story of metaphysical quest.

Ghost especially appealed to young white women, many of whom saw the film more than once (Travers 20). In fact, a female student in one of my classes that autumn claimed to have seen the film 18 times, while several other female students admitted watching it more than twice. Certainly the American female's seduction during that fall of 1990 was, according to Cynthia Enloe in *The Morning After: Sexual Politics at the End of the Cold War*, instrumental in legitimating a war, "framed by the contrast between the liberated US woman soldier" and her veiled counterpart regularly represented by the harem (170). Indeed, the "harem" of women represented in Oda Mae's household—dark, mysterious and multiple—are a dramatic contrast to the white, recognizable singularity of Molly's loft.

Enloe also notes that less than a week after the war began in January, American women had been lured into supporting the Bush administration's war through the guise of championing "our boys" (174–75).[4] This was a fairly astute observation about whose desire is really at stake in the film and its connection to other homefront heterosexual women similarly inhibited by the allusions to those Gulf soldiers who are also "always waiting" for them on the war front. The conflation tactics that were summoned to procure female support on the homefront (with harems and yellow ribbons), whether accidental or designed, underscores the desire of American foreign policy that, through romantic narrative, successfully constrained female objections to the military offensive.

After all, the ghost story is a productive venue for traditional existential questions about life and death, and the film *Ghost* included issues of sudden and unexpected loss, about dying young and for no good reason, about the heterosexual bonds of love beyond the grave, about the issue, no less significant, of guilt and innocence, all of which were crucial for Americans in the summer/fall of 1990 as departing reservists were relocating to the desert. Further, the existential questions continue to be framed by difference and propelled by the desire for a reclamation of innocence. Just as Sam sets about to expunge himself from any responsibility for his unexamined life through the assertion of a romantic objective—saving the girl and confirming his love—the United States sought to deflect any complicity for the hostilities in the Persian Gulf by calling for the support *not* of American foreign policy or American oil interests, but for the romanticized objective of saving the Kuwaitis for democracy. The reconstruction of power and legitimation is virtually contingent upon a long-standing trope of romantic quest.

In *Alice Doesn't: Feminism, Semiotics, Cinema,* Teresa De Lauretis crystallizes how the female position in narrative functions as terrain upon which the hero will stake his claim. It is the female body that represents difference and reflects a panoply of ideological and social relations that reinforce his status as hero and her status as tablet. The heterosexual male desire that is projected onto the female image by the male subject signifies a discursive system that denies a woman the subjectivity that is the consequence of representing one's self (1987, 10). As the representation of what she is not—in the Lacanian sense, the very absence or lack of maleness, literally the fetishized object of male desire—her own desire is hidden, buried, inaccessible to her while she signifies that of another.

Narrative discourse, according to De Lauretis, "circumscribes woman in the sexual, binds her (in) sexuality, . . . a political function in the service of cultural domination including, but not limited to, the sexual exploitation of women and the repression or containment of female sexuality" (1984, 25–26). This double entendre—representing the desire of another while displacing the woman's desire, and exploiting her as an object of male heterosexual desire at the same time her own sexuality is circumscribed—designates a cultural danger zone, in which female representation always risks the reproduction of and complicity with her subservience.

In *Ghost*, clearly the female is designated in opposition to the qualities of masculinity. Molly remains a virtual spectator and spectacle throughout the film. Her face and figure often fill the camera lens. She rarely does anything but cry and stare, unless it is to make an abrupt exit from the scene. Not much more than the object of Sam's nostalgic gaze, she contrasts Sam's character who takes action and continues to empower himself—of course, only for the purpose of protecting Molly, since she is wholly incapable of doing that for herself. Similarly, Oda Mae provides a contrast to the ethereal Molly with her psychic power, which Sam initiates, an ability to mediate the living and the dead. Prior to that moment her psychic ability is a well-elaborated con. Clearly if Molly is the epitome of the male gaze, Oda Mae is her twin. Black, wild, powerful, and despite her modest means, *not* in need of saving, the hardly visible adjunct to Sam's adventure.

Although De Lauretis works specifically with the technologies of film narrative, the issue of representation and difference extend into any number of narrative genres. Lydia Lui, for instance, indicates how the rape of women in Chinese literary narrative depicts not a calamity for a single woman or family, but an ideological offense of nationalistic proportion even when a female author wishes to displace it in order to critique its existence. According to Lui, "the female body signifies a woman's lack of control over her destiny, not so much because sexual desire is an animal instinct as because patriarchy determines the meaning of desire and chastity so it serves the interests of men" (53). Like De Lauretis, Lui's discussion about Chinese nationalist discourse shows that the appropriation of the female body to patriarchal interests is so common a narrative strategy, where a discourse of nationalism serves to deny "the specificity of female experience by giving larger symbolic meanings to the signifier of rape: namely, China itself is being violated by the Japanese rapist" (44). Even when a female writer intends to radically critique the meaning ascribed to women's bodies, the dominant discourse subsumes the female experience (59).

Similarly, Molly Jenson's body serves as a representative of American ideals. While both Sam and Molly are victims of corrupt banking desires, only Molly is still endangered, only Molly is still alive. Even though the banking scandal may have diminished faith in American institutions, Sam, a deceased privileged white man, is still empowered with the capacity to rescue the shattered American ideals, and restore them to that institution, by saving the girl, her body, the landscape of those fantasized ideals and by ridding the world of the perpetrators of corruption and self-interest. While this connection to nationalist discourse explains the film's interest in Molly, it does not fully elucidate the continued narrative focus upon the woman of color's body. It seems clear that she is not the embodiment of American ideals with her awkward walk, colorful costuming, and ethnic speech.

To clarify this relationship, I need to take a detour into complicated national discourse central to the notion of American freedom. In *Playing in the Dark*, Toni Morrison deconstructs the Africanist presence in the construction of an American national subjectivity (5). Like Lui, Morrison's argument centers on the spectacle of the slave's body in constituting American national identity as that of individual freedom. According to Morrison, "Africanism is the vehicle by which the American self knows itself as not enslaved, but free; not repulsive, but desirable; not helpless, but licensed and powerful; not history-less, but historical; not damned, but innocent; not a blind accident of evolution, but a progressive fulfillment of destiny" (52). Thus, the bodies of Africanist men and women form a register for American claims to freedom.

More specifically, in her reading of *Huck Finn*, Morrison claims that the novel's quest for personal freedom "has no meaning . . . without the specter of enslavement, the anodyne to individualism; the yardstick of absolute power over the life of another; the signed, marked, informing, and mutating presence of a black slave" (56–57). Again, the establishment of boundaries for the American self as white, "human," free, and Anglo-Saxon are comprehended through the presence *of* and *by* the Other who is *not* any of these things. Certainly Oda Mae's presence in *Ghost* is intended to contrast a similar set of white identities.

Jane Flax, in "The End of Innocence," explains how the representation of difference embodied in tidy Western dyads (male/female, white/black, rich/poor, good/bad) controls and erases those identified as Other in what she calls a "metaphysics of presence." Here the dyad, presented as a "natural" phenomenon, not socially constructed but a genuine consequence of essence acts as a gestalt of positive and negative poles. From the contrast of opposites, one side defines, while the other is defined; then, "[o]rder is imposed and maintained by displacing chaos into the lesser of each binary pair, revealing [the definer's] desire for control and domination . . . [since] to be different than the defining one is to be inferior and to have no independent character of one's own" (453). Thus, woman mirrors the absence of masculinity, the absence of strength, power, and control. Further, since the coupling is maintained as deriving from nature, not from culture, it is legitimated and becomes virtually invisible as a cultural assumption, which cements it to a system of domination by the haves over the have nots.

From within these dichotomized poles, those associated with the defining side constitute and maintain privileges over the subordinate side without bearing any responsibility for doing so, remaining essentially innocent of the acts of subordination (453). The adjacent corollary to Flax's thesis that the dyadinal configuration grants innocence to the powerful, by extension, renders the subordinated Other to serve the legitimation of her own subordination, and imposes upon the Other the "inherent" responsibility for what happens to them. Accordingly, this logic makes the Jew responsible for the holocaust, the African for American slavery, the poor for their deprivation, the beaten for their beating. Something in the very essence of the Other of what she does or does not do, says or does not say, reveals her culpability.

The innocence of the truth-seeker is, for Flax, at the core of epistemological desire. It is, however, the postmodern project that calls into question "the belief (or hope) that there is some form of innocent knowledge to be had" (447) and exposes the process of representation that constitutes it. Truth under the postmodern is "discourse dependent," that is, always apprehended by and through discourse (452); as such, truth, rather than endemic to the nature of critical inquiry, is constructed and invested with the self-interest of those who articulate and authorize it. This unmasking of truth-saying exposes the "desire to claim a position of innocence in which one person's clarity does not rest on the exclusion of an other's experience" (458).

Here, then, innocence formerly procured at the expense of the Other is permanently discredited, and responsibility commensurate with the level of power, influence, and privilege replaces it (458–59). Indeed under postmodern critique, no one can claim neutrality in the formation of social relations and the perpetuation of the status quo. No longer are upper-class white men seen as natural dominators, the unwitting recipients of their fate; instead, they are accessories to, if not conspirators in, the structuring of social relations that grant, sustain, and maximize their status.

In the face of a postmodern critique of ideological and narrative discourse, strategies to resurrect the lost innocence are being retooled; however, as the dyadinal units collapse, new formats or paradigms hasten to replace them. The signs of representation available to return the truth-sayer to the days of unencumbered privilege, power, and innocence continue to be proffered. The representations of Otherness proliferating in popular culture genres such as American film may provide a clue to the "new forms" that resurrect the ghost of innocence lost, masked as a progressive and tolerant social re-engagement.

In *Ghost*, the oppositions of right and wrong, white and black, male and female, truth and deceit proliferate and are sharply identified by Sam, who as the white dead, heterosexual male, is the moral center of the film. When Oda Mae turns over the money she obtains in order to thwart Sam's former friend, it is not because of her own sense of honesty or even her own sense of danger, but because Sam coerces her with fear of physical harm. She not only operates in opposition to Molly, but in opposition to Sam as well. She is self-interested while he, in contrast, is driven by a desire to save Molly and secure justice. His wealth, his privilege must in no way imply her poverty. She must retain her unworthiness and guilt, in order for Sam to remain innocent. In fact, if Sam appears to be responsible for her power, and ultimately for her righteous behavior, the audience will not recognize his connection to Oda Mae's economic impoverishment. By necessity, Oda Mae must not be innocent; otherwise, Sam must bear some guilt.

When representation is diversified by the same representational figure in a single narrative move that fosters a doubled, tripled, and even quadrupled sign of difference such as race, gender, class, and sexual orientation, as it does with Oda Mae in *Ghost*, it not only overdetermines the narrative stakes, it also obscures the relations of power that are being posited. The collapsing of signs, as Homi Bhabba suggests, conflates all oppression into a single form revealing the anxiety at the core national identity. According to Bhabba, "the fetishes of national discrimination and minoritization . . . reveal through their alien 'outsideness' the fragile, indeterminate boundaries of the national imaginary of the 'People-As-One'" (12). Because each configuration of oppression does not operate distinctively within the culture, catalyzing constituents by any single set of oppressive practices or representation is difficult. The effect of collapsing difference, however, manages to consolidate various constituencies, making possible the longed-for People-As-One of national identity.

Claudia Springer has studied the use of ethnic women's bodies in the third world investigation film, in "Comprehension and Crisis: Reporter Films and the Third World," in an attempt to understand how ethnicity structures the search for identity on the part of the protagonist, usually white and male. In the new unfamiliar environment of the third world, resplendent with violence and sexuality, the reporter/investigator finds himself (169) ill-prepared, distrustful, and radically questioning his American or western identity. Stranded among the miserable conditions and desperate inhabitants of a wholly different world, virtually determined, if not orchestrated, by American foreign policy, the protagonist struggles to redefine, if not regain his innocence.

Otherness in the third world is most often signified by the ethnic woman, who serves as a medium and landscape, through and upon which the hero's search is staked out: "Not only is the violence designed to destabilize the reporter and spectator, but is also a projection of the reporter's repressed desires onto the ethnic Other . . . who individually embodies the culture as a whole and evokes the reporter's simultaneous attraction and confusion . . . making the Other the enigma that propels the narrative" (Springer, 171).

The third-world woman embodies the mystery of the new environment and cues him about nature of this Other world. Her ultimate seduction by him, conflating gender and ethnicity, renders visually and erotically the pernicious exploration of a protagonist in re-establishing his own white male identity and rectitude (173–175). The significance of the enigmatic ethnic woman succeeds in enhancing ever more precisely the faltering innocence of the protagonist and the desire defined as American, white, male, and heterosexual to conquer and possess that Otherness (173): an Otherness of gender and ethnicity subsumed by the hero who "simultaneously possesses her body and her 'story,' making her transparent" (175).[5] Only then can an identity, besmirched by the exploitation of women and third world peoples, be reasserted. As the white American hero gains access to her Otherness across the terrain of heritage and body, the prospect of her desire to possess either for herself may be thoroughly appropriated to him. The colonizer takes possession of her history and her body in a single stroke. While both representations are feminized—woman and ethnic (as is often the position of the third world in respect to the first world)—his seduction constitutes in a single act the recognition by the third world and women, the vindication of his American integrity, and subsequently, his valid return to a state of innocence.[6]

Springer notes that in the investigation film, the narcissistic desire of the protagonist to be acknowledged does not hinge on the "fear that their voyeurism will be detected and their gaze returned," as it typically does in traditional film, but instead, upon the "fear that [their gaze] will not be returned" (174). Also like the protagonists whom Springer analyzes, Sam is investigating a world very different from the one he has come to know. His American capitalism is at least partially responsible for the runaway greed of his best friend and the subsequent violence of the black antagonist. It is also that same American domestic policy that has virtually erected the underworld he discovers after his death. It is also important to note in *Ghost* that while Sam's voice can be heard by Oda Mae, it is not until the end of the film that he himself can be seen by the living. Thus, Sam's final visibility to Molly and Oda Mae provides the needed Other's recognition. For having slain the proverbial dragons, he can "ascend" to his status as dead white hero, with the concurrence of the women, showered once again in the *white* light of power, privilege, and innocence via their returned look. Sam's metaphysical presence is now visible to the Other producing the narrative's ultimate restitution of equilibrium that resurrects his life and redeems his death.

As an ethnic member of an all-female household, Oda Mae enables Sam's quest. Indeed ethnicity is a key to his re-asserted innocence in her recognition of him.[7] Because of their difference, ethnic women are associated with the other side, the other world, however problematic.[8] The fearsomeness of their power is always easily cast. For what privileged people do not understand becomes, almost by default, the province of persons whom the privileged also do not understand.

In order for the white heterosexual male, whose self-identity has been compromised by the corruption of the historical setting, to return to an unspoiled, unsoiled innocence against postmodernism's disruption of privilege, someone else must mediate. Someone who is not privileged must assent to, even be instrumental in, the return to privilege of the dominant group. Though Oda Mae's power to mediate is determined and revealed by Sam, her consent to mediate is absolutely essential for the narrative to gain legitimacy. As the subaltern, whose talent and power is appropriated by Sam, Oda Mae is the perfect (or as Goldberg portrays it, the *near* perfect) agent for bringing to fruition his posthumous textual and sexual desire by the very spectacle of her difference.

Of course, the assumption simultaneously arises that ethnic women are the only ones daft enough to believe in ghosts in the first place. Nevertheless, there is something more insidious about the recourse to difference here. As a "scam artist" Oda Mae is *not* innocent ("Whoopi Goldberg," 59). She, like the villains of the film, makes a living by dishonest means. Once again, she is the absence of what Sam is. Having lived an ostensibly honest life, his fiduciary incompetence is moderated by the "outlaws" that inhabit the film, including Oda Mae. Oda Mae provides the balm for his unwitting culpability in his best friend's crime.

In part, what makes the film more interesting has mainly to do with Goldberg's sabotage of that function. In his review, Stanley Kauffman remarked that Goldberg's portrayal is executed with an "unremitting sledgehammer touch" (30). While Kauffman may not have intended his remark as a tribute to Goldberg's resistance, I think it inevitably evolves as precisely that. If Goldberg is heavy handed, it is out of instinct since little in what she is scripted provides anything close to the spoof she inevitably manages with her burlesque of the role. She unravels the fabric of Oda Mae's invisible desire by visually and aurally deconstructing it, parodying what is the tacit dismissal of her desire to stay alive, get rich, or get away.

The film gestures to a desire for Oda Mae when she obtains free money from the bank, resulting from her agreement to help Sam. Of course, her hysterical babble when she discovers how much money is available to her, legitimates a stereotypical white belief that Others do not know what to do with great wealth when they get it.[9] Even as she sputters and chatters at Sam's insistence that she get rid of the money, her stylized shock disrupts the scene. In this way, she uproots the counterfeit choice Sam offers that if she keeps the money, she can be traced and the heavies will come after her again. The choice is an artificial one, of course, for anyone acquainted with Oda Mae's deprivation. There is often very little difference between being killed by guns or by the insistent battle to survive for the Oda Maes of America. Her desire, which is always invisible, is buried further by posing the either/or complication as a real choice.

Goldberg is no doubt aware of the sham of choice used to dismiss Oda Mae.[10] In a parody to this serious co-optation of class (i.e., dispensing the dangerously won money to a white charity, white church, white women), Goldberg nearly torpedoes the whole narrative. The "sledgehammer touch" mimics the elimination of desire and exposes the problematics of co-optation. Through exaggerated twists, turns, and dialect, Goldberg caricatures the role she is expected to play, that nods to the dismissal of lower class, black, ethnic, female lack. Utterances that clearly mark her as Other as she hands the check over to the greedy nuns are exploded by the physical humor, in which she holds so tenaciously to the check that the nuns must literally wrench it from her hands. Goldberg "signifies," as Gates maintains, thereby drawing out the scene and likewise, the desire that is being so neatly discharged.

There are several opportunities for the film narrative to neutralize Oda Mae's desire and power. Surely the most ostentatious is the visual deletion that occurs near the end of the film. Tania Modleski's interpretation of the flirtation with the physical union of white and black women points out that the white female and her lost white male lover's reunion is made possible simply by "obliterating" the black female body (132). This extremely political manifestation, whether overt as it is in the film or veiled as it is in social practice, reinforces the stereotypical designation and determination of black women by white dominant culture. While Modleski poses a second more resistant reading in which the white man stands in the way of the union of white and black female (134), the more likely audience reception of the visual move is the one that reinforces an already familiar scenario in which black bodies, once they have served their purposes for white subjects, are simply erased from the picture.[11]

Oda Mae, having served her purpose of providing virtually the physical space for the romantic fantasy to take place, is no longer necessary to the film, to the trajectory of the plot, so she virtually disappears. Having metaphorized how male power dispatches female desire, by literally insinuating the male body into the union of white and black women, the film celebrates, in the guise of single desire, our culture's compulsory heterosexual and racist economy, as well as its pressing anxiety over identity.

Even Sam's subsequent impotence following this scene, in which he is unable to summon his new unearthly powers in Molly's defense, belies and reinforces a standard male anxiety about ethnicity and femaleness. The scene is set up earlier in the film when Oda Mae is taken over by a black, male ghost with identical reactions. Possessing this black female body is apparently a castrating experience for male ghosts. Certainly the familiarity of the implications fulfills audience expectations. A more critical representation of this anxiety occurs in *Schindler's List* (1993) when Goeth, the cruel camp director, defends Schindler who has injudiciously kissed a young Jewish girl. To a disapproving superior investigating the incident, Goeth explains, "They [Jewish women] cast a spell on you, you know." Indeed, lured by an encounter with the multiplied Otherness, any red blooded white man can no longer resist, nor, as in Sam Wheat's case, stand. By entering Oda Mae's body, the film reiterates a representation of slave history inscribing black women into white male erotic fantasy, fear, and practice. While Sam loses his erect-ness (foreshadowed earlier, when the clay phallus falls preceding love-making with the white woman), the castration is only temporary.

Such castration secures the audience's confidence that his interest in the black woman is strictly as a means to the white woman, who is really no woman at all but a fetish. Still the reverberation of what is being staked out across the black female ethnic presence is a staggering, even ingenious, strategy for sublimating all difference in the interest of Sam's justification. Oda Mae permits the dispossession of her *self* again for the white couple, and at this point, there appears to be no need for the narrative to pose even an artificial choice for Oda Mae, so dominant is the white heterosexual imperative in American culture. White women, after all, can't take care of themselves, everybody knows that. It is best not to think about whether Oda Mae is better off having been summoned to participate in this quest. Asking such a question is simply precluded by the invisibility of any other desire. In actual fact, Sam's obsession nearly kills both women.

Molly's penchant for large phallic sculptures aside (and perhaps this is the film's way of implicating Molly in a desire of her own), she functions as a mere reflection of her partner's ghostly image. She has no part in the bank swindle nor, we might add, any stake in Sam's revenge. Except for her physical loss of her provider/lover, she is more endangered by his machination of ghostly revenge than helped by it. The presumption of the film script goes virtually unnoticed, so entrenched are the assumptions about women and ethnic people. Although we laugh at Goldberg's spoof of ethnicity, which virtually steals a major part of the film, in the end, we witness her easy erasure to heterosexual romance—a male fantasy of rescue for the idealized, never realized, white female icon while the only female power in the film, manifested by Oda Mae, ultimately disintegrates.

We are asked to believe that this is what the women want, long for, need. Oda Mae wants nothing more than to help the white woman save her economic future from which Oda Mae has been excluded, or if we can't buy that, then she helps because she has inadvertently been snared by the heavies and needs to get them out of her hair. Of course, we know white women want nothing more than to be saved by white men, whatever the cost.

A closer look at the cosmology of *Ghost* indicates the innocence/guilt trajectory of the plot line, in which innocence is rewarded with life and light, while culpability, portrayed in the death of the perpetrators, is charged with total separation and darkness—dare we add, blackness. While both of the villainous men fall into the clutches of those fierce black shadows immediately following death, Oda Mae's blackness and initial dishonesty make her story easily dismissed. By leaving her fate and, to some extent, the white woman's, unaddressed, we can only sense her end. Only because Oda Mae's desire does manage to spill out in Goldberg's stylizing, her position as a proponent of the same epistemology is not quite complete.

In resurrecting the lost innocence, *Ghost* was unbelievably successful. Yet in terms of a full recuperation, Goldberg gives the film a much needed reality check. Oda Mae probably believes that what goes around comes around, but it is doubtful that she believes in innocence at any level.

Simple as its plot appears, *Ghost* is literally overstuffed with signification, that marks and reinscribes Otherness in the service of dominant American politics. In its posing of women and ethnic others, the film reveals its veiled narrative desire to reassert a white, American, heterosexual male identity that has been sullied by current ideological critiques of imperialism and colonization. Like Springer's investigation films, the structural elements that conflate difference add up to a complex epistemological desire to return white male American identity to a state of innocence and privilege, following the breakdown of banking trust and in the absence of any clear American objectives in the Gulf War.

NOTES

1. Patricia White's analysis of the ghost thriller indicates the American audience's level of anxiety about lesbianism, and perhaps female sexuality itself, that the thriller genre conceals just beneath the surface of the filmic discourse.

2. Again, for an indication of the breaking news about the government's part in the scandal see "Stop Bribery on Capitol Hill."

3. Actually, my "funniest moment" preceded Swayze and Moore's big lovemaking scene to the tune of "Unchained Melody," when her clay wheel-play, a remarkably long, narrow structure and viewed from a high-angle shot so clearly resembling an ejaculating penis. Unintentional "pun" or not, more than a few viewers noticed the resemblance, including the writers of *Naked Gun 33 1/3* who later spoofed the sequence. Significantly, it is Swayze's character who inevitably topples her creation to begin the love scene, for the female artist's work must always be displaced by the desire of the male partner.

4. Another female student remarked to me after the discussion of the film in class, which took place during the war, that if one really thought about it, Molly would find it difficult ever to fall in love again, knowing that Sam was always waiting for her.

5. Springer's article also considers films in which the eroticized Other is male, such as *Cry Freedom* and *The Killing Fields*, which, she suggests, veil a homosexual desire by the men, while assuming a heterosexual viewpoint (173).

6. See Cynthia Enloe for a discussion of the phenomena of configuring the developing world as feminized and signifying passivity to the intrusiveness of the first world, configured as masculine and active.

7. Ethnic indicates for me what Ella Shohat suggests as "more than sentimental traces of the customs and cuisine of the old country. . . . far from being a unitary topos. . . . [rather] a spectrum of identities and differences all ultimately involving questions of inequalities of power . . . [and] a changing set of historically diverse experiences situated within power relations" (216). In addition to, but not exclusive of, racial, gender, and

class differences, Oda Mae designates some cultural preferences related to the occult that are not convergent with race, but not necessarily opposed, either. She remarks as one point that she has the "gift" like her mother, meaning the gift to communicate with the dead.

8. Traditionally, when it comes to "other world" knowledge, ethnic women are the experts. Julie Cavner's portrayal of a psychic in Woody Allen's short segment, "Oedipus Wrecks," in the film *New York Stories* (1988) illustrates the complex. Woody's lover in that film is initially the eternal gentile, Mia Farrow, until his Jewish mother intervenes and he inadvertently turns to Cavner's character to exorcise his mother's influence from his life. In such a short film with so traditional an Oedipal theme, Allen's character is allowed to remain innocent, provoked by his *mother* and eventually Cavner's character into doing the very thing he hopes to avoid—marrying his mother, thus, the title "Oedipus Wrecks."

9. Though I have no statistics on this, it seems to me that African-Americans read this particular bit of stylizing as parodic of Euro-American stereotypes or what Henry Louis Gates identifies as "signifyin'," which is a form of verbal and at times performative resistance by which the minority discourse draws "on 'arbitrary substitution' freely, to disrupt the signifier by displacing its signified in an intentional act of will" (51) Although it is a standard white assumption that the underprivileged are incompetent in handling their financial affairs, the act of Whoopi's exaggerated response signals a slippage from that classic depiction.

10. In a "Whoopi Goldberg," the actress remarks, "There is a part of me that has always wanted to be a hero and Oda Mae permits me to play someone who becomes truly heroic" (59). The statement implies that Goldberg is cognizant of the sacrifice Oda Mae makes in foregoing her own interests for the interest of someone else. If her participation were less self-interested, the heroic component be genuinely asserted. That we do not marvel at her sacrifice results from the filmic manipulation that upstages her with Sam's seemingly altruistic desires..

11. Again, while White's article deals primarily with the ghost thriller/horror film, she makes an important point that the ghost story has been a productive conduit for the "representations of disruptive force of lesbian desire" (144).

BIBLIOGRAPHY

Ajami, Fouad. "The Summer of Arab Discontent." *Foreign Affairs* 69.5 (Winter 1990): 1–20.

"Battle of the Biceps," *People Weekly*, June 11, 1990: 86–89.

Bhabba, Homi. "Unpacking My Library Again." *The Journal of the Midwest Modern Language Association* 28.1 (Spring 1995): 5–18.

Cixous, Helene, & Catherine Clement. *The Newly Born Woman.* Minneapolis: University of Minnesota Press, 1986.

Corliss, Richard. "If It Worked Before, Do It Again." *Time,* July 30, 1990: 56–57.

De Lauretis, Teresa. *Alice Doesn't: Feminism, Semiotics, Cinema.* Indianapolis: Indiana University Press, 1984.

De Lauretis, Teresa. *Technologies of Gender: Essays on Theory, Film, and Fiction.* Indianapolis: Indiana University Press, 1987.

Enloe, Cynthia. *The Morning After: Sexual Politics at the End of the Cold War.* Berkeley: University of California Press, 1993.

Flax, Jane. "The End of Innocence." *Feminists Theorize the Political*. Ed. Judith Butler and Joan W. Scott. New York: Routledge, Chapman and Hall, Inc., 1992. 445–63.

Gates, Henry Louis. *The Signifying Monkey: A Theory of African American Literary Criticism*. New York: Oxford University Press, 1988.

Ghost. Dir. Jerry Zucker. Paramount Pictures, 1990.

Kauffmann, Stanley. "Books and the Arts: Midsummer Roundup." *New Republic* August 13, 1990: 30–31.

Lui, Lydia. "The Female Body and Nationalist Discourse: *The Field of Life and Death* Revisited." *Scattered Hegemonies: Postmodernity and Transnational Feminist Practices*. Ed. Inderpal Grewal and Caren Kaplan. Minneapolis: University of Minnesota Press, 1994. 37–62.

Modleski, Tania. *Feminism Without Women: Culture and Criticism in a Postfeminist Age*. New York: Routledge, 1991.

Morganthau, Tom, Thomas, Rich, & Clift, Eleanor. "The S&L Scandal's Biggest Blowout." *Newsweek*, November 6, 1989: 35–36.

Morrison, Toni. *Playing in the Dark: Whiteness and the Literary Imagination*. New York: Vintage Books, 1992.

Novak, Ralph. "Picks and Pans: Screen-*Ghost*." *People Weekly*, July 23, 1990: 8.

"Oedipus Wrecks." Dir. Woody Allen. *New York Stories*. Touchstone. 1988.

Shohat, Ella. "Ethnicities-in-Relation: Toward a Multicultural Reading of American Cinema." *Unspeakable Images: Ethnicity and the American Cinema*. Ed. Lester D. Friedman. Urbana: University of Illinois Press, 1991. 215–250.

Springer, Claudia. "Comprehension and Crisis: Reporter Films and the Third World." *Unspeakable Images: Ethnicity and the American Cinema*. Ed. Lester D. Friedman. Urbana: University of Illinois Press, 1991. 167–189.

"Stop Legal Bribery on Capitol Hill." *Business Week*, December 4, 1989: 134.

Travers, Peter. "The Year in Movies." *Rolling Stone*, December 13, 1990, 19–22.

White, Patricia. "Female Spectator, Lesbian Spector: *The Haunting*." *Inside/Out: Lesbian Theories, Gay Theories*. Ed. Diana Fuss. New York: Routledge, 1991. 142–172.

"Whoopi Goldberg Talks about Her Role in 'Ghost,' and Blasts Critics Over Her Film Choices." *Jet*, August 13, 1990: 58–60.

Chapter 7

Meridel Le Sueur, Reportage, and the Cultural Situatedness of Her Rhetoric

James M. Boehnlein

Out of the critical temper of the thirties came a type of writing that sought to capture the immediacy of the Depression experience while critiquing existing institutions or ideologies. Documentary reportage, or imaginative nonfiction, emerged as an important genre during the thirties as it provided social realists of the decade a means by which an aesthetic could emerge with a critical sociopolitical commentary. Its power lay in its ability not only to inform people, but to move people. James Agee's *Let Us Now Praise Famous Men* is one of the most prominent examples of the era. During the thirties, however, one Midwestern woman, Meridel Le Sueur, wrote some of the most important and influential reportage of the day. Adopting elements of fiction, emphasizing character, carefully selected detail and image, and narrative line, Le Sueur's use of documentary reportage evoked class and gender debate in significant, feminist ways. In order to capture the "dignity of actuality" so prevalent in the majority of thirties reportage, Le Sueur employed a rhetoric which, according to Kenneth Burke, was a mode of appeal essential for bridging the conditions of estrangement natural to society (146). Burke's observations about the ubiquity of rhetoric in human situations assist in explaining why reportage offered a unique glimpse into thirties America. Burke argues that the more complex a situation is, the greater the need for rhetorical devices when that situation is communicated. Rhetoric is not merely a calculated use of language and linguistic resources. It is also a means toward achieving social cohesion (146).

Social cohesion, "communal sensibility," and solidarity—all concerns of the socialist feminists of the decade—found expression in documentary reportage (Hedges 9). In this chapter, I hope to show that Le Sueur's reportage of the thirties employed a rhetoric of cultural situatedness which empowered her community by raising political and social consciousness. To this end, I will study the rhetoric of a selected depression-era piece—"Salvation Home"—as it demonstrates the use of documentary style while evoking cultural and social debate.

Born in 1900, Meridel Le Sueur grew up in a socialist home that was frequented by prominent members of the Socialist Party, the IWW, and the Nonpartisan League. She remembers Eugene Debs, Bill Haywood, Joe Hill, as well as Emma Goldman and Lincoln Steffens. Le Sueur's mother, Marion Wharton, was in her own right an activist: while raising three children she also, until well over the age of seventy-five, pursued an active career as a feminist and a socialist.

Le Sueur was exposed to the Midwestern tradition of radical dissent through both her mother and stepfather, Arthur Le Sueur. A socialist lawyer, Arthur Le Sueur met Marion while both were teaching at the People's College, a correspondence school for workers in Fort Scott, Kansas. The Le Sueurs were leading participants in the reform movements of the time—their involvement with the IWW, for example, figured prominently in Meridel's development as a worker-writer and belief in the artist as activist and revolutionary.

Le Sueur's early years after quitting high school in 1916 were spent in Chicago, where she studied dance; in New York, where she studied drama while living in a commune with Emma Goldman; in Hollywood, where she worked as an extra in the silent film industry; and in San Francisco, where she worked in restaurants and factories. Although the years between 1917 and 1928 were uncertain, she increasingly devoted more time to writing. She began to contribute to labor and left-wing journals and to write book reviews and short stories. *The Worker, Masses,* and the San Francisco *Call* were just three radical journals that published her earliest efforts at writing. Le Sueur's life during the twenties was hardly the glamorous life of the flapper. Always sensitive to society's ills, she remembers the twenties as years of political persecution and repression, especially for women (Hedges 9). Like many feminist activists of the time, Le Sueur was saddened by the sudden apathy among women and former suffragettes who had enthusiastically endorsed feminist issues.

As for many writers, the thirties were years of intensely satisfying work for Le Sueur. In a time of unprecedented economic crisis, political activists believed that radical social change was a real possibility. Furthermore, a sense of being a part of a collective effort of shared revolutionary goals and expectations sustained and inspired Le Sueur. Consequently, she belonged to a number of Leftist organizations: the John Reed Clubs, the *New Masses, Midwest Magazine,* the Workers Alliance, and the Writers Project of the WPA. Her association with other women was nourishing too. For a time, Le Sueur lived in communes with women with whom she shared her earnings from magazine writing. The experience contributed to her reportage about women in the thirties, and to her novel *The Girl,* which describes a group of women who have banned together to survive the Depression.

A Minneapolis truckers' strike in 1934 signaled another breakthrough for Le Sueur. Her participation in a sympathy-walkout resulted in one of her most important pieces of reportage, "I Was Marching." Here she describes her participation in the collective strike effort, presenting a sense of "fusing with a larger reality" (Hedges 9). She believed that she actually merged with others as if "a new reality were coming into being" (Hedges 9). Her reportage about unemployment, labor unrest, strikes, and the lives of women contains that combination of deep sympathy and absorbed attention to detail most characteristic of her thirties writing.

During the thirties, then, Le Sueur moved on to produce work "in which she was expressing her passionate feeling of connection and union through explorations of the political, economic, and social realities of life in the depression" (Hedges 8). The Great Depression was for Le Sueur and other writers the crucible in which was tested what Le Sueur called "communal sensibility." Furthermore, Le Sueur's feminist and class concerns were indeed supported by the subversive and critical temper of the Communist Party. She was capable of linking ideology and agency, the capacity to exert power. Her rhetoric embraced utterances as both reflections on and participants of experience.

Le Sueur, who joined the Communist Party as early as 1924 and has never left it, is today the most prominent female literary figure in the Communist Party of the United States of America (Pratt 247). As Robert Shaffer have demonstrated, the Party supported women writers. This certainly was no less true of Le Sueur. Her relationship with the Party provides a pattern by which to evaluate her role as a "socialist feminist" during the thirties. Moreover, Le Sueur's use of reportage conflated the agency/ideology opposition, so clearly the focus of aesthetic-social criticism of thirties radical literature.

Elaine Hedges' introduction to *Ripening* (1982), the first major anthology of Le Sueur's work, concludes that the Party was supportive:

But in the larger context the Party had much to offer Le Sueur. While it was antithetical to the spirit of some of her work, it was also helpful and supportive, and it provided a political theory and program of action to which she could commit herself while at the same time retaining the freedom to be critical. . . . What mattered was "communal solidarity," and if this in the thirties was part reality and part hope, it was reality and hope that she shared with innumerable others. (14–15)

The emphasis that Le Sueur placed upon "communal solidarity" was grounded in the understanding that ideology without action could never help change society. Indeed, she voiced the concern of many colleagues when she insisted upon the contextualization of ideological positions.

Nowhere was this concern made more evident than in her address to the 1935 American Writers' Congress, "Proletarian Literature and the Midwest." Both an important historical document as well as a literary manifesto, Le Sueur's address sought to intersect sociopolitical concerns with an aesthetic of engagement. It called for regionalism as a site of analysis of proletarian writing. For Le Sueur regional studies were equated with cultural studies. Writing by the working class can only be understood when read in light of its place or situatedness in a particular culture.

Le Sueur, then, envisioned a new literature that was informed by a contextual aesthetic. She espoused writing which was "never burdened with the old tradition in literature from the old world." Moreover, she fostered the emerging Middle Western mind, "finding a place, sensing a new and vigorous interrelation between himself and others" (*American Writers' Congress* 136). In many respects, she challenged the East Coast bourgeois literary circle as the privileged site of analysis. Because the Midwestern mind had experienced most acutely the struggles of the Depression, it was better prepared to address issues germane to a proletarian and socialist aesthetic.

This critical stance suggests that working-class art is created and experienced in group situations—not, as Paul Lauter points out, "in the privacy of a study, but in the church, the hall, the work site, the meeting hall, the quilting bee, or the picket line" (840). It is thus rooted in the experiences of a particular group of people facing particular problems at a particular time. It is not conceived as timeless and transcendent, nor does it often function in such modes.

The "instrumental" character of working-class art is, therefore, important to perceiving the aesthetic theory that informs it. By invoking the Midwest as the cultural site of analysis for this literature, Le Sueur privileged its status as literature whose objectives are "inseparable from the goals toward which the lives of the workers directed them" (Lauter 841). It is literature which at once "influences people's behavior" while "persuading readers to adopt particular beliefs" (Vicinus, *The Industrial Muse*).

The publication in 1939 of Meridel Le Sueur's "Salvation Home" represents an integration of those themes and rhetorical features that she developed in most of her thirties pieces. As a piece of reportage, "Salvation Home" depicts the lives of pregnant women in a home run by a local welfare agency. Again, these women, who feel the indifference and violence of their men, reassure each other by living through their personal struggles and by renewing their commitment to life and to the future.

"Salvation Home" explores that relationship between sex and power which informs most of Le Sueur's reportage during the late thirties. She uses this home for pregnant women as a "political forum" in which the Workers Alliance and, by extension, a sense of "communal sensibility" are supported. The scene in "Salvation Home" in which the girl communicates in writing with the deaf Alice is one of her most poignantly effective. It captures Le Sueur's ability to grace personal experience with meaning and empathy. Moreover, this scene represents a nexus point in Le Sueur's reportage where ideology, aesthetics, and rhetoric form a telling commentary about the contestatory nature of identity.

Indeed, Le Sueur uses scenes such as this to establish the identity of these two women, an identity borne of struggle and opposition.

From a rhetorical perspective, Le Sueur coalesces "inner world" with "outer world." She employs an "emancipatory" rhetoric that constructs identity: the Demeter and Persephone myth informs the very words that express Le Sueur's intentions. Moreover, "Salvation Home" uses a rhetoric that links "understanding" with "strategy": Le Sueur's words attempt to expose the disempowerment experienced by these women while enacting the very changes she proposes.

Reportage like "Salvation Home" and those written by Le Sueur throughout the thirties begin with some form of opposition and end in self-actualization or self-understanding. This dominant thematic shift parallels her use of a sociocognitive rhetoric which merges understanding and strategy, the constative with the performative. Her use of the "word" or "utterance" is meant to effect change. This over-arching feature of Le Sueur's sociocognitive rhetoric positions her use of language well within the rhetorical tradition advocated by Kenneth Burke, Mikhail Bahktin, Walter Beale, and Jurgen Habermas. Each sees language as a multi-faceted and multi-variant construct which embodies a goal-directed use of the word. "Speech" and "action" become one.

This rhetorical stance recommends itself to reportage because of the highly goal-directed purposes behind imaginative nonfiction. If sociocognitive rhetoric is indeed the holistic negotiation of truth and justice within an interpretive community, then reportage, which seeks the truth and justice among various communities, represents the clearest instance of any genre to mirror its rhetoric. Genre and rhetoric become one. Reportage for Le Sueur proved to be an appropriate narrative/journalistic form for the altered reality of depression-era America, an era of intense social change. Sociocognitive rhetoric with its pragmatic and goal-directed features embodies that reality as well.

Meridel Le Sueur's rhetorical legacy, then, finds expression in language which moves beyond pure linguistic utterance and toward linguistic engagement. Rhetoric and ideology merge by recognizing that both "foundational" and "anti-foundational" epistemologies can synthesize without neglecting each other's ability to empower. In other words, the "social" and the "cognitive" perspectives can indeed be treated simultaneously. The sociocognitive project allows for pure utterance as such to coalesce with the gritty realism of the "lifeworld." This merging, then, of poetics with politics as evident in Le Sueur's use of sociocognitive rhetoric in her reportage is her rhetorical legacy. Significantly, Le Sueur's writing and concern for gender and class issues anticipated current debate in which rhetoric and ideology figure prominently.

In general, the rhetorical legacy that Le Sueur's depression-era writings about women have embodied views rhetoric, then, as a form of cultural critique. Likewise, as a form of feminist discourse, her writings construct gender and identity in their response to social division and oppression. Her use of sociocognitive rhetoric within reportage is a form of "communicative action" which expresses both an understanding of issues as well as a means of altering oppressive conditions. Current feminist theory reveals a similar type of rhetorical sensitivity that Le Sueur has so forcefully advocated. Feminist theorists such as Nekola, Rabinowitz, and Benhabib have appropriated a form of sociocognitive rhetoric which can help develop perspectives that can take into account strategies of resistance that women may construct in opposition to subjugated positions. To this end, Meridel Le Sueur's rhetorical legacy reveals a sustained effort at developing an alternative epistemology as the basis for an alternative feminist discourse.

Knowledge-making is the basis of any rhetorical construct. This axiom supports this project's claim that the sociocognitive theory of language use is grounded in an epistemological framework that is heavily influenced by the word as phenomenon. Le Sueur's "lifeworld" reportage intersects with social opposition in order to evaluate a dominant and oppressive culture. This dynamic generates new knowledge and creates a means by which feminist identity can be classified. This form of engaged knowledge is a corrective to the Enlightenment tradition of metaphysical knowledge-making which has failed to support feminist theory.

In her article "Postmodernism and Political Change: Issues for Feminist Theory," Nancy Hartsock argues that an alternative to the universalizing tendencies of the Enlightenment tradition would be the recognition of the "ad hoc contextual, plural, and limited" features of a "situated knowledge" (16). Hartsock believes that because feminist theory can no longer rely upon an Enlightenment epistemology of totality, theorists need to offer an alternative epistemology that more adequately addresses knowledge-as-phenomenon issues which so inform an anti-essentialist feminism. The notion of "situated" or "engaged" knowledge is key to understanding how an epistemology can yield insight into the "marked subjectivities" or identities of gender-charged subjects.

But what are the characteristic features of these "epistemologies of marked subjectivities"? Hartsock answers this question by arguing that "these epistemologies grow out of an experience of domination": "It must be recognized that the historical creation and maintenance of the dominance of Euro-American masculinist culture requires a series of renamings and redefinings" (24). She believes that the dominated and marginalized are forced to inhabit multiple worlds (26). The material conditions of existence generate the epistemologies of subordinate groups. "One must also recognize," Hartsock avers, "that these situated knowledges are at once available to members of oppressed groups and at the same time represent an achievement in the face of dominant ideologies" (26).

Hartsock's position is remarkably similar to Le Sueur's standpoint as both a feminist and socialist during depression-era America. The women in her thirties reportage represent the marginalized and subordinate. Their experiences develop knowledge and subjectivity borne less from an Enlightenment tradition than from engagement in the "lifeworld." Hartsock supports this type of "knowledge-making" as she argues, "For Western (white) women, the experience of life under patriarchy allows for the possibility of developing an understanding both of the falseness and partiality of the dominant view and a vision of reality which is deeper and more complex than that view" (27).

Le Sueur's merging of the "self" with the "social" in her documentary expressions is actually the development of an "epistemology of marked subjectivities," to use Hartsock's terminology. The particular historical, social, and economical contexts that informed Le Sueur's reportage about women helped create a form of knowledge-making. The dominant shift from opposition to self-actualization, characteristic of much of her reportage, qualifies as a means by which "marked subjectivities" and knowledge-making intersect.

Thus, the epistemological framework out of which Le Sueur operated as a feminist and socialist resonates with the current feminist position that "the knowledges available to multiple subjectivities [identities] have different qualities from that of the disembodied and singular subject of Western political thought" (Hartsock 28). From Le Sueur's point of view, this notion is evident in her belief that political identity is dialogic, which, for Le Sueur, is a "relationship of interdependence" (Schleuning 86). Each is part of the other. One cannot understand or isolate, or analyze anything separately. The implication for Le Sueur's political identity or "marked subjectivities" is that knowledge-making and identity cannot be determined separate from the collective, or outside of the circle (Schleuning 86).

Thus, Hartsock's and Le Sueur's epistemologies are similar:

Most fundamentally, these are situated knowledges—that is, they are located in a particular time and space. . . . As an aspect of being situated, these knowledges represent a response to and an expression of a specific embodiment. The bodies of the dominated have been made to function as the marks of their oppression: we are not allowed to pretend that they do not exist. (Hartsock 29)

Because situated, these knowledges cannot be other than social and collective. As Hartsock notes, "Those of us that Euro-American masculinist thought marked as Other cannot but experience the world collectively since our stigmatized identities are formed as members of groups" (29). This notion of "group" identity at once resonates in Le Sueur's own theory of "communal sensibility" which so informed her reportage about women during the Depression. As noted elsewhere in this project, Le Sueur's women would begin their experiences isolated and find solace of self-actualization among fellow women. "Salvation Home" is noteworthy for its reassuring belief that meaning can never be isolated and abstract; it finds expression and significance in the group.

The shape of these knowledges are evident as well "by attending to the features of the social location occupied by dominated groups" (Hartsock 29). These knowledges express multiple and often contradictory realities; they are not fixed but change with the changing shape of "the historical conjuncture and the balance of forces" (Hartsock 29). Although these knowledges are both critical of and vulnerable to the dominant culture, they are also contained within it. This notion of knowledge-making as a voice(s) of opposition is highly congruent with Le Sueur's belief that in struggle, a new behavior emerges. Le Sueur supports an "engaged knowledge" that encodes human behavior. This concept echoes another quality of "marked subjectivities" and epistemology:

The knowledge of marked subjectivities opens possibilities that may or may not be realized. To the extent these knowledges are self-conscious about their aspects and assumptions, they make available new epistemological options. The struggle they represent and express, if made self-conscious, can go beyond efforts at survival to recognize the centrality of systematic power relations; they can become knowledges that are both accountable and engaged. (Hartsock 30).

Attention to the epistemologies of situated knowledges can allow for the construction of important alternatives "to the dead-end oppositions set up by Enlightenment epistemology" (31).

Therefore, to develop an alternative epistemology, both Le Sueur and Hartsock believe that the chance of power relations and the development of subjectivities must be grounded in the experience of the dominated and the marginalized. Le Sueur's reportage about women during the Depression feature such an epistemological and self-actualizing project. Indeed, Le Sueur's writings anticipate current feminist theories which deny the privileged Enlightenment construct. Her works, like those of current feminists, refigure aspects of engaged or situated knowledge: They recognize knowledge as conditioned by location; they accept the multiple and contradictory nature of their reality; they avoid a descent into a particularistic relativism; and they embrace knowledge as limited and changing (Hartsock 32). Likewise, this notion of "situated knowledges" demonstrates a means by which language privileges women's accounts of their experience. This form of aesthetics figures prominently in Le Sueur's works. As a proletarian writer, she believed that the goal of art "was to bring the reader and writer together once again, in an encounter with the experience of human interrelationship in a social environment" (Schleuning 121). Through engagement with the artist the observer is drawn into art and participates in art.

This leftist aesthetic, which Le Sueur embraces, finds expression in current feminist thinking about the function of language because it shifts from the ahistorically conceived subject to the examination of discourses grounded in historical struggles of oppositional groups. Le Sueur argues that the word should be defined in "social" rather than formalistic terms (Schleuning 116).

Indeed, Le Sueur's "situatedness" would necessitate a discourse ethic which privileges essentialist tendencies within the historical struggles of oppositional social groups. The potential advantage of a discourse ethic of this kind consists in an ongoing dialogue between formal and pragmatic discourse for interpreting needs, defining situations, and pressing claims.

These aspects of "situated knowledges" illustrate Le Sueur's modernity and the similar struggles of oppressed women of two very different periods of American history. The dominant standpoint of both generations is oppositional and contestatory, out of which emerges an identity that acknowledges the contextual, limited, and engaged features of knowledge-making.

BIBLIOGRAPHY

Bahktin, M. M. *The Dialogic Imagination.* Austin: University of Texas Press, 1986.
Beale, Walter. *A Pragmatic Theory of Rhetoric.* Carbondale: Southern Illinois University Press, 1987.
Benhabib, Seyla. "The Generalized and the Concrete Other." *Praxis International,* 5 (1986): 402–424.
Burke, Kenneth. *A Rhetoric of Motives.* Berkeley: University of California Press, 1969.
Habermas, Jurgen. *The Theory of Communicative Action.* Boston: Beacon Press, 1984.
Hart, Henry, ed. *The American Writers' Congress.* New York: International, 1935.
Hartsock, Nancy. "Postmodernism and Political Change: Issues for Feminist Theory." *Cultural Critique* 14 (1989–90): 15–33.
Hedges, Elaine, ed. *Ripening: Selected Works of Meridel Le Sueur 1927–1980.* New York: The Feminist Press, 1982.
Lauter, Paul. "Working-Class Women's Literature." *Feminisms.* Ed. Robyn R. Warhol and Diane Price Handl. New Brunswick: Rutgers University Press, 1991. 837–856.
Le Sueur, Meridel. "Proletarian Literature and the Midwest." *The American Writers' Congress.* New York: International, 1935. 135–138.
Le Sueur, Meridel. "Salvation Home." *New Masses.* January 10, 1939. 19–20.
Nekola, Charlotte and Paula Rabinowitz. *Writing Red: An Anthology of American Women Writers, 1930–1940.* New York: Feminist Press, 1987.
Pratt, Linda Ray. "Women Writers in the CP: The Case of Meridel Le Sueur." *Women Studies* 14 (1988): 247–64.
Schleuning, Neala. *America: Song We Sang Without Knowing.* Mankato, Minneapolis: Little Red Hen Press, 1983.
Shaffer, Robert. "Women and the CP in the USA: 1930–1940." *Socialist Review* 9 (1979): 73–118.
Vicinus, Martha. *The Industrial Muse.* New York: Barnes, 1974.

Chapter 8

Maternity and the Masses: Drama, the Media, and Jane Martin's *Keely and Du*

Ann C. Hall

In his 1993 review of the Hartford Stage production of Jane Martin's *Keely and Du*, *New York Times* critic Ben Brantley praised the playwright's ability to dramatize the abortion debate because "the prospect of America reaching a happy consensus on abortion is about as likely as unconditional harmony in the Middle East." Murders at abortion clinics, recent vetos and veto overrides on late-term abortion legislation, as well as limits on the protests by pro-lifers substantiate Brantley's prediction and perhaps explain the media's own reluctance to cover, participate in, or facilitate discussions regarding the issue. Heated debates, reports, and news items about abortion from both sides of the issue appear, but abortion rarely rates an extended discussion or "mini-series."[1] In many ways, the abortion debate has gone underground, so the appearance of *Keely and Du* is unique. The play not only offers both sides of the issue, it does so in a detailed and compelling manner.

Part of the problem is that the abortion issue is about women, and media representations of femininity in general have never been noteworthy as far as feminists have been concerned. Representations of motherhood have been particularly troubling. On the one hand, media representations of the maternal have often reflected the mood swings of a manic-depressive patriarchy, alternatively presenting motherhood as a life-force and cultural mainstay to its opposite, a destructive, subversive, and subterranean force.[2] On the other hand, feminists themselves continue to struggle with the question of motherhood, since the maternal role is often the primary site of female oppression and the reproduction of patriarchy.[3] The question of abortion clearly highlights and complicates the dilemma of female representation in patriarchal culture, so the relationship between the media and the abortion debate will always be strained. During the late nineteenth and early twentieth century, for example, newspapers, at the height of their popularity, ran ads for abortionists and abortifacients, as well as reports and editorial condemning the practice.[4]

Contemporary media are in similar positions: television stations may cover pro-life or pro-choice demonstrations that are interrupted by revenue-generating commercials from a pro-life or pro-choice perspective. Even the media's attempts at objectivity have political, cultural, and social ramifications. That is, by presenting "both sides," particularly the extremes and therefore most dramatic or newsworthy moments, the media have effectively commodified and manufactured the abortion debate into a controversial, nearly taboo topic, a subject capable of inspiring as much fear—but ironically less coverage—as child abduction narratives that have gained tremendous airtime. One effect of such coverage is that audiences conclude that the issue is overwhelmingly irresolvable; only the extremists are involved or openly discuss the issue. The position of the media becomes not only appealing but a model for response—somehow removed from the fray, serenely observing or recording the chaos from a pristinely removed technological vantage point. The ramifications of such a stance are silence and apathy. Who wants to be involved with this issue, even among friends, when it is so volatile? A discreet and persistent silence surrounds the issue in many powerful circles, from liberal middle-class discussions to the Republican Party's national convention in 1996 during which candidates were encouraged to express but not debate their views on abortion.

Admittedly, the media is not entirely to blame for the cultural reticence. As Laurie Shrage notes:

Disagreements about the meaning of abortion reflect disagreements not only about the meaning of fetal life but about the meaning of life itself and how it should be lived by women and others. Yes these larger philosophical disagreements implicit in disagreements over abortion are often overlooked by standard philosophical approaches to abortion. (58)

The abortion debate is valorized because of these deeper concerns, but, ironically, these concerns are precisely the reason people are unwilling to discuss the issue. In other words, when people debate abortion, they are "defending a *world view*—a notion of what they see as sacred and important" (Luker 7). Discussions about such issues are clearly time-consuming, frequently hostile, at best philosophical, and incapable of miniaturization into byte-sized formats. And yet, it is precisely because abortion represents these deeper, philosophical, existential views that it should be discussed, perhaps not in the hopes of resolving the abortion conflict, but, more realistically, in order to identify, analyze, and examine the assumptions that underlie abortion in order to discover common ground, shared views, or persistent misunderstandings. Shrage, for example, argues that both pro-life and pro-choice groups agree that femininity is a "social construct" (69), a construct that could potentially be reorganized "in a way that reflects that we value children and the work of those who care for them" (66). Such an opportunity will not be realized if people are unwilling to address the debate out of a fear of conflict, a fear that the media perpetuates through its lack of coverage.

Theatre, which has historically presented issues that popular venues were reluctant to address, has also been silent on the abortion debate. Few modern or contemporary plays make it their central topic.[5] The appearance of Martin's *Keely and Du*, which does, is a refreshing addition to the theatre's silence and the media's superficial handling of the debate. By representing both sides of the issue in significant ways, by exposing some of the underlying assumptions about the issue, and by oscillating between pro-life and pro-choice views, the play promotes discussion and engages, rather than alienates, audiences. As a result, the play creates Brechtian "new media": media that will "not only serve as instruments for heightened perception, but also a means of critically examining that very perception" (Wright 87). The play-as-new-media succeeds where the mass media do not.

In a matter of moments, Martin's work quickly establishes one of the more important arguments in the abortion debate, the distinction between the rights of the mother and the rights of the fetus. In the play, a radical pro-life group, Operation Retrieval, kidnaps a young woman in order to save the fetus she is on her way to abort. The woman, Keely, is quickly drugged, handcuffed, and prevented from obtaining the abortion she seeks. As she awakens, her keeper, Du, explains the situation to her, not with expository references to the kidnapping, the group responsible, or even the sparse surroundings they inhabit, but instead by bluntly telling Keely that she will have her baby.

Admittedly, this opening image is an unflattering one for the pro-life cause, but the play deliberately and explicitly articulates its concerns—the life of the fetus is equally important, if not more, important than, the mother's. Further, the play may aim at objectivity, but it does not always reach its goal, a limitation that actually works to the play's advantage. By avoiding the objective stance of the contemporary media, the play, as will be seen throughout this discussion, engages the audience in significant and deeply emotional ways as a result of its temporary biases. Pro-lifers, for example, might fault the play for its extreme representation of their position, while pro-choice advocates might commend it for its accurate depiction of the ramifications of the pro-life stance: the "mother is literally reduced to a holding vessel" (Kaplan 14).[6] But this stance is not static.

The play defends the pro-life stance by having every character refer to the fetus throughout the play not as "cells," which Keely does only once, but as a "baby" (17). Later in the play and the pregnancy, Keely even listens to the heartbeat. As clearly as Lennart Nilsson's photographs during the mid-sixties documented the gestation of the fetus, these references movingly establish the existence of human life in Keely's body and Keely's attachment to the baby, despite her wishes to abort (Kaplan 14).[7] The pro-life's sense of urgency over this issue is presented; this group is attempting to save human life.

Just as clearly, though, the play establishes the complex needs of the mother in contemporary society. Keely is poor, caring for her aged father, isolated in her struggle, and, finally, pregnant as a result of a rape by her estranged husband. As Walter, the patriarch of Operation Retrieval, tells her, she was chosen for this very reason because "rape has always been understood as the extreme edge of abortion policy" (18). For Walter, the question of rape is about fetal rights; but for feminists, the question of rape is an extreme representation of the reality of femininity in patriarchal culture. Women do not control sex under any circumstances:

> Sexual intercourse, still the most common cause of pregnancy, cannot simply be presumed coequally determined. Feminism has found that women feel compelled to preserve the appearance—which, acted upon, becomes the reality—of male direction of sexual expression, as if male initiative itself were what we want, as if it were that which turns us on. . . . Rape—that is, intercourse with force that is recognized as force—is adjudicated not according to power or force that the man wields, but according to the indices of intimacy between parties. The more intimate you are with your rapist, the less likely a court is to find that what happened to you was rape. . . . Abortion policy has never been explicitly approached in the context of how women get pregnant, that is, as a consequence of intercourse under conditions of gender inequality; that is, an issue of forced sex. (MacKinnon 354)

By including a character who has been brutalized and impregnated by her husband, then kidnapped by Operation Retrieval, Keely may not only serve Walter's political purposes, but feminists' as well. As a "typical" woman, Keely offers a frightening representation of femininity within a patriarchal system. Every effort that she has made to free herself from her husband, her poverty, and her own self-abusing beliefs about herself has been thwarted, ignored, or denied.

Walter and Du offer compassionate responses to her victimization by giving her the choice either to keep the baby and take their financial support or give the baby up for adoption. Such a response is more than many governmental, social service, or individual agencies provide today. While "extraordinary levels of vigilance" are expected of and taken on by pregnant women, "neither the father nor the state nor private industry is held responsible for any of the harms they may be inflicting on developing fetuses, nor are they required to contribute to their care" (Bordo 83). Clearly such altruism is hardly blameworthy; and through the play, it may even prompt pro-life organizations and individuals to begin to lend or improve such assistance to pregnant women, mothers, and children.

Like many, Walter and Du believe that economic burdens are the chief reasons for abortion. Underlying this belief, as the play so clearly demonstrates, is their faith in the maternal instinct. Keely will want to mother her child; she will "fall in love with" her baby (19). Maternal instincts are natural and inherently nurturing. As one critic notes, our culture assumes that women are "always already to be mothers, if only the conditions are right" (Willis 81).

The play, however, illustrates that motherhood is far from simple and instinctual. To borrow a phrase from Margaret Drabble, we witness "the Armageddon of maternal instinct" (qtd. in Wilt 34). Ironically, it is through Walter and Du that the play undercuts the beliefs they espouse. Whether they notice it or not, they spend an incredible amount of time educating Keely on this "instinct." They frequently bribe her with treats or momentary freedoms if she will only read anti-abortion treatises or books on infant development and mothering.

If this image is too subtle, Keely makes it clear that there is more to motherhood than economics and *Parents* magazines; it is frequently the moment when many women suddenly sense, realize, or intuit the existence of patriarchal oppression and subsequently take it out upon the children. During one discussion, for example, Keely challenges Du's platitudes, saying, "My sister-in-law, she threw her baby on the floor. You think 'in love with your baby' is all that's out there?" (19). She even exposes Walter's less than altruistic attitude toward her and her baby. She claims that he cares nothing for the baby; it is his "little political something" (38). Legitimized abortions are a national embarrassment for a country that claims to care about women, children, and the unborn, and Keely's outbursts highlight the inadequacies of much of the pro-life rhetoric to account for the reality of female experience, a view that challenges the stereotypical and cultural representations or interpretations of maternal instinct.

In the midst of this patriarchal oppression is Du, the older woman who takes care of Keely during her kidnapping. Initially, she appears to be nothing more than a puppet of the patriarchy. She also appears to be a pro-choice version of a pro-lifer: one of the many "benighted victims of social conditioning that prevents their own views from authentically reflecting their own genuine needs and deepest beliefs" (Tribe 239). But as the play progresses, we learn that Du is more than a male impersonator; she is a capable, independent woman who has had her own share of hardship. As a young woman, she was bartered between her father and her husband. Her marriage was loveless, her children her only comfort. Suddenly, everything changed. God, she says, turned her husband "into a firebrand and an orator and a beacon to others, and I fell in love with him and that bed turned into a lake of flame and I was, so help me, bored no more, and that's a testimony. There is change possible where you never hope to find it, and that's the moral of my story" (35). And here is the essential difference between Keely and Du. Du is optimistic; experiences in her life have led her to believe that "change is possible," that there is hope, and it appears to be the defining differences between the pro-life and pro-choice positions.

Du's optimism, admittedly, has been tempered by the pain of her nursing work, experiences that led her to conclude that abortion is horrifying for both mother and child:

They tear the babies, they poison them with chemicals, and burn them to death with salt solution, they take them out by Cesarean alive and let them die of neglect or strangulation, and then later on these poor women, they cut their wrists or swallow lye, and they bring them to me because I am a nurse. Over and over. Little hands. Little feet. (39)

For Du, the abortions concretely stop all potential for change and either human or divine intervention, for out of the destruction of "little hands" and "little feet" comes further destruction.

One of the great successes of the play is this portrayal of a pro-life woman who has made her choice based on her own experience. And as the play progresses, the two women grow to love and care for one another in significant ways. Out of their differences, they forge a bond; they generate new life, ironically a very palpable symbol of Du's own optimistic approach to life. Importantly, one of the first arenas in which they begin to establish a connection is through their irreverent attacks on the pompous male leader of Operation Retrieval.

What Du does not understand, however, is the depth of Keely's anger over the rape and the other injustices in her life, as well as her own self-loathing. She tries to tell Du: "I'm so angry and fucked up, I just can't do it. I dream of how it happened over and over all the time. I'd be angry at the baby, I think so. I'd hurt the baby sometime and might not even know it, that could happen. If I had a baby, my first one, and I gave it away, I'd just cry all the time, I would" (40).

Keely's monologue not only illustrates the plight of women in patriarchal systems, but also communicates an opposing view of the maternal instinct. Here, for example, Keely believes that the greater abuse to the baby would be birth, the lesser, the abortion. Such reasoning is clearly a threat to a culture that prides itself on its humane treatment of its citizens, for Keely clearly believes that her baby is safer dead than alive.

Du misreads Keely's maternal instincts and makes a fatal mistake at the end of the play. As a result of her mystical belief in the power of motherhood, she and Walter arrange for Keely and her estranged husband, Cole, to meet. Cole has supposedly gone through a treatment program for domestic violence under the auspices of Operation Retrieval. In a matter of moments, Keely has bitten Cole, and he is about to beat her senseless. While Walter and Du remove him from the room, Keely takes the opportunity alone, not to escape, but to abort her child with a coat hanger. This very graphic depiction of female desperation leaves little doubt about the lengths to which women will go to abort.

Tellingly, the men depart, leaving Keely to die. She is literally nothing without the fetus now; in fact, she is a liability, since her existence will surely bring about legal prosecution. Du, however, remains with Keely and saves her life, an ennobling action that illustrates and affirms her commitment to life.

While we may not endorse either female character's perspective on abortion, the relationship that develops between the two women throughout the play is admirable, and their struggles to define themselves and their relationship to motherhood is compelling. Each is human, and each has something to offer the other. Keely offers the harsh reality of female sexuality in a patriarchal system, a system the permits domestic violence, that entangles motherhood with economics, identity, and oppression, and a system that offers no support to women, whatever their reproductive status. Du, on the other hand, offers hope; she is an optimist who has experienced redemption on earth and who believes that it awaits us all, if we are patient and life-affirming. Most importantly, the play avoids the stereotypes that the members of pro-life and pro-choice groups are apt to make about the female members of the opposing group. In many ways, the play consciously dramatizes the admonitions made by Ginsburg:

> Many feminists assume that anti-abortion activists are dupes of organized religion or conservative politicians, thus denying pro-life women the possibility of being active, rational members of society. On the other hand, some anti-abortion activists are convinced that pro-choice women are selfish and promiscuous, devoid of any moral concern. Each side, viewing the other as the personification of evil, renews itself through its vision of the opposition. A more fruitful approach recognizes women on both sides as social actors who respond to and reshape the ideological and material circumstances of their lives. (173–74)

The women have built a relationship together under the worst circumstances and on the basis of one of the most difficult issues of our time.

The final scene takes place in a prison visiting room. Du has been prosecuted for kidnapping, and she has suffered a stroke. Keely brings her gifts, companionship, and a resurrection of the maternal through its absence. She tells, Du, for example:

> So, I went to a Judd concert. You know that one that sings without her mother now . . . (*she stops*) . . . without her mother now. I don't know, I left. People, they're about half screwy, you know. People who go to concerts? There was this guy next to me, he was smoking grass, right out there, had a little girl on his lap, maybe two. (*She tears up.*) Had a little girl on his lap. So. I don't know. I don't know. Anyway . . .
> (*The conversation burns out. They sit. Du looks directly at her. They lock eyes. The pause lengthens.*)
> Du: Why?
> Keely: (*Looks at her. A pause.*) Why?
> (*They sit. Lights dim*) (70)

Keely's return to the maternal marks and highlights her own anxiety over the abortion, as well as highlighting the play's ambivalent representation of motherhood.

Ironically, Keely's maternal feelings are still present through the absence of her child, the absence of the mother-daughter relationship in the defunct country-western team of the Judds, and the absence of a maternal or paternal sensibility in the story about the joint-smoking father and his daughter. Through such a conclusion, the play, like the abortion issue itself, forces us to examine our own and our culture's expectations regarding motherhood. Through the play and the abortion issue, we are forced to address   sexual stereotypes, the relationship between sexuality and politics, and numerous cultural myths surrounding our supposed commitment to family values. The play concludes with a very complex but important question, what do we do when we construct motherhood in our culture? Clearly, the play illustrates that there is slippage between our cultural expectations regarding motherhood and the life experience of women, but a more specific answer is not born. Like the entire abortion question itself, the play presents complexities without closure, perhaps in the hope of generating further discussion, ideas, and consideration for the maternal in patriarchal culture. [8]

NOTES

1. See Faludi (112–168; 400–454). Also see the following authors for some examples of the frustrations of both pro-life and pro-choice groups regarding abortion coverage: Leo, Byrne, Sharpe, and Olasky's "The War on Adoption."

2. See Williamson, Irigaray, Honey, and Sochen.

3. See Horney, Irigaray, Chodorow, Kaplan, and Luker for varying ideas on motherhood and feminism.

4. See Tribe and Olasky's *The Press and Abortion*.

5. Eugene O'Neill's *Abortion* (1914) is one of the only dramas that deals with the issue directly. Works such as Lorraine Hansberry's *A Raisin in the Sun* (1959) and Ntozake Shange's *For Coloured Girls Who Have Considered Suicide When the Rainbow is Enuf* (1976) are some of the few dramas that even mention the issue. Judith Wilt's book discusses abortion in contemporary novels and short fiction, while also pointing out that there are no new plots. From *Oedipus* to *Beloved*, the question of infanticide continues.   Her book, though, offers important discussions about the political ramifications of abortion and childbirth in African-American culture, a culture that at one time had to consider the birth of children into slavery. Miriam Claire offers similar conundrums regarding births in Nazi death camps.

6. For discussions on the disappearance of the mother in the abortion debate, see Shrage and Willis, as well as Kaplan.

7. It is interesting to note, as Caroline Whitbeck does, that many hospitals, even those that are pro-life, do not bury any fetus under 500 grams (394).

8. According to Jon Jory, the Artistic Director of Actors Theatre of Louisville and the director of the original production, the play is about "forgiveness on several levels." In this way, the concluding questions between the two women also prompt the audience to wonder if the two will remain friends, if Du can forgive Keely. While forgiveness is clearly an issue in the play, Jory's comments minimize the controversial and important issue of the play, an issue that makes the play so important to the modern dramatic canon

and feminism.

During the 1994–95 theatrical season, four productions of *Keely and Du* were performed throughout the midwest. According to Geoff Nelson, the Artistic Director of The Contemporary American Theatre Company (Columbus, Ohio), he chose the play because it tried to "present a balanced view of the issue" and because it offered "strong roles for women." Artistic Director Brian Fonseca of the Phoenix in Indianapolis praised the play and its courage because the theatrical experience is "so immediate. In two or three years, the issue will be distilled for television and film." And while none of the audience members seemed to change their minds about the issue, the play challenged them in significant ways. During some performances, for example, audiences would applaud when Keely bit her abusive husband. And one pro-life viewer said that while the play made her angry at times, she thought other pro-life proponents should see the play because it illustrated how cliched some responses seem to women considering an abortion.

Jane Martin, by the way, is thought to be a pseudonym for Jon Jory or a pen name for Jory and a group of writers, a rumor that Jory himself denies: Jane Martin "honestly feels, for whatever reason, that she couldn't write plays if people knew who she was and what she was."

BIBLIOGRAPHY

Bordo, Susan. *Unbearable Weight: Feminism, Western Culture, and the Body.* Berkeley: University of California Press, 1993.

Brantley, Ben. "Two Women Find an Odd Bridge Across Abortion-Debate Divide." *New York Times.* December 11, 1993: 13.

Byrne, Jeb. "The News Media and Abortion." *Commonweal,* October 25, 1991: 601–604.

Chodorow, Nancy. *The Reproduction of Mothering: Psychoanalysis and the Sociology of Gender.* Berkeley: University of California Press, 1978.

Claire, Miriam. *The Abortion Dilemma: Personal Views on a Public Issue.* New York: Plenum, 1995.

Faludi, Susan. *Backlash: The Undeclared War Against American Women.* New York: Anchor Books, 1991.

Fonseca, Brian. Interview. June 26, 1995.

Ginsburg, Faye. "The Body Politic: The Defense of Sexual Restriction by Anti-Abortion Activists." *Pleasure and Danger: Exploring Female Sexuality.* New York: Routledge, 1984. 173–188.

Honey, Maureen. *Creating Rosie the Riveter: Class, Gender and Propaganda During World War II.* Amherst: University of Massachusetts Press, 1984.

Horney, Karen. *Feminine Psychology.* New York: W. W. Norton, 1993.

Irigaray, Luce. *This Sex Which Is Not One.* Trans. Catherine Porter. Ithaca, NY: Cornell University Press, 1985.

Jory, John. In "Is Kidnapping for Jesus a Moral Right?" By William Henry III. *Time,* November 29, 1993: 71.

Kaplan, E. Ann. *Motherhood and Representation: The Mother in Popular Culture and Melodrama.* Berkeley: University of California Press, 1984.

Leo, John. "Is the Press Straight on Abortion?" *U.S. News & World Report,* July 16, 1990: 17.

Luker, Kristin. *Abortion and the Politics of Motherhood.* New York: Routledge, 1992.

MacKinnon, Catherine. "Privacy v. Equality: Beyond Roe v. Wade." *Ethics: A Feminist Reader.* Eds. Elizabeth Frazer, et al. Oxford: Blackwell, 1992. 351–363.

Martin, Jane. *Keely and Du.* New York: Samuel French, 1993.

Nelson, Geoffrey. Interview. 26 June 1995.

Olasky, Marvin. "The War on Adoption." *The National Review,* June 7, 1993: 38–44.

Olasky, Marvin. *The Press and Abortion: 1838–1988.* Hillsdale, NJ: Lawrence Erlbaum Associates, 1988.

Sharpe, Rochelle. "States of Confusion." *Ms.* July/August 1992: 83–85.

Shrage, Laurie. *Moral Dilemmas of Feminism: Prostitution, Adultery, and Abortion.* New York: Routledge, 1994.

Sochen, June. *Enduring Values: Women in Popular Culture.* New York: Praeger, 1987.

Tribe, Laurence. *Abortion: The Clash of Absolutes.* New York: Norton, 1990.

Whitbeck, Caroline. "Taking Women Seriously as People: The Moral Implication for Abortion." *The Abortion Controversy: A Reader.* Eds. Louis P. Pojman and Francis Beckwith. Boston: Jones and Bartlett, 1994. 384–407.

Williamson, Judith. "Woman Is an Island: Femininity and Colonization." In *Studies in Entertainment.* Ed. Tania Modleski. Bloomington: Indiana University Press, 1986. 99–118.

Willis, Ellen. *No More Nice Girls: Countercultural Essays.* Hanover: Wesleyan University Press, 1992.

Wilt, Judith. *Abortion, Choice, and Contemporary Fiction.* Chicago: University of Chicago Press, 1990.

Wright, Elizabeth. *Postmodern Brecht: A Re-Presentation.* New York: Routledge, 1989.

Section III

The Backlash

Chapter 9

Misogyny and Misanthropy: Anita Hill and David Mamet

Katherine H. Burkman

David Mamet's play *Oleanna* (1993) was greeted by the critics as a play about sexual harassment that called up the Anita Hill/Clarence Thomas hearings during which a black lawyer accused a black nominee to the Supreme Court of sexual harassment. Frank Rich, for example, writes in the *New York Times:*

A year later, a mere newspaper photograph of Anita F. Hill can revive those feelings of rage, confusion, shame and revulsion that were the country's daily diet during the Senate hearings on Clarence Thomas. . . . Enter David Mamet, who with impeccable timing has marched right into the crossfire. "Oleanna," the playwright's new drama at the Orpheum theater, is an impassioned response to the Thomas hearings. It could not be more direct in its technique or more incendiary in its ambitions. (11)

Although the circumstances are a bit different in the play from the Hill/Thomas hearings covered by the media, in that the players are white and the setting is a university at which an undergraduate student accuses a professor of sexual harassment, the dramatic situations are analogous: a male career is at risk because of the accusations of a woman. Clarence Thomas went on to the Supreme Court. John, in Mamet's drama, loses all in the fray. Paradoxically, Anita Hill's credibility has increased enormously since the televised hearings in which she played a losing role,[1] and for many she has become a heroine who has raised the awareness in this country of the subtle workings of sexual harassment in the workplace. Conversely, although John is defeated by Carol in the Mamet play, many audiences have cheered him on as a hero when he physically attacks her at the climax of the drama. Despite the fact that Mamet claims to have written the play before the Hill/Thomas hearings, his drama has evoked a conservative political backlash in their wake.[2] His creation of a stereotype of the politically correct parallels the stereotypes of Hill that were used to undermine her credibility. By exploring the misogynist underpinnings of *Oleanna*, one is able to see more clearly the misogyny at the heart of the Hill/Thomas drama and to understand the close relationship between misogyny and misanthropy.

"Imagine," Frank Rich writes in his review of *Oleanna*, "eavesdropping on a hypothetical, private Anita Hill-Clarence Thomas confrontation in an empty room, and you can get a sense of what the playwright is aiming for and sometimes achieves" (12). Since Mamet finally gives us a character (Carol) who is out to destroy John if he does not capitulate to her demands, Rich's suggestion here becomes almost more pernicious in his use of the play to interpret the hearings than the play itself may be. While Rich doubtless does not intend the conclusion that can be drawn from his invitation to our imagination, he nevertheless suggests an analogy that would condemn Hill as a malicious destroyer of men. To be fair to Rich, he vacillates, complaining that Carol is not a fully developed character, in that she is "presented alternately as a dunce and a zealot" (12), but he is reluctant to label the play sexist as I do here because he rightly sees that Mamet is attacking "fanatics like Carol who would warp the crusade against sexism that abridges freedom of speech and silences dissent" (12). What finally does make this a sexist play, however, is the stereotyping that contributes to a backlash against women, not those who fanatically insist on political correctness, but those who, like Anita Hill, insist on being treated like a person and not like prey in a power game.

In a series of essays edited and introduced by Toni Morrison, *Race-ing Justice, En-gendering Power: Essays on Anita Hill, Clarence Thomas, and the Construction of Social Reality*, a large array of scholars from the fields of english, history, political science, and law explore ways in which power politics and the media worked to deflect the issue of sexual harassment that Anita Hill brought forth and to construct an imaginary Anita Hill who fit into an illusion of social reality that suited those who backed Thomas. The construction of social reality extended as well to Thomas, so that the distasteful drama in which an ambitious and conservative black woman reluctantly made public her accusations against a former black employer who was nominated for one of the most important offices in government, could be presented as a soap opera that met criteria for racial and gender stereotypes necessary to the confirmation of Thomas and to the Bush agenda for his nomination.

As Toni Morrison herself points out in her Introduction to the book, Senator Danforth introduced Thomas as a person who laughs because a laughing man is a "clearly understood metonym for racial accommodation" (xiii), one that would hardly be appropriate in the introduction of any other nominee or member of the high court. This stereotyping of Thomas as a black man was continued in his presentation of himself as the victim of a "high-tech lynching," a sympathetic portrayal that evoked both his innocence and white guilt.

At the same time, however, that Thomas and his supporters presented him as an innocent black man, they also presented him as essentially raceless. Had he not lived out the Horatio Alger myth of rising out of the mire of his origins, thereby leaving them behind? Had he not also married a white woman and embraced a political agenda that rejects the kind of affirmative action that helped him leave his blackness behind? There had been much consternation before the Hill/Thomas hearings about Thomas' attack on his sister for accepting welfare, given the context that came to light about his privileged position compared to hers, but this proved merely to be a prelude to the tarnishing of Hill's character in a way that also called upon him to play the black victim one minute, the whitened achiever the next.[3]

Claudia Brodsky Lacour points out that as Thomas coopted the role of victim from Hill, "managing to conceal misogyny with claims of 'racism'" (152), he was using language to mask rather than refer to reality (154). Anita Hill herself understood the process that was deflecting the hearings from the exposure not only of Thomas but of the issue of sexual harassment in the workplace. "I resent the idea that people would blame the messenger for the message rather than looking at the content of the message itself and taking a careful look at it, and fully investigating it," she noted (quoted by Pemberton 187). In the process of smearing Hill, it did not much matter which image was used since one minute she was accused of being a lesbian, another of being a spurned woman. "Any demonic narrative will do in a pinch, even two or three, it simply depends upon what demon is most effective in making the sense of the world that power requires" (Lubiano 343).

The blaming of the messenger involved a series of ploys for stereotyping Hill. In one such ploy she was cast as a black female traitor to the race, conniving with whites for the black man's ruin (Painter 204). Another ploy, according to Nancy Fraser, was to construct her as "functionally white," so that Thomas could singly play the role of racial victim (605). Other stereotypical assumptions included branding her as whore or slut and as spurned and unstable. "There was no way," writes Painter, "for Hill to emerge a hero of the race, because she would not deal in black and white. By indicting the conduct of a black man, Hill revealed the existence of intraracial conflict, which white Americans find incomprehensible and many black Americans guard as a closely held secret of the race" (Painter 213).

Mamet's method of stereotyping in *Oleanna* provides a frightening parallel to the stereotyping methods employed by those Thomas supporters who were trying to destroy Hill's credibility. He gives us an innocent appearing woman in Act I, who turns out to be a vicious and inhuman destroyer in Acts II and III. And to complement the suggestion that Hill is being used by massive forces of the left to destroy an innocent man, (David Brock's contention about Hill in his best-selling *The Real Anita Hill: The Untold Story*), Mamet presents us with a character who is clearly a willing tool of forces who are merely using her to

destroy the also innocent appearing John. In his cogent analysis of Dinesh
D'Souza's *Illiberal Education*, James Phelan points out the dangers of
demonizing the "other side" in what he considers the unfortunate use of the
metaphor of culture wars (266n1). The "demonization" of political correctness
in Mamet's play becomes the means to a more general attack on feminism that
blurs the issue of sexual harassment that the play also purports to investigate.

Despite wearing a mask of innocence, Carol's manipulations of John are
present from the beginning of Mamet's play. Rather than making a frontal
attack, she begins her assault indirectly by commenting on his personal
telephone conversation with his wife that opens the play, a conversation about
the house they are buying. "What is a 'term of art'?" (2) is her opening line,
and once he agrees to attempt to answer that question rather than address the
issue of her presence in his office, his fate is sealed. He does not, it turns out,
know.   Uncomfortable about her intrusiveness into his private life, and
accurately noting her anger about the failing grade he has given her, John is
very shortly taken in by the role that Carol plays of the student struggling to
understand.

The only definite evidence we have that Carol probably is not able to pass
John's course comes from a line of her paper that he reads to her: "I think that
the ideas contained in this work express the author's feelings in a way that he
intended, based on his results" (8). If Carol cannot express herself clearly on
paper, however, she is very clear with John about the fact that she must pass the
course and begins a subtle line of intimidation. She has, she assures him, done
everything that he has instructed her to do, including the buying of his book and
even the reading of it. But when he responds to these assertions by insisting that
he is not her father, she is offended. If he cannot understand her paper, she, it
turns out, can't understand his book, which she quotes to him in what amounts
to a mirror reflection of his quoting of her paper. She has not made herself clear
to him, but he, she asserts, has not made himself clear to her and what she wants
is to understand, to be taught.

Although many reviewers and audience members are taken in by Carol's
con, much as John is—all the more reason to give him sympathy at the end—
Mamet offers many clues to suggest that Carol is far from innocent; she is rather
playing a socially constructed role of the innocent. Carol attacks John for not
being clear either in his usage of words in his telephone conversation with his
wife, in his own book, and in his response to her work. She draws him in by
agreeing that he is correct, she is stupid (although reminding him that she comes
from "a different *social*" and "a different economic" background (8). She thus
not only draws on his sympathy but on his guilt as well; he insists that he has
not called her stupid and has in fact called her intelligent, but she is quite right
that he has implied that she is hopeless and stupid after quoting her paper: "You
said, 'What can that mean?' (*Pause*) 'What can that mean?'. . . (*Pause*)" (13),
she reminds him.

Actually, the person who comes to mind here is not Anita Hill at all but Clarence Thomas. It is Thomas who portrayed himself as rising from a different (lower) economic background and class than that of the senators who questioned him and who met any objections to his undistinguished record at his hearings for confirmation with counter-charges of racism designed to make his questioners feel sympathy and guilt. But just as Carol cleverly turns John into the villain, so Thomas succeeded in convincing a large majority of the American people that Hill was the liar and the villain. Now, when audiences of Mamet's play come to see that Carol is merely playing the victim, the temptation is to compare her not to Thomas but to Hill and to take the suggestion of Thomas's backers that Hill merely presents herself as the victim while in truth, like Carol, she is a stereotypical conniving woman. Carol becomes the "type" of the "real Anita Hill" that Hill's detractors, finding her dignity unpalatable, require.

When John tries to excuse himself to attend to the buying of a house that the telephone calls he receives are about, Carol hooks him into her problems by suggesting that he would prefer his own comforts to her because she is insignificant. John says, "and though I wish I had the time, this was not a previously scheduled meeting and I . . ." (13).

> CAROL: . . . you think I'm nothing. . .
> JOHN: . . . have an appointment with a *realtor*, and with my wife and . . . .
> CAROL: You think that I'm stupid. (13)

Soon John, though he insisted earlier that he was not her father, goes on to play that very role. "'I' m talking to you as I'd talk to my son. . . . I'm talking to you the way I wish that someone had talked to me. I don't know how to do it, other than to be *personal*, . . . but . . . " (19).[4] Being personal for John involves sharing with Carol his own plight as one who was labeled as stupid, his own sense of failure. "Why would you want to be personal with me?" (19), Carol asks in seeming innocence after almost demanding that he be so, which of course becomes grist for her mill when she accuses John of sexual harassment and rape.

Not only does Mamet portray Carol as cleverly manipulating John, so that he actually puts his arm around her in a comforting way (a gesture she later uses against him), but he also portrays her as playing upon his guilt so that he soon believes it is all his fault that she is not succeeding. Carol senses his vulnerability very early in the play when she observes that he has a need to fail upon which she then proceeds to capitalize. He confesses to her that people continually called him stupid in his childhood.

> CAROL: And what did they say?
> JOHN: They said I was incompetent. Do you see? And when I'm tested the, the, the *feelings* of my youth about the *very subject of*

> *learning* come up, and . . . I become, I feel "unworthy," and "unprepared" . . .
> CAROL: . . . Yes.
> JOHN: . . . eh?
> CAROL: . . . Yes.
> JOHN: And I feel that I must fail. (*Pause*)
> CAROL: . . . but then you *do* fail. (*Pause*) You have to. (*Pause*) Don't you? (17–18)

Having cleverly diagnosed John's need to fail, Carol moves in for the kill.

Mamet, however, is out for bigger than misogynist game here.   His essentially misanthropic agenda is at work as he shows us that Carol may be calculating and destructive but that on some level she is right about John. The play is essentially about how the politically correct meets the pontifically patriarchal. For the fun of the play, if fun there is, involves a kind of doubling of the characters which makes Carol despicable in her political correctness but partially correct nevertheless. John may not have raped her or sexually harassed her in any literal way, but Mamet portrays him as more interested in his purchase of a new house and all it represents than in an educational system in which he does not believe. With a fragile but inflated ego, he plays into Carol's hands by offering simply to give her an A and tutor her in a more "personal" way that will really teach her something.   While one may view such a suggestion generously, one may also view it cynically, as Carol does, as a patronizing gesture from one who does not respect either the system or her.

The doubling of the characters becomes increasingly clearer, not only from the way Carol throws John's implied accusation that she is stupid back at him, but by the way they both speak in truncated sentences, not finishing words, echoing each other's fragmentation.

> CAROL: What gives you the *right*. Yes. To speak to a *woman* in your private . . . Yes. Yes. I'm sorry. I'm sorry. You feel yourself empowered . . . you say so yourself. To *strut*. To *posture*. To "perform." To "Call me in here . . . " Eh? You say that higher education is a joke. And treat it as such, you *treat* it as such. And *confess* to a taste to play the *Patriarch* in your class. To grant *this*. To deny *that*. To embrace your students.
> JOHN: How can you assert . . . How can you stand there and . . .
> (51)

Although Carol may be distorting somewhat what John intended, her diagnosis of his behavior is not that far off. Power is the issue and they are virtual twins in their desire to possess it.

When John seems finally to hear how demeaned and powerless Carol has felt and suggests that he might learn, might change, Carol presents her list of books which her group wishes to be banned in exchange for recanting charges, a list that includes his book. At this moment John becomes the absolute hero, Carol the absolute villain. Carol's behavior is politically correct in the worst sense of the phrase, and John's behavior is politically heroic in his refusal to acquiesce— there are limits to his desire for tenure, for a new house, for a safe life. He accepts the loss of his job.

Mamet's final turn of the screw, however, solidifies the characters' unpleasant twinship. When John learns from another telephone conversation that Carol and her group have accused him of battery and attempted rape, he loses control and throttles her, calling her a "little *cunt*" (79). But as the audience applauds, doesn't Carol make her final point, take her final victory? She has provoked him into the very assault of which she has accused him. She has known her man, and his use of the four letter word suggests just how sexist his anger is.

In a play that in its gaps leaves some essentials untold, the drama of Harold Pinter comes to mind, and Pinter, clearly attracted by the play, has directed it in London, but the real influence here would seem rather to be Lillian Hellman. In her play, *The Children's Hour*, a perverse child accuses two teachers of a lesbian relationship, driving one to question the motives of her friendship with the other and kill herself. In *Oleanna*, Carol's accusations drive John to the violence which Carol accuses him of already having performed. This is not so much the stuff of mystery as of melodrama, in which evil does its nasty work.[5]

In the melodramatic world of *Oleanna*, in which the evil woman destroys the foolish man, there is finally, in true misanthropic fashion, no debate. The pair are almost equally unattractive, alike, doubles. Education becomes a con akin to the real estate con of Mamet's *Glengarry Glen Ross* or the film world con of *Speed the Plow*. Everything is a house of games as it is in Mamet's film of that name, and the winners come out looking like losers as well. When life is nothing but a power game, in which a misguided feminist seeks to ban books and a stereotypical, myopic professor resorts to fisticuffs, the issues (honesty, integrity, and decency) of the Hill/Thomas hearings are lost.

Jonathan Cole's analysis of Mamet's *Oleanna*, which he makes in the context of a discussion of the future of universities, emphasizes the danger of such a loss and of submitting as John does in the play to Carol's agenda out of a misguided sense of fairness. When Carol accuses John of mocking the system that supports him, she gets to the heart of why she is able to change the definition of the word rape from his understanding of it to hers. Mamet, Cole astutely notes, does not really see much "net gain or loss" in what becomes a "transfer of power and a shift of terms" (21). Cole warns us of such a cynical view: "many of us believe in the ideals of meritocracy, organized skepticism, rationality, objectivity, and truth and wish to preserve them. To agree that there have been violations of the basic principles does not require their abandonment" (22).

In Mamet's cynical world-view the issues get dangerously blurred, much as they were in the Hill/Thomas hearings. Harvard sociologist Orlando Patterson's reasoning about the Hill/Thomas hearings suggests such a blurring. According to Patterson, "Thomas's sexual taunting of Professor Hill was defensible as a 'down-home style of courting,' one that black women are accustomed to and apparently flattered by" (qtd. in Crenshaw 421–22). Hill was expected to take Thomas' kind of sex talk as flirtation so as not to tarnish the black male, be he ever so tarnished by his own betrayal of his race. We can all see in Mamet's play what a good hearted fellow John really is, a bit foolish perhaps, but surely in the patriarchal "culture" of his world, acting as many a professor does.

Patterson blurs the issues dangerously with his cultural defense and Mamet blurs the issues dangerously, in my estimation, by pitting stereotype against stereotype, finally stacking the cards in John's favor. Like Thomas, John may not be exceptional, but hey, guys, let's give the poor slob a break. In the classroom?   On the Supreme Court?   Down with the politically correct, especially if they are women! Like Thomas, Mamet offers us a sense of "shared guilt" in the "symbolic body of the lynched man" and a way to assuage that sense of guilt.

By quite literally changing the subject of the inquiry from sexual harassment to racial victimage, Thomas deploys a dissembling, displaced form of guilt. He evokes a painful memory of ritualized male racial violence to displace the patriarchal "guilt" endemic to gendered relations—sexual harassment—within the workplace. In this metaphor of transference Thomas activates a primal guilt—between men—which can be assuaged by a pious commitment to the myth of the "common culture," and an invitation to join the plural world of "individuals"—both ethical acts easily accomplished in the elevation of Clarence Thomas to the Supreme Court. . . . By creating a familial frame for Hill's charges, by substituting the lynched man for the abused woman, Thomas refuses to acknowledge the place from which Hill speaks—sexuality in the workplace—as he addresses himself to the common culture of fathers and brothers. (Bhabha 248)

Mamet's appeal in his drama is to just such a common culture. By presenting us a victim, or lynched man, he subtly denies any just claims that the more "monstrous" Carol may have against the patriarchal bombasity of his vapid character.

Deborah Tannen objects to a play that manipulates us into feeling "good about a man beating a woman" and Mark Alan Stamaty makes much the same point when he describes the play as "Rambo meets P.C." (qtd. in "He Said . . . She Said" 6). When he goes on, however, to describe John's final violence as "cathartic, an explosion of the humanness suffocating inside both of them," I think he misses his own point. It is Rambo-style explosion that we witness, just about as inhuman as violence comes. Ellen Schwartzman, Vice President of the Student Government Association at Barnard College, perhaps puts it most convincingly.   Objecting to the play as "the consummate rejoinder to the controversy surrounding the Thomas-Hill hearings," she finds that "Mr. Mamet's treatment of sexual harassment does a disservice to the subject's seriousness. . . . In his version of the Thomas-Hill hearings, Mr. Mamet presents a plot devoid of ambiguity, while perpetuating a myth prevalent in American culture: harassment exists in the mind of the victim alone" (qtd. in "He Said . . ." 6).

One may ask, however, why Mamet should be held to political correctness in a play which audiences are finding electrifying on stage? What then happens to Shakespeare and *The Merchant of Venice* or Chaucer and his antisemitic prioress? Susan Brownmiller, for example, admits to being not entirely comfortable with a play that rather traditionally puts the blame on a woman, but comes down on its side despite its misogyny. "Was Strindberg guilty of misogyny in 'Miss Julie' or Ibsen in 'Hedda Gabler'?" she asks. "Absolutely. But can you name a half dozen better parts for female actors?" (qtd. in "He Said . . ." 6). The assumption, however, that Ibsen's or Strindberg's plays are misogynist is a questionable one. Despite his intentions, Miss Julie comes off with much more dignity and sympathy than Jean in Strindberg's play, and despite her often despicable behavior in *Hedda Gabler*, the heroine is portrayed as an anguished woman trapped in a patriarchal world that has made her both miserable and vicious. Hardly misogynist on the authors' parts. An unflattering portrait of a woman is by no means misogynist in its own right. A flat, stereotypical portrait of a woman out to destroy a man, is. But even such a portrait might be forgiven if the Hill/Thomas hearings were not so fresh in all of our minds. By seeming to comment on those hearings, the play becomes part of a backlash that is not so much politically incorrect as it is, albeit unconsciously, an easy escape for a society that has indeed indulged in a high tech lynching, not of Thomas but of Hill.

Since what Anita Hill presented to the senators and the country was misogyny, and they did not wish to hear her, clothing her in stereotypes that permitted them not to listen, one cannot help but look at the misanthropy that controlled the whole. George Bush's cynical nomination of an undistinguished but ultra-conservative black man was a gamble. His hope that Thomas would appeal to the black community who would prefer a black conservative to a white, shows not only a contempt for women that is part of the rightist agenda that Thomas adheres to, but a contempt for men and women, black and white. If as Stansell suggests, Thomas's "contempt for Anita Hill came clothed as a black man's brave stand against racism" (266), Bush's contempt for the American people, black and white, with his nomination of Thomas, also came clothed as a president's stand against racism and was, in my estimation, the single most cynical and misanthropic act of his tenure in office. The details of the selling of Thomas, complete with a hasty swearing in to forestall new evidence the press had uncovered from being released that Jane Mayer and Jill Abramson have amassed in their *Strange Justice: The Selling of Clarence Thomas* (350), not only serve to tarnish Thomas's image but also to undermine the "reality" of the image of Hill presented in the best-selling *The Real Anita Hill: The Untold Story*, by David Brock. Fortunately, despite the immediate political results, the drama of Anita Hill is far from over and her contributions to the awareness of sexual harassment in our country are immense.[6] That the best Mamet can do with his gift for plot twists and his wonderful ear for dialogue, is a clouding of the issues in a misogynist and misanthropic play, puts him a little in the position of the foolish professor whom he has presented as a bumbling hero. Perhaps Carol's flunking paper may be used as a final comment on the play. "I think that the ideas contained in this work express the author's feelings in a way that he intended, based on the results" (8).

NOTES

1. "A year after the hearings the public's perception of who was telling the truth had undergone a sea change. . . a Wall Street Journal/NBC News poll taken in October 1992 found that 44 percent of registered voters said they believed Hill, while only 34 percent found Justice Thomas credible" (Mayer and Abramson 352).

2. In an interview with Mamet conducted by Richard Stayton just before the play's pre-New York opening in Cambridge, Massachusetts, Stayton, who notes Mamet wrote the play before the hearings, writes: "Since his play dramatizes the very themes the Senate Committee was investigating, Mamet marveled that 'I might be doing something right'" (7). Such a reaction is a measure of both Mamet's and Stayton's political naivete.

3. Thomas's invocation of racial oppression virtually immunized him to public interrogation about the gendered elements of his self-presentation" (Stansell 260).

4. Ann C. Hall suggested (in conversation) that when John becomes personal with Carol by comparing her to his son, he is actually unsexing her. Does she then, according to Hall, become one of Mamet's "offspring, a male version of a woman?"

5. David Richards writes in the *New York Times*, "By purposefully withholding information about his characters, Mr. Mamet forces us to chart our own path through the play with only our speculations and prejudices to guide us" (II.1:5). I don't find this kind of Pinter-like mystery in the play at all. Mr. Mamet plays upon our prejudices without leaving anything essential out.

6. It is distressing to read the reviews of Harold Pinter's English production of Mamet's play, which tend to cheer the defeat of Carol as the embodiment of what they consider rampant political correctness at American universities. "Am I glad I no longer teach in an American university? You bet," writes Benedict Nightingale in *The Times*. Those reviewers (Sheridan Morley in the *Spectator*, Michael Billington in the *Guardian*) who saw both the New York and English productions found the latter to be much stronger and more balanced. But aside from the assumption that the play was an accurate picture of life in American universities rather than a depiction of American stereotypes, several of the British reviewers seemed more amused than disturbed by the cheering of the audience when John physically attacks Carol. "For it is not every day you witness the enlightened liberal audience of the Royal Court Theatre applauding the sight of a middle-aged man kicking the living daylights out of a gauche young woman," writes Jack Tinker in the *Daily Mail*. As with several of the American reviews, even the recognition of misogyny was not a deterrent to enjoyment. Clive Hirschhorn writes in the *Sunday Express*, "Clearly inspired by the senate hearings on the Anita F. Hill-Clarence Thomas case, Mamet's play is a deeply misogynist piece that is as manipulative

as the actions of his vengeful heroine," but he finishes his review by calling the play "Riveting" (745).

BIBLIOGRAPHY

Bhabha, Homi K. "A Good Judge of Character: Men, Metaphors, and the Common Culture." *Race-ing Justice, En-gendering Power: Essays on Anita Hill, Clarence Thomas, and the Construction of Social Reality.* Ed. Toni Morrison. New York: Pantheon Books, 1992. 232–249.

Billington, Michael. *Guardian.* July 7, 1993. Quoted in *Theatre Record.* XIII:13. 740.

Brock, David. *The Real Anita Hill: The Untold Story.* New York: The Free Press, 1993.

Cole, Jonathan R. "Balancing Acts: Dilemmas of Choice Facing Research Universities." *Daedalus* 122 (Fall 1993): 1–36.

Crenshaw, Kimberle. "Whose Story Is It, Anyway? Feminist and Antiracist Appropriations of Anita Hill." *Race-ing Justice, En-gendering Power: Essays on Anita Hill, Clarence Thomas, and the Construction of Social Reality.* Ed. Toni Morrison. New York: Pantheon Books, 1992. 200–214.

Fraser, Nancy. "Sex, Lies, and the Public Sphere: Some Reflections on the Confirmation of Clarence Thomas." *Critical Inquiry* 18 (1991–92): 595–612.

"He Said . . . She Said . . . Who Did What?" *New York Times.* November 15, 1992, sec. 2:6.

Hirschorn, Clive. *Sunday Express.* Quoted in *Theatre Record.* April 7, 1993: 745.

Lacour, Claudia Brodsky. "Doing Things With Words: 'Racism' as Speech Act and the Undoing of Justice." *Race-ing Justice, En-gendering Power: Essays on Anita Hill, Clarence Thomas, and the Construction of Social Reality.* Ed. Toni Morrison. New York: Pantheon Books, 1992. 127–155.

Lubiano, Wahneema. "Black Ladies, Welfare Queens, and State Minstrels: Ideological War by Narrative Means." *Race-ing Justice, En-gendering Power: Essays on Anita Hill, Clarence Thomas, and the Construction of Social Reality.* Ed. Toni Morrison. New York: Pantheon Books, 1992. 323–61.

Mamet, David. *Oleanna.* New York: Vintage Books, 1993.

Mayer, Jane, and Jill Abramson. *Strange Justice: The Selling of Clarence Thomas.* Boston and New York: Houghton Mifflin, 1994.

Morrison, Toni. "Introduction: Friday on the Potomac." *Race-ing Justice, En-gendering Power: Essays on Anita Hill, Clarence Thomas, and the Construction of Social Reality.* Ed. Toni Morrison. New York: Pantheon Books, 1992. viii–xxx.

Nightingale, Benedict. *The Times.* Quoted in *Theatre Record* July 1, 1993: 744.

Painter, Nell Irvin. "Hill, Thomas, and the Use of Racial Stereotype." *Race-ing Justice, En-gendering Power: Essays on Anita Hill, Clarence Thomas, and the Construction of Social Reality.* Ed. Toni Morrison. New York: Pantheon Books, 1992. 200–214.

Pemberton, Gayle. "A Sentimental Journey: James Baldwin and the Thomas-Hill Hearings." *Race-ing Justice, En-gendering Power: Essays on Anita Hill, Clarence Thomas, and the Construction of Social Reality.* Ed.Toni Morrison. New York: Pantheon Books, 1992. 172–99.

Phelan, James. "Narrating the PC Controversies: Thoughts on Dinesh D'Souza's *Illiberal Education.*" *Narrative* 2 (1994): 254–271.

Rich, Frank. "Mamet's New Play Detonates the Fury of Sexual Harassment." Rev. of *Oleanna*, by David Mamet. *New York Times*. October 26, 1992: C2:4+

Richards, David. "The Jackhammer Voice of Mamet's 'Oleanna' " *New York Times*. November 8, 1992: II,1:1 and 5.

Stansell, Christine. "White Feminists and Black Realities: The Politics of Authenticity." *Race-ing Justice, En-gendering Power: Essays on Anita Hill, Clarence Thomas, and the Construction of Social Reality.* Ed. Toni Morrison. New York: Pantheon Books, 1992. 251–67.

Stayton, Richard. "AND THEN HE CREATED WOMAN." Fanfare. *Newsday.* October 25, 1992:7.

Tinker, Jack. *Daily Mail.* Quoted in *Theatre Record* July 7, 1993: 741.

Chapter 10

Oprah Winfrey's *Scared Silent* and the Spectatorship of Incest

Rosaria Champagne

Sexual abuse of children is common (best estimates: at least one girl in three, one boy in ten). It is not overreported but vastly underreported (best estimates: under 10 percent of all cases come to the attention of child-protective agencies or police). False complaints are rare (best estimates: under 5 percent of all complaints). Most victims do not disclose their abuse until long after the fact, if ever. Though many suffer long-lasting psychological harm, the great majority never see a therapist.

—Judith Herman, "The Abuses of Memory"

THE FALSE MEMORY SYNDROME FOUNDATION

As of 1996, cultural representation of incest survivors takes place against the context of what I would argue is an anti-feminist political backlash from the False Memory Syndrome Foundation (FMS),[1] a backlash targeted against incest survivors and their therapists. The popular press has, of course, extensively debated the issue of false memory, and many writers, like the authors of the 1994 edition of *The Courage to Heal*, have detected rampant anti-feminism and misogyny in the rhetoric of the Foundation. Take, for example, the following passage from the FMS Foundation Newsletter (October 1993) which accuses feminists of "totalistic thinking":

Emerging political movements almost always exaggerate their "oppression" and attack the powerful and the rich. That is par for the course. In the FMS phenomenon, victimization has become the ideal, the preferred state. Women . . . redefine their personalities and reinterpret their pasts to meet that ideal. Celebrities lead the way. To maintain their new image, "victims" become more and more cult-like in their behavior. They must cut themselves off from their families in order to maintain their image. (6)

To the False Memory Syndrome Foundation, women who come out as incest survivors and who choose to separate from abusive family systems are merely "lost." Under the column "Retractor Notices," we find that "Elizabeth Carlson has prepared yellow ribbons for family and friends to wear until the children lost to false memories return. The funds will be used to support the efforts of the retractors through the National Association Against Fraud in Psychotherapy" (6). The section concludes by giving the price and address to write to for these ribbons. Of course, we all remember that the yellow ribbon also represented support of George Bush's display of American macho in his attack on Kuwait in January 1992.

After 21 states changed the statute of limitations regarding incest charges (Goleman 6) and have extended the law around the window of the survivor's memory instead of the incest-event itself, an organization called the False Memory Syndrome Foundation, directed by Pamela Freyd, a mother who claims to have been "betrayed" by a 30-something daughter's accusation of childhood sexual abuse, began to challenge the viability of survivor's memories. While a spokesperson from the FMS Foundation told me that as an apolitical, objective research group, they are "not in the business of condemning individual memories" (June 2, 1993), this claim would seem to be contradicted by the institutional consequences of the FMS Foundation.[2] In spite of the fact that the American Psychological Association has rejected the construction of "false memory" as a syndrome and that Judith Herman, author of *Father-Daughter Incest* and *Trauma and Recovery* and a psychiatrist who specializes in incest has dismissed the FMSF as "an advocacy group for people whose children have accused them of sexual abuse" ("Abuses of Memory" 3), I would argue that the Foundation poses a very real threat to feminist therapists and their clients.[3]

This chapter examines the political spectacle and spectatorship of incest survivors in two critical contexts: 1) in the False Memory Syndrome Foundation, a "family values" organization with over 6000 members that has institutionalized this current public backlash against incest survivors and 2) by Oprah Winfrey's popular television documentary, *Scared Silent: Exposing and Ending Child Abuse*, aired on three major networks simultaneously in October 1992. I wish to take up both projects together for two reasons. First, Oprah Winfrey's documentary was conceived as a response to the backlash; indeed, the growing backlash unwittingly made possible the popularity and seduction of the incest narratives in the mass media. Second, despite the fact that *Scared Silent* is progressive in some respects, there are some eerie convergences in the ideological projects of the two.

According to the FMS Foundation stationary, "False Memory Syndrome describes a situation in which a person acquires a memory that is not true but which seems very vivid and real to the person who has it. The memory comes to dominate the life of the person to the detriment of the person and the people involved in the memory." When a Foundation spokesperson returned my phone call, she defined "false memories" as those repressed memories that emerge in therapy and which cannot be corroborated by "evidence."[4] False Memory has become a syndrome, she explained, because of over-zealous underqualified therapists who rely on *The Courage to Heal* by Ellen Bass and Laura Davis especially its point that "if you think you were abused and your life shows the symptoms, then you were" (22).

The promotional packet the FMS Foundation sends to parents who feel themselves "falsely accused" includes: a worksheet defining the "syndrome," the history of the foundation, and its mission; an order form for Eleanor Goldstein's and Kevin Farmer's *Confabulations: Creating False Memories, Destroying Families*, which "tells the stories of 20 [FMS Foundation] families in their own words, includes interviews with therapists and provides analysis of the impact of the Recovery movement, New Age and radical Feminism in regard to false memories" [*The False Memory Syndrome Phenomenon* 41; half of the book's proceeds from Foundation members goes back into the Foundation]; a xeroxed page of supposedly damning quotations from *The Courage to Heal*, which the FMS Foundation calls "the Bible of the Incest-Memory Recovery Movement" and "a political statement that preaches anger and revenge"; newspaper articles supporting and describing the FMS Foundation collected in a packet entitled *The False Memory Syndrome Phenomenon*, a conference bulletin (with opportunities to purchase papers) from this year's FMS Foundation conference; a recent *FMS Foundation Newsletter*; and xeroxed essays written by members of the FMS Foundation Professional Advisory Board.[5]

The FMS Foundation began when "a group of families and professionals" responded to "the growing wave of accusations of incest or sexual abuse brought on by adults who recovered 'memories' of events that families and people involved in the memories claim *just could not have happened*" (FMS stationery, back page, my emphasis). The power and politics that buttress this position that parents are the final arbiters and truth-tellers about sexual abuse are undercut by the assertion that "the Foundation aims to provide accurate information on current research about the nature of human memory." As a 1992 pamphlet published by the Foundation defines the problem:

Increasingly throughout the country, grown children undergoing therapeutic programs have come to believe that they suffer from "repressed memories" of incest and sexual abuse. While some reports of incest and sexual abuse are surely true, these decade-delayed memories are too often the result of False Memory Syndrome cause by a disastrous "therapeutic" program. False Memory Syndrome has a devastating effect on the victim and typically produces a continuing dependence on the very program that creates the syndrome. False Memory Syndrome proceeds to destroy the psychological well-being not only of the primary victim but—through false accusations of the incest and sexual abuse—other members of the primary victim's family.

A primary function of the Foundation is to help "the secondary victims (those falsely accused) to establish reliable methods to discriminate between true and false claims of incest and abuse charges, and the psychological and other reasons they are made, including the intentional or unwitting suggestion of therapists and therapeutic programs" (1992 pamphlet). Nowhere does the Foundation cite methods for or concern about establishing "reliable methods to discriminate between true and false claims" made by accused parents. The Foundation currently "provide[s] information on legal rights, and access to legal counsel, to alleviate or remedy damage done by such accusations resulting from False Memory Syndrome" (1992 pamphlet) and in the future, hopes to "provide financial assistance to families who need help in paying for polygraph tests, counseling, or legal services" (1992 pamphlet).

According to the Foundation, 92.2 percent of false accusations are made by 30-something daughters against middle and upper-middle class families. In this same May 1993 newsletter, a recent legal coup is proudly announced:

Texas therapists have been told that: 1) Their psychological and psychiatric records may be subpoenaed; 2) They may have to bear the expenses of an attorney to file protective orders, unless the client is willing to pay; 3) Personal information may be explored in court if it appears in mental health records.

One Texas attorney has suggested that this ruling might potentially lead to a situation in which a therapist's expert testimony in a child custody case might be discounted as biased if records reveal that the therapist was abused as a child. (13)

While accused parents are the victims, 30-something feminist therapists are the "perpetrators" of this new False Memory Syndrome. Feminist therapists are called "flakes" and "fanatics" who have created a "trendy . . . sex abuse industry" which "attracts a lot of people making statements about themselves or others that are patently invalid" (Taylor "What if," 19). The Foundation hopes to appeal to the "community ethics" of therapists and challenge any therapeutic practice that does not find resolution in family restoration. For believing incest survivors means failing to grant the nuclear family the power to define the truth. It is the breakdown of the nuclear family which prompts Pamela Freyd to ask: "Does a therapist have a professional responsibility for the impact of her or his diagnosis on the relationship of the client with her or his family or for the impact on the lives of others who are not directly her or his clients?" (2). The question, of course, is rhetorical.

The FMS Foundation employs its own version of "victim-politics" (a term it uses to characterize feminism). An excerpt from *Confabulations* makes this clear: "Since sexual abuse of a child is the worst crime we know of—to be falsely accused of such a crime is the worst thing that can happen to a person," (*FMS Phenomenon* 40). Setting aside the faulty logic (which suggests that each of two experiences is "the worst"), we might ask: under what system can a false accusation be considered even equivalent to childhood sexual abuse, which leads to post-traumatic stress disorder, a high rate of suicide attempts, and long-term psychological aftereffects?

Indeed, family vindictiveness rather than scientific neutrality birthed the FMS Foundation. Even though Foundation director, Pamela Freyd, claims to believe that sexual abuse can happen[6] she rejected the disclosure of one survivor: her daughter Jennifer—a 30-something feminist clinical psychologist (Freyd 26). Pamela and Peter Freyd, a step-brother and sister who married, have launched what appears to be a smear campaign against their daughter, creating in the process an institution which is fueled by the confusion, anger, and anxiety shared by other accused parents.

As for the daughter, Jennifer Freyd, she points out the irony of the fact that her disclosure of sexual abuse became the "proof" that she is an unreliable narrator of her own experience. She writes:

Is my father more credible than me because I have a history of lying or not having a firm grasp on reality? No, I am a scientist whose empirical work has been replicated in laboratories around this country and Europe. . . . Am I not believed because I am a woman? A "female in her thirties" as some of the newspaper articles seem to emphasize? Am I therefore a hopeless hysteric by definition? Is it because the issue is father-daughter incest and as my father's property, I should be silent? . . . Indeed, why is my parents' denial at all credible? In the end, is it precisely because I was abused that I am to be discredited despite my personal and professional success?" (30)

Not only does Jennifer Freyd's "personal and professional success" fail to authorize her credibility, but Peter Freyd's known hospitalization for alcoholism does not tarnish his authority over his daughter's narrative (Bass and Davis 490). And even Jennifer Freyd's ostensibly unwavering heterosexuality has not protected her from her father's "lesbian baiting" via e-mail. In explaining why the FMSF launched a heavy publicity campaign in the community in Oregon where Jennifer Freyd lives and works, Peter Freyd explained: "We have a lot of members not just from Oregon but with children who are in Oregon involved in rather radical feminist (often lesbian) cult-like groups"—and therefore, presumably, are not to be believed (Jennifer Freyd 26). Of course, Peter Freyd would never read the system under which a father owns a daughter's disclosure as "cultist." Indeed, nowhere in FMS literature will you find a survivor speaking outside the narrative of the father's law. The only "survivors" who speak are those who have recanted and who now see feminism and feminist therapy as "perpetrators."

Feminist therapy offers survivors the option to reject the tautological thinking that declares families of origin always already the final arbiters of truth. FMS backlash emerges out of the desire not to see the image of the survivor or hear her experience—that is, never to cast her in the role of the spectator of the transgression. It is important to the Foundation that the nuclear family's economic and social status not be jeopardized through "false accusations." Master narratives, though, are threatened, and it is the master narrative that the incest taboo holds in place (because the incest taboo has historically been a taboo against speech and image, not action).[7] "Survivor discourse" is really under attack.

SURVIVOR REPRESENTATIONS: THE SILENCED, CENSORED, AND DISCURSIVE

Remembering is a testament to surviving; only survivors remember.
—Rokele Lerner's *Affirmations for the Inner Child*

The popular media appear to believe that directly representing incest survivors is sufficient to establish their believability, as if letting the marginalized speak for themselves were all that is necessary to create an effective counterdiscourse. "Speaking from experience" allows neutral, context-free "truth" to seep through the web of oppression. But psychoanalysis teaches feminism that we cannot "fix" sexist politics merely by letting the survivor speak, as if speech floats freely in culture from unbiased paradigms and politically uncommitted frames of intelligibility. When the survivor speaks within the ideology of patriarchy—as in courts of law or television talk shows where the expert psychiatrist is strategically positioned to fetishize her pain— she does not have the language necessary to describe even to herself her experience of sexual violation. Hoping that the text of self-disclosure will re-write the context of patriarchy is wishful thinking. More egregiously, this wishful thinking can even foreclose the social change it seeks when the survivor's speech is absorbed by the master narrative that discredits survivors for having survived and denies legitimacy—and therefore political efficacy—to survivor discourse.

In "Survivor Discourse: Transgression or Recuperation?" Linda Alcoff and Laura Gray point out that survivor discourse functions neither as a social panacea (one that actually "ends" child abuse) nor as a political washout:

The very act of speaking out has become used as performance and spectacle. The growth of this phenomenon raises questions: has it simply replayed confessional modes which recuperate dominant patriarchal discourses without subversive effect, or has it been able to create new spaces within these discourses and to begin to develop an autonomous counterdiscourse, one capable of empowering survivors? (275)

Rejecting the two theoretically current solutions (the neo-Marxist rejection of all things personal or experiential, or the liberal Feminist embrace of the "pretheoretical" experiential as necessarily subversive), Alcoff and Gray recommend that we become the "theorists of our own experiences": "To become the theorists of our own experience requires us to become aware of how our subjectivity will be constituted by our discourses and aware of the danger that even in our own confessionals within autonomous spaces we can construct ourselves as reified victims or as responsible for our own victimization" (284).

This danger must, of course, be greater when confessionals occur within mass-mediated spaces. For if one of the primary ways one can become the theorist of her own experience is to control the production of knowledge that frames that experience, no one individual can "control" representation emanating from institutionalized apparati. Nevertheless, being the "theorist of one's own experience" appears to be Oprah Winfrey's desire in producing and hosting her television documentary, *Scared Silent: Exposing and Ending Child Abuse*. Oprah Winfrey presides over this documentary as an "out" incest survivor and as an ally of other survivors.

Scared Silent opens and closes with the voices of two survivors. The first image is that of a nine-year old white girl, Wendy, with red hair in pigtails, rocking in a rocking chair. Hardly able to open her mouth wide enough to shape the words, eyes cast down, she whispers: "He told me if I told anybody, he was going to kill me." The second image and voice is Oprah's. She "comes out" as a survivor, and then tells the camera: "We hope the stories of these abusers and their victims can help *all* the children and adults among us who have for too long now been scared silent." Her image promises to give voice and permission to Wendy and the other survivors on the show. Oprah "comes out" to establish herself in political solidarity with the other survivors. Her more important role in the documentary, though, is to "bear witness" to the stories of the other survivors. By bearing witness—this bestowing an important gift on the survivor of crimes committed in isolation and secrecy—and controlling the means of production, Oprah potentially delivers what Judith Herman calls the "first principle" of recovery: "the empowerment of the survivor." "The survivor," Herman writes, "must be the author and arbiter of her own recovery. Others may offer advice, support, assistance, affection, and care, but not cure" (*Trauma and Recovery* 133). The approach seems to work for Wendy, who at the documentary's end optimistically commands that other children: "Tell somebody. Tell anybody. Tell until somebody listens." Wendy's transformation establishes another of Herman's points: that the act of telling the trauma story transforms the traumatic memory from prenarrative disintegration to postnarrative integration (175). Importantly, though, it is not really the "telling" that empowers Wendy, but the "listening" that permits her another chance at psychological health, and being heard is not in any survivor's power to control.

The progressiveness of the documentary rests in its reinstatement of the reliability of the survivor. Nevertheless, this progressiveness is undercut by the overt heterosexism of the documentary. Some survivors tell their stories and many of them interpret the personal and political meaning of survivorship. Importantly, though, in too many cases, the "expert," who usually is a white male psychiatrist or psychologist, is cast in the interpretive role, and even when his interpretation supports the survivor's rights to be believed, he still robs her of the opportunity to invent her life's meaning. In *Scared Silent*, the privilege to make meaning of abuse follows traditional lines of cultural privilege: for example, as I will show, white heterosexual male perpetrators are given many more opportunities to remain "in charge" of their recovery than either white female or African-American female or male perpetrators.

Most important of all, I would argue that, like the FMS Foundation, *Scared Silent* is more deeply invested in the survival of the family than in the survival of the survivors. The documentary resolves the pain of survivorship by returning (at least in the cases of the white heterosexual men) to the same nuclear family that produced the conditions under which children are abused. Thus, while *Scared Silent* offers a politically progressive example of self-theorizing, its political impact is constrained by liberal notions of recovery. A closer look at each of the six perpetrators represented in *Scared Silent* suggests a relationship between cultural privilege and familial forgiveness.

Del, Eva, and Jan are members of a white upper-middle class family. Del, the father-perpetrator, molested his daughter Eva and stopped only when Eva told her mother—twenty years later—in an effort to rescue her younger sister from incest. Jan acted immediately and effectively; Del was removed from the house and prosecuted. But in the confrontation between Del and Eva (*Scared Silent* stages their first encounter since Del went to prison three years before), Del is allowed to remain the expert of his family's experience—both in spite *and because* of his role as perpetrator. In the absence of a moderator for this confrontation, Del takes charge. Eva says she "just wants some understanding," and in place of listening to Eva's needs—or discharging his own guilt and shame—he redeploys cliches of psychotherapy to establish himself the authority of his victim's prognosis for healing. When Eva expresses rage that Del "passed on" his own victimhood to her, Del warns her of her potential to similarly abuse her children by marrying a man just like dear old dad.

Finally, Del shuts Eva down (and shuts her up) with his tears and bratty insistence that the family stay together. When Eva was a little girl, Del bought her secrecy by threatening the break up of the family as the inevitable result of her disclosure; twenty years later, Eva seems fully capable of surviving family estrangement, but Del will not stand for it. The ultimatum with which he bought her secrecy earlier stands as a naked projection of his own castration anxiety, for what exactly is a heterosexual patriarch without a family to lord over? For the family of Del and Eva, reconnection does not heal Eva, but rather, restores the phallus to Del.

The second perpetrator represented is an African-American woman named Tasha. We see Tasha in a group therapy program facilitated by a white male expert. We learn that Tasha's brother brutally raped her and that the adults in Tasha's life neglected her. We also learn that she molested, raped, and physically abused her male cousins, in an effort to, in her words, "get back against guys." To force Tasha's accountability for molesting children, the white male expert and her fellow group members confront her viciously. They strip her down and she cries the shame and terror reflecting the double-bind of the perpetrating victim. The episode is filmed like a scene of political torture; Tasha's is the only face exposed; she sits crumpled up like a captive under a bright light; angry words are hurled from a mass of people made anonymous by black-out while she cries with shame and terror. She sits next to the white male expert whose posture and words provide "reason" and force "accountability," but not compassion. In the end, he declares that "Tasha will never be cured," but her release is made possible because she connected her experience of victim to her behavior of victimizing. Unlike Del, Tasha is released into a void; we do not witness any reconnection with a nuclear family, and her expert makes no such prognosis inevitable or even possible.

Jill, a white upper-middle class divorced woman, is a victim and perpetrator of severe childhood physical abuse. Jill "accidentally" murdered her son Roger by beating him with a curtain rod, then hurling it at him so that it punctured his eyeball and pierced his brain. Jill says: "I didn't think of myself as an abuser," and indeed only Roger's death "makes" her role as abuser real to her and to her family. Jill is alone, and her journey of healing has no future. Indeed, we learn that Jill's niece has just given up her baby for adoption fearing that she will pass on this legacy of abuse. The video captures Jill with her brother Dave searching through old family photos—six generations worth—tracing the abuse *back*, not recovering forward through familial reconnection.

George, a middle-aged divorced African-American male was physically abused as a child and went on to physically and psychologically abuse two wives and five children. He now lectures across the country on child abuse, focusing on the devastating effects of psychological and verbal abuse. Tracing his own abuse back to his mother and his mother's house, he returns home to confront his internal demons and talk with his own mother about her behavior. As George cries in front of his abuser, remembering how it felt to hear her declare him a failure and how it hurt to be beaten, his aged mother laughs nervously and dismisses his invitation to reconnect, explaining that "slapping a child upside the head" is just how things were done. We last see George preparing to give another lecture on child abuse. By lecturing to perpetrators and parents, George connects himself to the community, but the social text offers no familial immunity—or place to call home—for George.

Wendy, the strawberry-blonde who open the video but has a hard time opening her mouth wide enough to form the words she wants to express, is part of a working-class white family. Her father Brian molested her and stopped only when his wife, Roseanne, walked in to witness his abuse. Like Del, Brian serves a short jail term and then returns home. On the one hand, Brian seems more accountable than Del for his behavior: he looks Wendy in the eyes and says, "It was all my fault and it never should have happened to you." But Wendy, only twelve, seems unconvinced by her father's avowed guilt. Brian acknowledges that he stopped molesting Wendy only because his wife "caught" him; he also says that his healing—and the health of his family, in his view—is dependent on his reconnection with them.   Wendy and Roseanne seem simultaneously hopeful and leery: the final scene captures Roseanne vigilantly watching Brian and Wendy gardening.   The singularity of this act—the watchful and rescuing mother's gaze—suggests the terms under which Brian is "cured": when his wife polices his behavior.   Thus, like Del, Brian's recovery takes precedence over his victim's.

The final perpetrator featured is Patrice, a Hispanic woman who physically abused her children.   When she broke the leg of her two year old daughter, a children's services agency removed her children from her home.   After undergoing therapy and finding "a loving husband," Patrice, like the white men, is allowed to reclaim the social role she held before crossing the line of abuse. Rather than male privilege determining the perpetrator's right to a second chance, the prerequisite seems to be heterosexism—the institutional fodder for family values.   This message is emphasized by the closing message, delivered first by Brian and Del, all serving to promote the desirability of the reunited family.

Perhaps because heterosexuality and heterosexism condition survivor spectatorship in "Scared Silent," we find no lesbian representation here.   As Shana Rowen Blessing suggests in "How to Be a Political Dyke and an Incest Survivor at the Same Time, or, Why Are All the Dykes I Know Reading *The Courage to Heal?*"[8] there is a relationship between incest survivorship and lesbianism, although exactly what this relationship means is unclear.[9]   The imposition of traditional notions of family and gender renders impossible the solution to child abuse offered: to be "scared silent" is, in fact, a logical extension of the law of the father.   For the families represented in *Scared Silent*, incest stops only because mother's walk through closed doors—or daughters forge through them—and they all have the courage to act on what they see and remember.   Thus, *Scared Silent* fails to "end" child abuse because its liberal embrace of family values sanctions the father's ownership of his victim's healing as well as his own.

Nevertheless, as I have said, Oprah Winfrey's *Scared Silent* offers one important response to the FMS Foundation: by positioning survivors who are believed, Winfrey makes a space for survivor discourse.   This does not mean that Oprah Winfrey's position offers a "solution" to the reactionary politics of the False Memory Syndrome Foundation.

Totalizing theories—those that offer solutions—do not effect progressive social change.   For this reason, the problem of sexual abuse and its aftereffects cannot be "solved" by one person, one idea, one moment, one word, one wish, one master theory, or one television production.   Instead, politicized incest survivorship demands that we return a re-theorized notion of "experience" (contesting experience as an organizing category of personal identity and instead emphasizing the meaning made of experiences as one organizing category of political commitment) to a re-theorized notion of "social." This re-theorized social rejects the sociological determinism of neo-Marxism and reclaims the Lacanian concept of the symbolic order of culture, a move which allows us to repudiate the transparency of experience without rejecting the epistemological potential of personal experience. Such a move allows us to see that incest survivorship is not an identity, but is often claimed as such because of the cultural and psychological erasure of the crime and its aftereffects. Survivors face disbelief on the level of truth-value ("did it *really* happen") and import ("even if it did happen, it wasn't that bad"), and this disbelief confirms our worst fears—that the pathology of abuse resides within our bodies, not within our culture.

Thus, "survivorship" as I define it emerges when the experiences of sexual violation are made meaningful through the politics of feminism, with its analysis of heterosexism and on the oppressive nature of the family. Indeed, only by showing how the social makes the experiential discursively "real" and how our most private "experiences" take shape through and give meaning to the social can incest survivorship mean anything—political—at all.

NOTES

1. The FMS Foundation is located at 3401 Market Street, Suite 130, Philadelphia, PA 19104; it costs between $100.00 and $125.00 to become a member for a year; their phone numbers are: 215–387–1917 and 1–800–568–8882. An emerging organization called The Coalition For Accuracy About Abuse offers education and advocacy for survivors and allies and contests the false claims of scientific neutrality proffered by the FMSF. To find information about a local chapter of the Coalition, contact The Family Violence and Sexual Assault Institute, 1310 Clinic Drive, Tyler, Texas, 75701; 903–595–6600.

2. Other than member surveys and a structured questionnaire that only seeks to understand the family history as reflected by the point of view of the accused parent, the FMS Foundation has conducted no research to date as far as I can discern.

3. The False Memory Syndrome Foundation deceptively inflates its membership to include all phone calls received by its office. Thus, they declare in a recent newsletter that they have 13,000 members, when in fact they include as supporters researchers like me who contest their position. (They write: "If any other medical product had more than 13,000 complaints, it would be taken off the market. Not only is there no way to take 'therapy' off the market, there is no way for people affected by the therapy to have their complaints considered" [*False Memory Syndrome Foundation Newsletter*, May 1994: 1]).

4. Even "evidence" does not validate the survivor: "Physical evidence does not prove truth, merely that the memory has elements of reality. . . ." (Wielawski 3).

5. See essays by Dawes, Lief, Loftus, McHugh, and Meachum.

6. Pamela Freyd: "Do I believe children are sometimes abused by their parents? Absolutely. But to the degree that we are being asked to accept? Absolutely not."

7. As noted by Claude Levi-Strauss and extended by Gayle Rubin, the incest taboo functions to protect the patriarch's duty to exchange his daughter, to "traffic" her in a patriarchal marketplace—and an acceptable gift should be unused.

8. This essay is from a special edition of *Lesbian Ethics* that focuses exclusively on lesbian incest survivors.

9. Lesbianism can, of course, serve as a useful contradiction to those sexual abuses contained by normative heterosexuality. But for closeted lesbians, lesbianism can also function as a repetition of the incest narrative via homophobia and heterosexism, by closeting sexuality and thereby revisiting the isolation and secrecy that signifies victimhood.

BIBLIOGRAPHY

Alcoff, Linda, and Laura Gray. "Survivor Discourse: Transgression or Recuperation?" *Signs* 18.2 (1993): 260–290.

Bass, Ellen and Laura Davis. *The Courage to Heal*. Rev. edition. New York: Harper Collins, 1992.

Blessing, Shana Rowen. "How to Be a Political Dyke and an Incest Survivor at the Same Time, or, Why Are all the Dykes I Know Reading *The Courage to Heal?*" *Lesbian Ethics* 4.3 (Spring 1992): 122–128.

Dawes, Robyn M. "Biases of Retrospection." *Issues in Child Abuse Accusations* 1.3 (1991): 25–28.

False Memory Syndrome Foundation Pamphlet. Philadelphia: The FMS Foundation, 1992.

FMS Foundation Newsletter. 2 [4] (May 1993): 2.

FMS Foundation. Personal Interview. 2 June 1993.

FMS Foundation Newsletter. 2 [9] (October 1993): 6.

FMS Foundation Newsletter. 3 [5] (May 1994): 1.

FMS Foundation Stationary.

Freyd, Jennifer. "Personal Perspectives on the Delayed Memory Debate." *Family Violence and Sexual Assault Bulletin* 9.3 (1993): 28–32.

Freyd, Pamela. "True or False?" *Toronto Star*. May 18, 1992.

Goleman, Daniel. "Childhood Trauma: Memory or Invention?" *New York Times*. July 21, 1992. 6.

Herman, Judith. "The Abuses of Memory." *Mother Jones*. March/April 1993: 3–4.

Herman, Judith. *Trauma and Recovery*. New York: HarperCollins, 1992.

Herman, Judith, with Lisa Hirschman. *Father-Daughter Incest*. Cambridge, Massachusetts: Harvard University Press, 1981.

Lerner, Rokele. *Affirmations for the Inner Child*. Deefield Beach, Florida: Health Communications, 1990.

Levi-Strauss, Claude. *The Elementary Structures of Kinship*. Trans. James Harle Belle and John Richard von Sturmer. Boston: Beacon Press, 1969.

Lief, Harold I. "Psychiatry's Challenge: Defining an Appropriate Therapeutic Role When Child Abuse is Suspected." *Psychiatric News*. August 21, 1992.

Loftus, Elizabeth F. "The Reality of Repressed Memories." Unpublished essay, 1992.

Mayne, Judith. *Cinema and Spectatorship*. New York: Routledge, 1993.

McHugh, Paul R. "Psychiatric Misadventures." *The American Scholar* 61.4 (1992): 497–510.

Meachum, Andrew. "Perilous Journey: The Labyrinth of Past Sexual Abuse." *Philadelphia Inquirer*. February 13, 1992.

Meachum, Andrew. "Study Disputes Link Between Eating Disorders, Sexual Abuse," *Changes.* April 1993: 22.

Meachum, Andrew. "When Tales of Sexual Abuse Aren't True." *Philadelphia Inquirer,* January 5, 1992.

Meachum, Andrew. "When Therapists 'Find' Childhood Sexual Abuse." *Philadelphia Inquirer,* March 15, 1992.

"Retractor Notes." *FMS Foundation Newsletter* 2 [10] (November 1992): 6.

Rubin, Gayle. "The Traffic in Women: Notes on the 'Political Economy' of Sex." *Toward an Anthropology of Women.* Ed. Rayna Reiter. New York: Monthly Review Press, 1975.

Taylor, Bill. "Therapist Turned Patient's World Upside Down." *Toronto Star,* May 19, 1992.

Taylor, Bill. "True of False? The Psychiatric Community Knows Incest is Real, But Worries that When Over-Eager Therapists Uncover Repressed Memories that are False, Families Can Be Needlessly Torn Apart." *Toronto Star,* May 18, 1992.

Taylor, Bill. "What if Sexual Abuse Memories Are Wrong?" *Toronto Star,* May 16, 1992.

Wielawski, Irene. "Unlocking the Secrets of Memory." *Los Angeles Times,* October 3, 1991.

Chapter 11

Women Who Have Dared but Deterred Other Women: Hannah More and Beverly LaHaye

Veronica Webb Leahy

A few years ago, when I was researching eighteenth-century conduct literature for women (educational handbooks prescribing proper female education, manners, and behavior, and proscribing any conduct viewed as improper or inappropriate for, primarily middle class, women), I was struck by the fact that, although the majority of such works were written by men, women also wrote conduct literature—an act of self-assertion seemingly at odds with their advice that women be meek, submissive, and self-effacing. What surprised me even more was that a few of these women authors led anything but the quiet domestic lives that they were advocating for other women.

Sometime later, I read Susan Faludi's *Backlash* and was particularly interested in the section on the "Movers, Shakers, and Thinkers," in whom, Faludi claims, the 1980s reaction against feminism originated. As might be expected, many of these individuals were men, who made feminist women the scapegoats for their decline "in a felt sense of importance, influence, and power" (231), but Faludi also cites a significant number of women enlisted by the New Right "to handle the heavy lifting in the campaign against their own rights" (239). Faludi points out that the lives of some of these women presented an ironic contrast to the ideas they were busy disseminating about the need for "passive sequestered womanhood" and in the words of Phyllis Schlafly—a lawyer, author, and two-time congressional candidate—"the marvelous legal rights of a woman to be a full-time wife and mother in the house supported by her husband" (239).

Clearly, as Faludi also argues, the practice of enlisting women against women's rights is part of a time-honored tradition, but this tradition warrants scrutiny by feminists, and the contradictions inherent in the private lives and public stances of some of its exponents deserve particularly close examination.

What has motivated some women to become media figures in the battle against women's rights, and why has this practice persisted into the late twentieth century?

In recent years, various feminist critics have posited explanations for the behavior of eighteenth- and nineteenth-century female anti-feminists. Elizabeth Kowaleski-Wallace, for example, argues that "Many eighteenth-century literary women allowed themselves to be seduced by masculine literary discourse and by the apparently benevolent patriarch who was the bearer of that language" (11). She terms such women "'daddies' girls'" and claims that "they are worth our attention as *case studies in complicity*" (12). Nancy Armstrong, who asserts that educational handbooks that sought to define the female and the female role, and which proliferated in the eighteenth century, "severed the language of kinship from that of political relations, producing a culture divided into the respective domains of domestic woman and economic man" (60), contends that this division empowered women in their particular domain. As a consequence, according to Mary Poovey, "scorn of women's rights is anchored in . . . dread that, in gaining equality, women . . . will lose all power" (32).

Looking at twentieth-century examples of this phenomenon, Faludi implies that some of the same anxieties persist today. She says of the New Right women of the 1980s that they "were voicing antifeminist views—while internalizing the message of the women's movement and quietly incorporating its tenets of self-determination, equality, and freedom of choice into their private behavior." She explains that "The women always played by their men's rules, and for that they enjoyed the esteem and blessings of their subculture." Thus, "They could indeed 'have it all'—by working to prevent all other women from having that same opportunity" (256).

Traditionally, some of the most emphatic anti-feminist rhetoric from women has been expressed in the name of religion. Critics like Poovey have noted how, in the seventeenth century, Puritanism aggrandized women by "emphasizing the importance of the family as a unit of religious and social discipline," while at the same time emphasizing "the patriarchal family organization ratified by Scripture" and restricting "women's activity to narrowly defined domestic duties." Thus, according to Poovey,

Puritanism simultaneously reinforced the injunctions against the free expression of female desires *and* provided women a role that seemed constructive rather than destructive. The fact that women did not really acquire the equality that Puritan doctrines seemed logically to promise appeared to most women insignificant beside the acquisition of their new spiritual and socially meaningful role. (7)

In the eighteenth century, Evangelicalism, the heir to Puritanism, expanded the domain in which women could legitimately participate. Ministering to the poor, disseminating religious pamphlets, and teaching morality and decency in Sunday schools and religious associations were essentially selfless activities, requiring no "masculine" skills and devoted to celebrating the Holy Spirit rather than his humble agent. Indeed, in one sense women might be considered the primary beneficiaries of the reform movement, for such work gave both married and unmarried women a constructive vehicle for their talents and, in return, a heightened sense of their ability and self-worth (9).

In the twentieth century, evangelicalism continues to both limit and expand opportunities for women. Faludi offers the example of Beverly LaHaye, the founder of Concerned Women for America, formerly a self-described timid and dissatisfied housewife, who became an author, public speaker, and president for life of the organization "often described as the Moral Majority's ladies' club" (252). According to Faludi, LaHaye's awakening came in 1965 at a conference for Sunday school teachers,[1] which led her to consider how she might overcome her fears and express herself:

She wanted to assert herself and exert "strength," but she wanted to do it without challenging the church or threatening her husband. And she found she could, if she made it clear that she was seeking only "spiritual power." It was acceptable to crave authority by framing it as a desire for "access to the power of the Holy Spirit." No one in the evangelical community could object to her ambitions, as long as they were holy. (249–250)

One of the most notable eighteenth-century women whose life exhibited these contradictions was Hannah More, who, like Beverly LaHaye, found religion to be an acceptable rationale for expressing herself and for exercising power and control and who led an extraordinary life for a woman in that era, at the same time that she was deterring other women from doing the same. Although nearly two hundred years separate More and LaHaye, and opportunities for women have significantly increased since then, there is surprising correspondence between these two professed anti-feminists. It is instructive to examine their careers and their writing and the paradoxical way that evangelicalism enabled them to promote themselves at the same time that it required them to promote a stereotype of tractable domestic womanhood and to attack women who refused to pay lip service to the patriarchal model of family life.

HANNAH MORE

Hannah More was born in 1745 in Bristol, England, the fourth of five daughters of Jacob and Mary Grace More. The girls were largely educated at home by their father, a staunch Tory and high church Anglican, who was the headmaster of a school, and who "began to train his daughters to be teachers while they were still young" (Hopkins 13). According to Mary Alden Hopkins, "Mr. More was not altogether easy in his mind about educating his daughters because he shared the general belief that female brains were more delicate in texture than male and easily wrecked by book learning" (14). Nonetheless, the family viewed Hannah as something of a prodigy, and although "Mr. More may have had an antipathy to female pedants, he did his best to turn Hannah into one" (14–15).

In 1758, when Hannah's oldest sister Mary was nineteen, she and her sisters, Elizabeth, aged seventeen, and Sarah, aged fourteen, opened a young ladies seminary in Bristol; and they were later joined by Hannah and the youngest sister, Martha. The More sisters continued to run the school, which proved to be a successful and lucrative venture, until 1789, when they retired. Hannah, however, left the teaching staff in 1767, when she was twenty-two and became engaged to a wealthy middle-aged cousin of two sisters in the school, Edward Turner. The engagement lasted approximately six years, for Mr. Turner postponed the wedding three times, until finally Hannah broke off the engagement but was prevailed upon to accept an annuity of two hundred pounds as compensation from Mr. Turner—a sum which made her an independent gentlewoman.

In 1773, Hannah, who, like her sisters, decided never to marry, made her first of many visits to London and began to associate with the rich and the great, like Sir Joshua Reynolds, Samuel Johnson, David Garrick, Horace Walpole, and female "bluestockings" such as Elizabeth Montague and Mrs. Thrale; and to write poetry and plays, which enjoyed both popular and financial success. She is mentioned several times in Boswell's *Life of Johnson*, twice in relation to an episode in which Johnson is supposed to have criticized her for her "indelicate and *vain* obtrusion of compliment" (1328 and 949), although she became one of Johnson's intimate circle of friends. She also became an intimate of the Garricks, but after David Garrick's death, she turned against the theater, and her growing friendships with evangelical men and women led her into the campaign to abolish the slave trade and reform efforts among the poor and into writing works that were increasingly didactic and religious. According to Mitzi Myers, "After her conversion to Evangelicalism, she won international prominence as an educator, reformer, and magisterial arbiter of manners and morals, always specially concerned with the 'morals of my own sex' " ("Hannah More's Tracts" 265).

In 1789, at the urging of William Wilberforce, she and her sister Martha (known as Patty) started the first of many Sunday schools, eventually to be associated with schools of industry and women's friendship clubs, this one in Cheddar—where they cajoled and coerced the poor into a little learning and a lot of religion and engaged in philanthropic projects to improve the living conditions of the deserving poor. Meanwhile, she continued making annual trips to London and publishing works such as the *Cheap Repository Tracts* (begun in 1795), moral tales intended for the young and the lower classes; *Strictures on the Modern System of Female Education* (1799), an educational/conduct manual for young Christian women; and *Coelebs in Search of a Wife* (1809), a conduct book in the garb of a novel; in addition to more explicitly religious works.

Although she had always been viewed as sickly and frail and was long subject to headaches and bouts of illness, she outlived all her family, and died in 1833 at the age of eighty-nine, leaving a fortune of some thirty thousand pounds, largely earned from her writing. In her lifetime, she had led a very public life and was famed—and sometimes defamed—for both her writing and her evangelical activities. According to Hopkins, "Hannah believed destiny imposed one set of duties upon men and a completely different set upon women, although an exceptional woman might push her way a very short distance into what was essentially a masculine province" (48). She clearly viewed herself as an exceptional woman, but she appears to have held the generality of women in low esteem. Elizabeth Kowaleski-Wallace cites a passage of a letter from More to Horace Walpole: "To be unstable and capricious I really think, is but too characteristic of our sex; and there is perhaps no animal so indebted to subordination for its proper behavior as women" (41).

Both *Strictures on the Modern System of Female Education* and *Coelebs in Search of a Wife* are strongly religious works that at times read more like homilies than conduct books. In *Strictures*, nonetheless, More early states that "A female Polemic [even in religion] wanders nearly as far from the limits prescribed to her sex, as a female Machiavel or warlike Thalestris" (I:7). In More's theology, human beings are born in a state of corruption, and a persistent recognition of one's own fallen state, faith, divine grace, religious worship and prayer, and good works are necessary to be a true Christian. A recurring idea, illustrative of her political conservatism but paradoxical in light of her reform activities, is that "whatever is is right": a paternalistic God established the prevailing social order, and to question it is wrong, "for God himself is covertly attacked in many of the invectives against laws and governments, and the supposed unjust disproportion of ranks" (I:134). She attacks both Rousseau's idea of "natural" goodness and schemes for social reform " in which want and misery are considered as evils arising solely from human governments, and not from the dispensations of God; in which poverty is represented as merely a political evil, and the restraints which tend to keep the poor honest, are painted as the most flagrant injustice" (I:3).

More also assails Mary Wollstonecraft, "The Female Werter" (I:13), and derisively asserts:

To [the rights of man] have been opposed, with more presumption than prudence *the rights of woman*. It follows, according to the natural progression of human things, that the next stage of that irradiation which our enlighteners are pouring in upon us will illuminate the world with grave descants on *the rights of children*. (1:147)

She claims that

the imposing term of *rights* has been produced to sanctify the claim of our female pretenders, with a view not only to rekindle in the minds of women a presumptuous vanity dishonorable to their sex, but produced with a view to excite in their hearts an impious discontent with the post which God has assigned them in this world. (II:22)

She says of "female warriors" and "female Politicians," "I hardly know which of the two is the most disgusting and unnatural character" (1:6) and disavows all "desire to make scholastic ladies or female dialecticians" (1:187). She is critical of women who write novels, "those ever multiplying authors, that with unparalleled fecundity are overstocking the world with their quick-succeeding progeny" (1:188). And she claims that "The profession of ladies, to which the bent of *their* instruction should be turned, is that of daughters, wives, mothers, and mistresses of families" (1:107).

Most of the recommendations that she makes in *Strictures* are illustrated in the narrative *Coelebs*, in which Charles, a Christian young man, goes on an odyssey in search of the ideal wife—the archetype in his mind being Milton's Eve before the fall. After a series of encounters with unsuitable young women, each of whom personifies common female failings, Charles finds his future wife in the family of a close friend of his now deceased father: the Stanleys. The eldest daughter, Lucilla, who coincidentally has taken Milton's Eve as *her* model, embodies all the virtues that our hero wants in a wife. She is well-educated but no pedant, domestic, pious, chaste, modest, obedient, self-critical, self-denying, and totally unassuming. In addition to her household duties and reading, her time is taken up with charitable activities and gardening. Kowaleski-Wallace says of her, "Lucilla's attractiveness is enhanced by the fact that she almost—but not quite—fades into the natural background that produces her" (50). Mrs. Stanley tells Charles,

Lucilla is no prodigy dropped down from the clouds. Ten thousand other young women with natural good sense, and good temper, might with the same education, the same neglect of what is useless, and the same attention to what is necessary, acquire the same habits and the same principles. Her being no prodigy, however, perhaps makes her example as far as it goes, more important. She may be more useful, because she carries not that discouraging superiority, which others might be deterred from imitating, through hopelessness to reach. If she is not a miracle whom others might despair to emulate, she is a Christian whom every girl of a fair understanding and good disposition may equal, and whom, I hope and believe many girls excel. (II:9)

In fairness to More, it should be pointed out that while much of this is standard conduct book fare—to be found in the popular works of such male writers as the Rev. James Fordyce and Dr. John Gregory—there *are* differences in her prescriptions for women; and as Mitzi Myers has accurately pointed out, there is "unexpected congruence of the ideals and programs" ("Reform or Ruin" 333) in More's *Strictures* and Mary Wollstonecraft's *A Vindication of the Rights of Women*, a work which More claimed not to have read. Myers argues that critics tend to overlook "the positive redirections factored into the ostensible traditionalism of reformers like More" (331) and overaccent Wollstonecraft's iconoclasm, instead of noting that both women "challenge popular conduct book recommendations for feminine training and behavior—hide your wit, your learning, your health—and define themselves in opposition to the usual art of flattery, dissimulation, and manipulative pleasing" (335). They both agitated for educational reform for women. Although the framework of *Coelebs* is to demonstrate the kind of woman who will be desirable to a good Christian man, most of More's advice on the education of women is intent on producing women who will be principled and useful Christians, and, like Wollstonecraft, she recommends a more substantive education over the typical curriculum of accomplishments—music, drawing, dance, and so forth—given to young women. According to Myers, for both it is "God, however differently envisioned, who empowers what are essentially revivified spiritual ideals," and she says that "Evangelical spiritual egalitarianism, like feminism, offers a path to autonomy and transcendence of sex" (335).

Poovey, who examined the way in which women writers of the eighteenth and nineteenth centuries "thought of themselves as textbook Proper Ladies even as they boldly crossed the borders of that limited domain" (40), explains how Evangelicalism "provided women with practical opportunities outside their home." She explains that "because charitable work simply extended women's domestic activities into the neighborhood surrounding the home, this reform movement was one in which women could legitimately participate" (8–9). In the same way, writing texts for the moral improvement of others—particularly their own sex—offered women like Hannah More another acceptable forum for self-expression. Her earliest biographer—a man—is somewhat apologetic for the first part of More's career as a figure in society, poet, and playwright, but he waxes lyrical on the subject of her religious and moral writing: "But as her light tread proceeded along this beaten path, a new life of green and gay variety sprung up beneath her: surprising the senses with new colours and new odours, from products bursting into being in quick and endless succession. Her powers were inexhaustible" (Roberts 459).

Thus in engaging in the philanthropic activities among the poor and writing works of moral and religious instruction, More, like Beverly LaHaye after her, was able to assert herself and exert strength in ways that were socially acceptable yet hardly illustrative of the domestic ideal she endorsed—but at a high cost, not only to others but to herself.

Kowaleski-Wallace argues that "if Evangelicalism afforded middle-class women an opportunity for self-definition and self-advancement, that advancement also exacted its price: the perpetuation of an unequal class system" (86). She examines the way in which women like More and her sister Patty viewed the working class women, men, and children among whom they worked as "savages" and how they were controlled by a class politic that demanded "that they differentiate themselves from the rural poor" (72). She claims that part of their cultural work was to contain the disruptive energies of the poor, and *The Cheap Repository Tracts* were a tool in this endeavor, bearing "witness to a compulsion to control the narrative of the 'Other' as a way of defining one's own status" and functioning "within a discourse of middle-class self-definition and self-promotion" (81).

In the same way that More's philanthropic work facilitated "patriarchal class relations" (Kowaleski-Wallace 74), her conduct books were intent on affirming the value of patriarchal gender relations and roles. While More may have been more progressive than she was fully aware in her call for better education for women and her exhortations that women be active in charitable endeavors, she was also intent on containing women's disruptive energies and making them see the value of the domestic ideal. She writes in *Strictures*:

they little understand the true interests of woman who would lift her from the important duties of her allotted station, to fill with fantastic dignity a loftier but less appropriate niche. Nor do they understand her true happiness, who seek to annihilate distinction from which she derives advantages, and to attempt innovations which depreciate her real value. (II:22)

She asks her readers:

Is it not more wise as well as more honourable to move contentedly in the plain path which Providence has obviously marked out to the sex, and which custom has for the most part rationally confirmed them, than to stray awkwardly, unbecomingly, and unsuccessfully, in a forbidden road? (II:23–24)

And she states that "the most elaborate definition of ideal rights, and the most hardy measure for attaining them, are of less value in the eyes of a truly amiable woman, than "that meek and quiet spirit, which is in the sight of God of great price" (II:25).

Nonetheless, she never married, she did not live retired, and hers was not a meek and quiet spirit—a fact for which she seems to have paid a personal price. That she lived to be eighty-nine would suggest that she was constitutionally sound, but throughout her life she struggled with debilitating headaches and other disorders that may have been psychosomatic. Her letters and journals abound with descriptions of these episodes, and her journals reflect her own inner conflicts and the fact the religion did not bring her peace of mind:

Sunday, January 21.—Up late last night—much harassed all the week by worldly company. My temper hurt—heart secularized. I had looked forward to a peaceful Sunday—instead of this, an acute head-ache. Spent the day in bed—little devotion—no spirituality. Could not even *think* at all. (Roberts 255)
Sunday, 28th.—After a week of too much worldliness, my mind has somewhat recovered its tone in devout prayer in the night. I have also to-day prayed with more affection. I

have endeavoured to check my own spirit, by placing death before my eyes, and carefully reading Doddridge's last chapter—the dying scene.   When I read, the impression is strong, and my mind serious; but when the book is closed, the heart grows cold, and the world rushes in. (Roberts 317)

The world rushed in on Hannah More around 1800, when she became embroiled in a controversy that began as an attack on one of the Sunday school teachers she had hired and grew into an attack on More herself.   She was accused of "enthusiasm" or Methodism, disaffection to church and state, and sedition.   Pamphlets circulated caricaturing her life, her religious activities, and her character.   When the furor abated in 1803, she suffered a total collapse, which lasted for two years.   It is not a little ironic that a woman who believed she had devoted her life to the preservation of the status quo should have been attacked for trying to undermine it.

Although More's reputation survived these assaults, and she went on to produce the bulk of her religious and moral writings and to achieve fame at home and abroad—particularly in America—it is clear that religion not only empowered but also debilitated More—a seeming contradiction in a life full of contradictions.

BEVERLY LAHAYE

Beverly LaHaye's life exhibits many of the same contradictions.   Unlike More, she married and had children, but, exactly like More, she has become a public figure through her evangelical activities, which expanded into the political domain in 1979 when she founded Concerned Women for America (CWA), a pro-family women's organization "dedicated to such popular right-wing causes as antigay rights, antiERA, antiabortion, and proprayer in public schools" (Garrison 235).   In particular, LaHaye's organization is opposed to secular humanism and "radical feminism," which she blames for most of the ills in contemporary society (*The Restless Woman* 109).

LaHaye "had early experienced family instability stemming from the loss of a male parent."   Her father died when she was young, "and though her mother later remarried, the family had been forced to move several times, living in Missouri and Michigan before Beverly went away to college" (Garrison 234). In 1946, as a coed at Bob Jones University, she met Tim LaHaye, a conservative Baptist from Michigan, who had also lost his father at an early age, and she married him the following year.   After marrying, she dropped out of school to become a homemaker and pastor's wife, and the marriage produced four children: Linda, Larry, Lee, and Lori.

David Garrison suggests that the early deaths of their fathers was "doubtless a contributing factor to why [Tim and Beverly LaHaye] would later spend much of their lives crusading for a strong patriarchal model for the church and family" (234).   Settling in San Diego in 1956, the couple appeared on a weekly television program, *LaHayes on Family Life,* and over the years "expanded their family ministry through the publication of articles and books and a national lecture series called "Family Life Seminars" that began in 1972" (234). Despite this early public exposure Beverly LaHaye claims that she was " 'a fearful, introverted' housewife who clung her husband's side and was so shy that 'it was difficult for me to entertain in our home,' much less venture outside it" (Faludi 248).

Nonetheless, "when her youngest child was still in diapers, LaHaye went back to work, full-time, as a teletype operator for Merrill Lynch" (Faludi 249) to help out with family finances, and she hired a black single mother as a housekeeper. Faludi quotes LaHaye as saying of her job at Merrill Lynch, "I liked working there. It was kind of exciting. You had to get there at six a.m. because that's when the stock market opened in New York. They paid well. And I enjoyed it" (249). While this job may have increased her self confidence, the "missing dimension" in her life was supplied by Dr. Henry Brandt's message about the Holy Spirit in 1963. In the revised *The Spirit Controlled Woman,* LaHaye writes:

The fears and anxieties that possessed me were not from God: "For God has not given us a spirit of fear, but of power and of love and of a sound mind" (2 Timothy 1:7). This was exactly what I lacked! I needed power, love, and a sound mind to enable me to throw off my poor self-image and fear, step forward with new confidence, and let God do whatever He chose to do with my life. I knew my limitations and that I could only do this by turning the controls over to the Holy Spirit. (13–14)

Imbued with the Holy Spirit, Beverly LaHaye went on to author several books beginning with *The Spirit Controlled Woman* in 1976; to co-author with her husband a sex manual, *The Act of Marriage,* which not only taught "Christian men how to gratify their wives in bed, it informed them in no uncertain terms that an orgasm is every woman's right" (Faludi 251); to carry the "Family Life Seminar to more than fifty cities across America and into several foreign countries" (Garrison 235); to birth "a daily radio talk show . . . in the nation's capital that is now the largest of its kind led by a woman and is carried by almost every city in the nation" (Tim LaHaye in the Foreword to the revised *The Spirit Controlled Woman*); and, of course, to found Concerned Women for America, which in 1983 moved its headquarters to Washington D.C., "where she built up a twenty-six person Capitol Hill Staff, launched a five-attorney legal division to take on the courts and wielded a $6 million dollar annual budget" (Faludi 253). Today CWA has over 600,000 members, and since 1987 LaHaye has been president for life, creating what Faludi calls "a one-woman fiefdom" (253).

Despite this formidable list of accomplishments, Beverly LaHaye's message to every woman is to remain submissive to her husband (*The Spirit-Controlled Woman* 167). Like More's works, LaHaye's books are conduct manuals, strongly infused with religion. LaHaye is a fundamentalist Christian, who believes that God "has a plan, and using biblical citations, she sets out to tell women of God's plan for them (*The Spirit-Controlled Woman* 22).

The Spirit-Controlled Woman, her first book is a mixture of Hippocrates, pop-psychology, and religion, in which she divides all individuals into four basic personality types—claiming that they cannot be changed—and in which she advises "Martha Melancholy," "Polly Phlegmatic," "Clara Choleric," and "Sarah Sanguine" how to make the most of their strengths and overcome their weaknesses by cooperating with the Holy Spirit. The work is relatively innocuous, although it advocates a traditional patriarchal family structure and takes a few swipes at "choleric feminists" and "the anti-family excesses of the feminist movement" (68). However, as Faludi says, the work promises that "By tapping 'spiritual power,' . . . a fundamentalist woman could 'step forth in all confidence,' 'overcome her passivity,' and become 'a capable person' " (250).

Such advice, combined with her progressive views on female sexuality, early support of equal rights for women and pay equity, and condemnation of sexual harassment on the job, "may have read," according to Faludi,

as if Beverly LaHaye were on the verge of a feminist conversion, and one worthy of Germaine Greer. . . . Yet she was never prepared to take the final steps, which had the potential of separating her from her church, husband, and social universe. . . . Having attracted a huge following by telling women to "step forward in all confidence," she now mobilized her female army for a campaign to chase themselves home. (251–252)

If there were any doubts about this, *The Restless Woman*, written in 1984, would put them to rest. In this book, LaHaye mounts an assault on the feminist movement and feminists. However, most of the work is devoted to attacking "radical feminists," to establishing that feminism is a mental illness resulting from a flawed childhood, to claiming that feminism is destroying society, and to advising "restless" women that it is in their best interest to return to the traditional family unit (19). And, according to LaHaye and the sources she cites, damage to the family unit leads to virtually all other social problems.

In her assault on feminists, LaHaye attempts to demonize them (53). She uses Lundberg and Farnham's infamous 1947 work *Modern Women, The Lost Sex* to establish that Mary Wollstonecraft (whose work she has apparently not read) had an unhappy childhood and, therefore, "grew up to be a neurotic—a man-hater who sought vengeance by striking out at society" (qtd. in LaHaye, *Restless*, 49). She says the same of all subsequent leaders of the feminist movement: "These women are tragic victims of parental neglect. They have grown up filled with paranoia and impulsive hatred that drives [sic] them relentlessly toward their goals." Her conclusion is that "In a very real sense, these women are mentally disturbed" (85).

She also lists "the sick ideas espoused by the leaders of the feminist movement" and demanded by the liberated woman, who "is working to restructure both our economic system and our family arrangements":

She must have access to twenty-four-hour child care services; she must be given special privileges at work; she must be given government subsidies; she must be allowed to destroy her unwanted children; if she is a lesbian, she must have the freedom to adopt children or to be artificially inseminated through a "gay" sperm bank; she must be granted the right to marry another woman if she desires; she must have the right to be a combat soldier, even if she can't possibly compete with men in physical strength. (85)

Not content with misrepresenting feminist beliefs and goals, LaHaye also associates feminism—at least rhetorically—with some of the most reviled and feared elements in society:

Child pornographers, known to law enforcement officers as "pedophiles," seldom admit they need help. Instead of seeking professional psychiatric assistance, they form their own political/social organizations such as the North American Man-Boy Lovers Association. These organizations *reinforce* the psychopathic behavior of these men, giving them justification to continue in their sexual abuse of preadolescent children. This same tendency holds true in feminist organizations. (86)

In another passage, after recurring to the idea of the importance of the lessons parents teach children, she says, "In the study of the lives of mass murderers, dictators, or radical feminists, it becomes evident that their parents neglected to give them proper moral training" (139). In addition to pedophiles, mass murderers, and dictators (such as Stalin), through humanism, she also links feminism to Hugh Hefner (16–17).

In the latter part of the book, LaHaye provides anecdotal evidence of former feminists who "are either losing interest or are making a deliberate turn-around in their attitudes regarding family, God, and country" (124). She cites a letter from one such woman, "who had been influenced by Jane Fonda . . . voted for the radical Peace and Freedom Party, picketed with feminists, and smoked marijuana." LaHaye claims that "Following the feminist ideals of 'womanhood,' this individual had become an alcoholic, who had deserted her husband, had had several abortions, and ended up sterile, but, fortunately, her story has a happy ending, for she is "now a committed Christian" (124–125).

Much of this would be comical if LaHaye did not have such a wide following and if her activities were limited to the fundamentalist Christian community. Garrison credits Tim and Beverly LaHaye as being the man and woman most responsible for tagging "secular humanism" as the common enemy of the New Right, "for identifying this villain and popularizing the fundamentalist crusade against it" (233). Furthermore, he suggests that "Secular humanism is, in fact, less a national conspiracy than a heuristic device invented by [Tim] LaHaye," and that after using it successfully on the local level in an attack on public schools, the LaHayes "projected their secular humanist model onto the national and international arenas and found it to be equally useful there" (239). Beverly LaHaye uses a similar heuristic device, presenting the "radical feminist movement," which she identifies as an outgrowth of secular humanism, as a demonic and neurotic presence in society, opposed to family, God, and country, and, thus, creating an enemy against which she can rally women to work against women's rights. And, ironically, in the process, she has gained fame, power, and status on Capitol Hill as a woman to be reckoned with.

Clearly, there are a number of parallels between Beverly LaHaye and Hannah More. Both became prominent women—media figures—as a result of their evangelical and educational work and writings, primarily targeting women. Both produced written works that were very accessible—oversimplifying the issues, presenting feminism as the enemy of women, and seemingly validating their arguments with Scriptural references. Despite this reactionary rhetoric, both exhibited progressive tendencies in their writing about women and their injunctions to women. However, both, as professed Christian women and moralists who courted male approval, were apparently compelled to advocate a patriarchal model of family life, instructing women that their place is in the home. Nonetheless, neither woman followed her own injunctions, and each of them seems to have rationalized her public role with the explanation that she was doing God's work.

It is easier to justify More's behavior at a time when so few opportunities were available to women and feminist ideas reflected anything but mainstream thinking. In the latter part of the twentieth century, LaHaye's reactionary rhetoric seems more exploitative, and it is certainly more virulent, undoubtedly because feminism seems to represent a greater threat to patriarchy than it did two hundred years ago. Garrison ends his essay on the LaHayes on a monitory note, pointing out that

the academic world has dismissed them as fringe figures who, despite an immense popular following, offer little to the wider scholarly community and therefore should not be taken seriously; thus, the academic community will no doubt continue to ignore them, since all of their books have targeted lay Christian audiences and critical scholarships, until the agenda of the Christian Right, with many of the Lahayes' ideals, has become adopted national policy. (239)

Feminists and feminist scholars should not ignore figures like Beverly LaHaye. Evidently, no matter how far we think we may have progressed since the time of Hannah More, Christian fundamentalists continue to work against those gains, and, as *Backlash* amply illustrates, they had considerable success in the 1980s misrepresenting feminism and, as Faludi so aptly puts it, dressing "it up in greasepaint and turn[ing] its proponents into gargoyles" (xxiii) and re-presenting traditional ideals of womanhood, wifehood, and motherhood. Feminists need to be aware of this reactionary and anti-feminist rhetoric and to respond to it by accurately representing feminism and allaying women's fears and anxieties about feminism. We also need, as Faludi ably did in *Backlash*, to point out the contradictions between the lives and the dicta of those women who proselytize on behalf of patriarchy and attack feminism even as they take advantage of the opportunities that feminist activism has made possible. If we are successful, then in the future such attacks may (like Hannah More's name which has been passed on in a phrase) "not amount to Hannah More," which, in a final irony, means "not amount to a hill of beans" (Funk 124).

NOTE

1. In the revised edition of the *Spirit Controlled Woman*, LaHaye puts the year as 1963, when she "heard Dr. Henry Brandt, a Christian psychologist, give a message about the filling of the Holy Spirit and the effect it could have on my life" (13).

BIBLIOGRAPHY

Armstrong, Nancy. *Desire and Domestic Fiction*. New York: Oxford University Press, 1987.

Boswell, James. *Life of Johnson*. Ed. R. W. Chapman. London: Oxford University Press, 1976.

Faludi, Susan. *Backlash*. New York: Crown Publishers, Inc., 1991.

Funk, Charles Earle. *A Hog on Ice and Other Curious Expressions*. New York: Harper, 1948.

Garrison, David. "Tim and Beverly LaHaye." *Twentieth-Century Shapers of American Popular Religion*. Westport, CT: Greenwood Press, 1989.

Hopkins, Mary Alden. *Hannah More and Her Circle*. New York: Longmans, Green and Co., 1947.

Kowaleski-Wallace, Elizabeth. *Their Fathers' Daughters*. New York: Oxford University Press, 1991.

LaHaye, Beverly. *The Spirit-Controlled Woman*. New and Revised Edition. Eugene, Oregon: Harvest House Publishers, 1995.

LaHaye, Beverly. *The Restless Woman*. Grand Rapids, Michigan: Zondervan Publishing House, 1984.

More, Hannah. *Strictures on the Modern System of Female Education*. 2 vols. London: T. Cadell Jun. and W. Davies, 1799.

More, Hannah. *Coelebs in Search of a Wife*. Philadelphia: Thomas & William Bradford, 1810.

Myers, Mitzi. "Hannah More's Tracts for the Times: Social Fiction and Female Ideology." *Fetter'd or Free*. Ed. Mary Anne Schofield and Cecilia Macheski. Athens, Ohio: Ohio University Press, 1986.

Myers, Mitzi. "Reform or Ruin: 'A Revolution in Female Manners.'" *A Vindication of the Rights of Woman*. 2nd ed. Ed. Carol H. Poston. New York: W. W. Norton & Company, 1988.

Poovey, Mary. *The Proper Lady and the Woman Writer*. Chicago: The University of Chicago Press, 1984.

Roberts, William, Esq. *Memoirs of the Life of Mrs. Hannah More*. London: R. B. Seeley
    and W. Burnside, 1838.
Wollstonecraft, Mary. *A Vindication of the Rights of Woman*. 2nd ed. Ed. Carol H.
    Poston. New York: W. W. Norton & Company, 1988.

Chapter 12

Elizabeth Tudor and Diana Spencer: Claiming an Image; Reclaiming a Life

Anne Marie Drew

While this article was in the process of publication, Princess Diana was killed in a car crash. And the media shared the blame for her death, a death which caused a cacophony. The media tripped over themselves trying to ascertain their own part in her death. The Earl of Spencer, in his stunning eulogy, accused the media of killing her.

As reprehensible as the media's actions are, still, the fact is inescapable: Diana Spencer used the media to her advantage. That advantage turned tragic. In revising this article, I faced the grim task of turning all of my present tense references to Diana into past tense references. Initially, the last line of the article began with the words: "Presumably, Diana Spencer has several remaining decades to maintain her image." Now that presumption has been shattered. Diana's image, like Elizabeth Tudor's, moves into the historical realm.

Grotesque though it may be, the following sketch clearly indicates the minimal progress made regarding female representation. Under a large caption which reads "O.J.'s England Photos," there are four cartoons depicting various aspects of Simpson's 1996 trip to England. One cartoon illustrates O.J. and Prince Charles on a golf course. Simpson is supposedly giving Chuck a few golfing pointers, and the cartoon's caption reads: "Helping Chuck with his swing." The golf clubs both men are gripping, however, are not putters or nine-irons. They are axes. Thick-handled, Renaissance axes, with broad, menacing blades. Perfect instruments for controlling troublesome wives. The sick humor of the cartoon sharply yokes the Renaissance and our own times. Violence, ridicule, manipulation were and continue to be the socially approved method for dealing with women who are perceived as troublesome, who refuse to subscribe to others' expectations. Through an examination of Elizabeth Tudor and Diana Spencer, it becomes clear that while the treatment of women has been unfortunately similar across the centuries, both women managed to affect some changes and gain some control, using the media to achieve their ends.

While Henry VIII had only two of his six wives beheaded, he stands as the Renaissance symbol of a man whose control of women extended to the very breath he took from them. His daughter, Elizabeth, the child of one of those beheaded wives, Anne Boleyn, grew into the kind of woman her father abhorred: strong-willed, independent, and powerful. No matter how fiercely independent she was, however, Elizabeth, like all royal women, was trapped. Her friends, romances, fertility, even her fingernails, were monitored by a curious and self-serving public. From the beginning of her conscious life, Elizabeth Tudor understood that her power emanated from and was sustained by the public's image of her. Perhaps no other royal English woman since Elizabeth so understood the power of public image as did Diana Spencer, Princess of Wales.   Writing after her death in *The New Republic*, Andrew Sullivan suggests, "Perhaps no royal member since Elizabeth I created a regal iconography of such sensual power, or subliminally trapped us into an enduring fascination with her glamour" (46). Certainly Victoria indulged the public's adoration, and the current Queen Mother enjoys a unique hold on the British people. Nonetheless, Diana Spencer, in her short life, learned, as Queen Elizabeth II never has, that the media can be a strong ally. How awkward did the perennially stuffy and dowdy Queen Elizabeth II appear in the days immediately following Diana's death, initially refusing to address the nation. The first Elizabeth, however, had an uncanny knack of putting forth a self-chosen public image. A similar skill formed a central part of Diana's character. Throughout her tragic journey from blushing bride to somber ex-wife to "A candle in the wind," Diana never lost the loyalty of the British people. Of course, some like Camilla Parker Bowles referred to her as "that ridiculous creature." Still others viewed her as a not-too-bright clothes horse who was an embarrassment to the crown. Even when she tackled serious issues like unexploded land mines, her critics labeled her interests as trivial. The charge of "trivial" appears all the more absurd in light of the 1997 awarding of the Nobel Peace Prize to those who seek to abolish land mines.   Such criticism notwithstanding, Diana Spencer knew how to weather criticism and live on the devotion of her loyal supporters.

Early on in the public life of both of these women, there came a public event that cemented an indelible image in the minds of the English people. For Elizabeth it was her coronation. For Diana, it was her wedding to Prince Charles. The almost sacramental nature of both events captured countless hearts and imaginations. Subsequently, when both women endured image-threatening media crises, they tacitly evoked their hold on the British people generated by the singular public spectacles of a coronation and a royal wedding. When Elizabeth faced the mysterious death of her favorite's wife, Amy Robsart Dudley, she was able to stare down her accusers, in part, by reminding them of her virginal devotion to England. Similarly, in the aftermath of the publication of Andrew Morton's book, *Diana: Her True Story*, Diana survived by holding fast to her position as the mother of heirs to the throne. In crisis, neither Elizabeth nor Diana, could control what was written, what was whispered, what suspected. They could, in some very real measure, control their public images.

Elizabeth's coronation and Diana's royal wedding offer clear examples of royal women finding strength and power through a media event. With several noteworthy features in common, the two events occurred very early in the public life of both women. They are repeatedly referenced as turning points in the lives of the women and England. And most importantly, for present purposes, the events created permanent and beloved images of Elizabeth and Diana, images that became sources of strength for these beleaguered women.

On her Coronation Day, Elizabeth was very much in control of her image. As the young virgin Queen riding triumphantly into London, she used her image, with all its echoes of her father, Henry VIII, to control her subjects' view of her. Her vibrant red hair evoked her spectators' strong memories of their beloved king, Great Harry, whose own distinctive red hair added to his legendary appearance. Intentionally letting her long hair fall loose and free onto her shoulders and down her back, the young woman was signaling two important facts: The loose hair was the traditional mark of a virgin and the red hair, of course, formed a strong link with her father, a man who had once labeled her "illegitimate." As the queen rode triumphantly into London to ascend the throne, her virginity was intact. She had survived the treacherous fall of her mother; the deaths of her brother and sister; the aborted attempt by Lady Jane Grey's family to usurp the throne. She was young and pretty and at her coronation she used those attributes to win favor. Throughout her reign, she fostered these coronation day images.

The red hair and the virginity ultimately assumed almost mythic significance. Although Elizabeth never spoke of Anne Boleyn's fate, she knew that the sins of the mother were suspected in the daughter. A succession of her intimate acquaintances—Anne Boleyn, Katherine Howard, Thomas Seymour— had been executed for their perceived sexual indiscretion. The disaster with Thomas Seymour, when as an inexperienced and lonely adolescent, she indulged an older, ambitious man's flirtatious attentions, had come perilously close to staining her reputation. The Seymour affair seemingly reinforced Elizabeth's incipient awareness that sexuality fostered a loss of power and death. The accounts of the adolescent Elizabeth giving in to the flirtatious sexuality of an older man suggest the precarious nature of Elizabeth's reputation. Christopher Hibbert describes Seymour's advances to Elizabeth:

Seymour did all he could to intrigue and excite her. He romped with her and her ladies in that boisterous way which allows lasciviousness to pass for foolery. . . . He would tease Elizabeth and buffet her, striking her on the back of the buttocks familiarly. He would come into her bedchamber . . . in his nightgown and slippers, and either cautiously lift or snatch back the curtains and make as if to jump on her. . . . On one morning at least he tried to kiss her in bed. (30)

When Elizabeth subsequently heard her behavior described by those who sought to discredit her, she learned, sooner than did her unfortunate mother, that reputation and image must be closely guarded. She would come to "castigate herself for her shameless behavior which had led, indirectly, to Thomas' death" (Luke 24). Some people close to the throne wanted to believe that Elizabeth and Thomas's close relationship was part of a plot to seize the throne. And while Elizabeth was able, barely, to clear her name, Thomas was not so lucky. His political enemies put him to death, using his proximity to Elizabeth's person as evidence of treasonous ambitions. Perhaps the distortions of Elizabeth's personality in old age did result, in part, from this Seymour incident, an incident that fostered her inability to resolve the need for intimacy with the attendant loss of power. At the very least, her relationship with Thomas Seymour taught her that virginity was power.

So, on her coronation day, she flaunted her medically certified virginity. She orchestrated her day to be a spectacle of mythic proportions, not only signaling her chastity with her loose hair, but signaling her regal status by her choice of fabric and jewels. Given Renaissance sumptuary laws, only royalty could wear the costly raiment Elizabeth selected. Paul Johnson, in his book *Elizabeth I,* recounts the spectacle:

Elizabeth herself had four state dresses made: one for her procession through the city, of twenty-three yards of gold and silver, with ermine trimmings and silver-and-gold lace coverings. . . . She had two other state dresses of crimson and violet velvet, and changed her outfit twice during the ceremony. She had a crimson velvet hat, decorated with gold and pearls, and silk and gold finely meshed stockings. (68)

Not content to rely on appearance alone to win the day, Elizabeth used her extraordinary people skills to win the hearts of her people. One subject said of the event, "If ever any person had either the gift or the style to win the hearts of the people, it was this Queen. All her faculties were in motion, and every motion seemed a well-guided action; her eye was set upon one, her ear listened to another, her judgment ran upon a third, to a fourth she addressed her speech" (Somerset 65). How easy to visualize Elizabeth, regally dressed, hair flowing, moving about her subjects, beginning the media blitz that earned her every superlative name from Good Queen Bess to Gloriana.

In subsequent years when celebrations of her accession surpassed all other holidays, she allowed pamphlets and prayer books to be written. Songs were composed, sermons preached, plays performed. As long as people imaginatively returned to the coronation day image of a regal virgin, she controlled their loyalty. Discussing the royal image in *The Cult of Elizabeth*, Roy Strong maintains that the Elizabethan monarchy "demanded the development of an elaborate ritual and ceremonial with which to frame and present the Queen to her subjects as the sacred virgin whose reign was ushering in a new age of peace and plenty" (114). Eager though she was to establish her link with her father's past, Elizabeth was doubly eager to break with the tyranny of the previous reign of her sister, Bloody Mary.

One of the most dramatic ways in which Elizabeth broke with her sister's legacy was in her refusal to accept the hand of her former brother-in-law, Phillip II of Spain. When his wife, Mary Tudor, died, Phillip assumed that Elizabeth, her younger, prettier sister, would be glad to marry him for dynastic and personal reasons. Elizabeth, with a shrewd wisdom that belied her years, denied Phillip's proposal. Not only had Phillip proved a cruel and worthless husband to Mary, his Catholicism made him repugnant to much of England. Further, Elizabeth was already articulating the position that would form her legacy: "And in the end this shall be for me sufficient, that a marble stone shall declare that a Queen, having reigned such a time, lived and died a virgin" (Williams 66). She would not yield control of her person, her image, to anyone. As Susan Frye writes in *Elizabeth I: The Competition for Representation*, "In order to preserve her body as inviolable—virginal, unassaulted, sanctified—Elizabeth perpetually had to negotiate control of as much of the material world as she could muster" (107).

Elizabeth's control of her material world was severely tested two years into her reign with the death of Amy Robsart Dudley, the wife of her beloved favorite, Robert Dudley. Robert and Elizabeth had been friends for years and had both been political prisoners in the Tower in Mary's reign. Upon her accession, Elizabeth named him Master of the Horse. Their shared interests— horses, theatre, politics—made them good friends. Their mutual physical attraction bonded them further. While no one can ever prove the exact nature of Elizabeth's relationship to Dudley, the chemistry between them was evident to all who saw them together. Many assumed they were lovers. Thus, when Robert's wife died mysteriously at her country home and her body was found at the bottom of a flight of steps, Elizabeth's credibility came under attack. The suggestion was made that "Amy had first been murdered and then her corpse deposited at the foot of the steps in hopes of diverting suspicion of foul play. Suicide was also put forth as a possibility" (Somerset 91). Even a verdict of suicide would harm Elizabeth because many believed Elizabeth's open affection for Amy's husband made the unfortunate woman despondent enough to kill herself.

As word of Amy's death spread through England and the Continent, the reaction was vicious. Mary Stuart laughed shrilly and said, "The Queen of England is going to marry her horsekeeper who has killed his wife to make room for her" (Luke 122). Nicholas Throckmorton reported from Paris, "One laugheth at us, another threateneth, another revileth the Queen" (Luke 122). At Amy's death, Elizabeth sent Robert away from court, from her, and ordered a full inquiry into the death. Keenly aware that her cousin Mary Queen of Scot's behavior under the similar circumstances, had irreparably damaged her own reputation, Elizabeth guaranteed her own behavior was beyond reproach. Dudley, Elizabeth's dearest love, was banished from court. The Queen ordered an independent counselor to investigate the circumstances of the unfortunate's Amy's death. Robert returned only after the death was ruled accidental.

Elizabeth, determined to escape the suspicion that she and Robert planned Amy's death, acted firmly and decisively. She ordered the court into mourning and planned an elaborate funeral. All foreign thrones and local concerns knew that she was saddened by Amy's death and concerned about its mysterious circumstances. Elizabeth's power prevailed. When Robert did return, more grateful than ever for his easy access to the throne, Elizabeth remained firmly in control. She ardently loved this man, cherished and sought his company, pined for him in his absence, but she did not marry him. He was one of many suitors she rejected. As Susan Frye suggests, Elizabeth's own poems signal the monarch's awareness of her power:

> When I was fair and young, and favor graced me,
> Of many was I sought, their mistress for to be;
> But I did scorn them all, and answered them therefore,
> Go, go, go seek some otherwhere!
> Importune me no more!
>
> How many weeping eyes I made to pine with woe,
> How many sighing hearts, I have skill to show;
> Yet I the prouder grew, and answered them therefore.
> Go, go, go seek some otherwhere!
> Importune me no more . (109)

The stanzas indicate Elizabeth's clear understanding of the power inherent in virginal unavailability.

Until she lapsed into the coma preceding her death, Elizabeth tightly gripped her image as desirable virgin. As Elizabeth aged and time wreaked its merciless havoc on her appearance, her vanity grew. Her wigs, her clothes, her jewels all were designed to disguise the withered monarch. As her beloved friends and advisers died, as she watched Burleigh, Leicester, and even Essex face death, Elizabeth withdrew into the terrors of lonely old age. Indeed, Essex's greatest treason, in some ways, was not the threat to dethrone the Queen but his bursting into her private chambers unannounced and seeing the ugly, old woman she had become. Neville Williams describes the almost unthinkable scene on that September morning when an impetuously desperate Essex stormed into the Queen's bedchamber: "She had only just risen and was scarcely dressed, so that Essex saw her as no man had ever seen her before: without her wigs and rouge, bare of jewels and the great ruff, with none of the trappings of regality, so that she appeared a rather ugly woman of sixty six" (233). As he gazed at the face of the withered woman who was his Queen, he snatched away her ability to control his image of her, thereby signing his own death warrant. In his gaze, Essex understood that Elizabeth was a "rapidly aging, tired and lonely old lady kept going by a will of iron and unflagging determination" (Strong 54).

Elizabeth's vanity has become almost as legendary as her virginity and with good reason. She closely guarded both. As she grew older, the Queen's control of her portraiture became almost vicious. As she lost teeth and hair and youth, she consigned to the castle dumpster any official portrait that even hinted at these natural losses. Never losing the understanding of the importance of image that was manifest at her coronation, Elizabeth continually crafted public perception of her. As her power and assurance grew, she fastened her hair and demanded regal portrait poses. After her famous Tutbury appearance, she willingly perpetuated the image of herself, the Queen, in armor.

However, even Elizabeth was not omnipotent in her attempts to control her image. She had limited power, at best, over the pamphleteers, the pulpiteers, the poster makers. True, she could and did shout from a church pew to a preacher who offended her, "Do not talk about that" (Hibbert 90). She could order Phillip Stubbs' hand cut off when, in a misguided attempt to prevent Elizabeth's marriage to Alencon, he published his earnest pamphlet, "A Gaping Gulphe wherein England is like to be swallowed" (Jenkins 232). But she could not stop the relentless, forward moving curiosity of the public that fed off every new rumor, that hungered after a glimpse of her. Both in England and abroad the curiosity about the Virgin Queen created an enormous audience and market for any royal image.

Diana Spencer's image, of course, was and is a market unto itself. Like Elizabeth I, she gained strength from the public's fascination with her, a fascination that was first epitomized by the enduring spectacle of the royal wedding. Just as the coronation spectacle served Elizabeth well, centuries ago, Diana's image as the blushing English rose dressed in a fairy tale gown is embedded in England's national memory. That picture of youth and beauty and promise will not fade. After her death, *Time* magazine started using pictures of Diana at the wedding as part of their advertising on CNN. The ad, a generic commercial meant to highlight *Time's* reporting, mentions the indelible image of Diana on her wedding day.

By the time Diana actually married Charles on July 21, 1981, her transformation into an image had already begun. Although more English and more royal than her husband, her English bloodlines going all the way back to the Tudors, Diana's employment history was almost unbelievably modest. A nanny and a maid, she never drew attention to herself. When she married she began to understand both the power of the media and her own participation in that power. Her triumphant carriage ride on her wedding day was much like Elizabeth's coronation. She was a vetted virgin with youthful good looks and a warm heart. She captured public imagination. Ralph Martin, writing in his book,

Charles and Diana, comments on the wedding: "It was almost too perfect. The Prince was handsome, his Cinderella was not only beautiful but fresh and unsophisticated and even—although it was impossible to believe—pure" (7). The image pressed into universal memory was that of a happy bride. David Cannadine, writing in his book *Rituals of Royalty* maintains that "the wedding of the Prince of Wales and Lady Diana Spencer, with its blanket television coverage and its global audience of hundreds of millions, provided the most convincing illustration yet of the view that all the world's a stage" (7). But, to extend further Cannadine's Shakespearean illusion, all was not well.

On her wedding day, when Diana rode in the carriage that so unfortunately wrinkled her beautiful gown, she already knew she was in trouble. The warning signs were everywhere. Prince Charles was not in love with her. He remained deeply committed to Camilla Parker Bowles, his great love and mistress of many years. Despite Diana's fears and her knowledge of the presence of Bowles in Charles' life, Diana walked down the aisle of St. Paul's and married Charles, thereby embracing a matrimonial nightmare. Diana's gown, a closely guarded fashion secret, provided a tacit symbol of what lay ahead. For all its originality, the dress presented an unexpected problem. The "dressmakers realized too late that they had not taken the size of the coach into consideration when they had designed the ivory silk dress with its 25 foot long train. In spite of all of Diana's efforts it was badly crushed" (Morton *True Story* 94). As the wedding photos make very clear, the beautiful gown resembled an unironed cotton hanky. The fairy tale was wrinkled.

The media's love affair with Diana after the wedding is well documented. Her transformation from virgin bride to blushing newlywed to pregnant princess to young mother took place under the glare of flashes. And while the strains of such attention were visible, the public's love fed on such exposure. To maintain her strongest card—the British people's affection—Diana needed to be visible. As her face appeared on tabloids and fashion magazines; as radio stations sponsored Diana look-alike-contests; as book after book about HRH The Princess of Wales rolled from the presses, Diana became an industry. And she gained a measure of authority by using the media attention to her own advantage. But behind the pretty face and the public adulation, a beleaguered young woman was collapsing. Faced with an indifferent and congenitally self-centered husband and treated as a troublemaker by the Windsors, Diana suffered bouts of bulimia and severe depression leading to several suicide attempts.

Finally, when the facade of her life became too unbearable, the young woman remained strong enough to play her trump card—the world's affection for her. As she prepared to separate from Charles, the Princess did not hinder Andrew Morton's access to her family and friends as he wrote *Diana: Her True Story*. Diana's actions, a stunning departure from the crown's typical handling of the media, created the intended result. The world believed that Morton's book contained the truth. Subsequently, by allowing television cameras to film her visiting Morton's sources, her friends, Diana reaffirmed the public's belief. The book was, for Diana, her true story. Indeed, after her death, Morton made clear Diana's active participation in the book. His revelations caused an uproar of course. But Morton's revelations evidenced the Princess' understanding of the media's power. Certainly, she knew the revelations about her emotional instability might cause criticism, yet she also believed in her own ability to weather that criticism.

The hysterical onslaught created by Morton's book caused Diana some tense public moments. But the British people's sympathy lay on her side. Morton's descriptions of failed suicide attempts and bouts of bulimia notwithstanding, his portrait of a beleaguered princess is a sympathetic one. She became, in the words of Anthony Holden, "the world's most popular princess, cruelly neglected by her husband, and schemed against by his coterie of cronies. . . . She [came] to represent, express and affect aspirations of the collective subconscious. Diana is . . . another Joan of Arc . . . a feminist heroine" (50). Like the young Elizabeth who relied on her country's affection when she weathered the controversy surrounding Amy Dudley's death, Diana, in crisis, gained strength from her public image as another Joan of Arc.

To be sure, there are those who failed to see Diana as anything more than a vain, spoiled, demanding woman. Camilla Parker Bowles, who reportedly encouraged Charles to choose Diana as a bride because she was just a "little mouse" and not an emotional threat, referred to Diana as "that ridiculous creature." Diana's lack of academic success and her lack of intellectual rigor made her a source of ridicule among Charles's friends. Indeed, Charles felt perfectly free to walk away from his pregnant wife after she hurled herself down a flight of steps to prevent him from attending a polo match. When asked about the incident, Charles replied, "Oh, she just wanted attention." Charles failed to realize the power of such an image—the image of a pregnant, sobbing Princess of Wales lying in a crumbled heap at the bottom of a flight of stairs. In such a state, she was, to Charles, neither Joan of Arc nor a fairy tale princess. She was merely a nuisance.

Unlike John F. Kennedy who had the grace and self-confidence to quip, "I'm the man who accompanied Jacqueline Kennedy to Paris," Charles failed to accept the accolades bestowed on Diana. He resented her good works, the public's enduring affection for her, and her refusal to disappear quietly.

Even though she did not escape the negative comments of those who portrayed her as willful, selfish, and immature, Diana did manage to use the media to stay afloat, albeit temporarily. Temporarily, at least, she used the media to resist the Palace's attempts to control her. Diana's image did get tarnished, of course. During her November 1995 BBC interview, she acknowledged both her infidelities and her culpability in her failed marriage. Her critics used such admissions to solidify their views of her. Still, her hold on the public's imagination and affection remained strong.

The worldwide outpouring of grief at Diana's death graphically portrayed the intensely powerful hold she had on our imaginations. The pundits have repeatedly said that without her image, she'd have been nothing. That without pictures there would be no Diana. Nevertheless, it is mandatory to note: Diana helped to fashion those pictures.

In eulogizing his sister, Earl Spencer said, "It is a point to remember that of all the ironies about Diana, perhaps the greatest was this—a girl given the name of the ancient goddess of hunting was, in the end, the most hunted person of the modern age" (11). But Diana knew how to use the hunt to her advantage, and although she was eventually hounded to her death, she did reclaim her life by refusing to succumb to someone else's image of her. Rather she chose to create her own.

Her death and funeral gave us memorable pictures: a demolished car, a flag-draped coffin, two young princes with heads bowed. These images will remain forever. However, like Elizabeth, Diana will be remembered most for her life, not her death. Just as the ultimate idiosyncrasies of Elizabeth's old age, do not erase the powerful image she created in her lifetime, so too, the image of Diana's flag-draped coffin will not erase the young, blushing bride. While both women lived, they fought fiercely to reclaim their own images in order to reclaim their own lives.

BIBLIOGRAPHY

Cannadine, David. Ed. *Rituals of Royalty: Power and Ceremonial in Traditional Societies.* Cambridge, England: Cambridge University Press, 1987.

Frye, Susan. *Elizabeth I: The Competition for Representation.* New York: Oxford University Press, 1993.

Hibbert, Christopher. *The Virgin Queen: Elizabeth I: Genius of the Golden Age.* New York: Addison Wesley, 1991.

Holden, Anthony. *The Tarnished Crown: Diana and the House of Windsor.* New York: Random House, 1993.

Jenkins, Elizabeth. *Elizabeth the Great.* New York: Coward, McCann, 1958.

Johnson, Paul. *Elizabeth I.* New York: Holt, Rinehart, and Winston, 1974

Luke, Mary M. *Gloriana: The Years of Elizabeth I.* New York: Coward, Mcgann and Geoghean, 1973.

Martin, Ralph. *Charles and Diana.* New York: Putnam, 1985.

Morton, Andrew. *Diana: Her True Story.* New York: Pocket Books, 1992.

Somerset, Anne. *Elizabeth I.* New York: Alfred Knopf, 1991.

Spencer, Earl. "Brother's Eulogy for Diana: The Very Essence of Compassion." *New York Times* 7 September 1997: 11.

Strong, Roy. *The Cult of Elizabeth.* Berkeley: University of California Press, 1977.

Sullivan, Andrew. "The Princess Bride." *New Republic* 22 September 1997: 46.

Williams, Neville. *All the Queen's Men: Elizabeth and Her Courtiers.* New York: Macmillan, 1972.

Index

About the Contributors

James M. Boehnlein received his Ph.D. from Miami University in American Literature and Rhetoric and Composition. He has published a book, *The Sociocognitive Rhetoric of Meridel Le Sueur*, and a number of articles, book reviews, and the like. He is currently an assistant professor of English at the University of Dayton. He is also working on a book on advanced composition and a reprint of a 1936 novel, Leane Zugsmith's *A Time to Remember*.

Katherine H. Burkman is a Professor Emeritus from Ohio State University. She has published widely in the area of modern drama. Most recently she has co-edited a collection, *Pinter at Sixty*. Another collection which she co-edited, *Staging the Rage*, is forthcoming. Currently she runs a women's theatre group called Women at Play. They are scheduled to perform a stage version of *Mrs. Dalloway*.

Rosaria Champagne, Ph.D. teaches at Syracuse University. Her book, *The Politics of Survivorship: Incest, Women's Literature, and Feminist Theory*, was recently published.

Anne Marie Drew is an Associate Professor of English at the U.S. Naval Academy. She also directs Masqueraders, a theatre group on campus. She received her Ph.D. from Ohio State University. She has written on Beckett, Shakespeare, Gray, Pinter, and Shaw. She is currently at work on a collection of midshipman letters from 1845–1971.

Carol E. Dietrich, Ph.D., is Dean of General Education at DeVry Institute of Technology in Columbus, Ohio. Her research interests include writing assessment, faculty development, nineteenth-century American literature, poetry, and theology.

Grace A. Epstein, Ph.D. is an assistant professor of literature, creative writing, and women's studies at Stephens College. She has several publications on women and the media in various professional journals and anthologies. She is currently at work on a book about narrative form in the novel, *Textual Hysteria: Narrative Desire in the Feminist Novel*. She also writes short fiction and drama.

Jean Gregorek is a Ph.D. candidate in English at Ohio State University and is currently employed as an assistant Professor of Literature at Antioch College. She is in the process of finishing her dissertation, "The Character of Culture: Self-help in Nineteenth-Century Britain." Her research interests include theories of gender and sexuality and many forms of nineteenth- and twentieth-century popular culture. She has published reviews in *The Journal of American Folklore* and contributes occasional articles on issues of feminism and popular culture to arts periodicals.

Ann C. Hall is currently chair of the Division of English at Ohio Dominican College and president of the Harold Pinter Society. She has published articles on feminism, drama, and medieval literature, as well as a book, *A Kind of Alaska: Women in the Plays of O'Neill, Pinter, and Shepard* (1993).

Julia Keller is the television critic for *The Columbus Dispatch* and a recent Nieman fellow. She received her Ph.D. from Ohio State University for her work on Virginia Woolf and biography.

Veronica Webb Leahy received her M.A. and Ph.D. from Ohio State University where she was a teaching associate and lecturer. She was an Associate Professor of English at the Josephinum Pontifical College, and she is currently chair of the English Department at Columbus School for Girls.

Susan E. Lorsch received her Ph.D. from Brown University and is now an Associate Professor of English at Hofstra University. Her field of specialization is the development of the novel, particularly British fiction. Most recently she has written on contemporary fiction, and she is currently at work on a book on feminist artist novels.

Judith Roof is Professor of English at Indiana University. She is author of *Reproductions of Reproduction: Imaging Symbolic Change* (1996), *Come as You Are: Narrative Sexuality* (1996), and *A Lure of Knowledge: Lesbian Sexuality and Theory* (1991) and co-editor of *Who Can Speak? Authority and Critical Identity* (1995) and the forthcoming *Staging the Rage: Misogyny in Modern Drama*. She is currently working on a book on Eve Arden, Thelma Ritter, and Mary Wickes.

ISBN 0-275-96156-7

90000>

EAN

9 780275 961565

HARDCOVER BAR CODE